Indian Government and Politics

Dr. Manoj Sinha

Indian Government and Politics

ISBN 978-93-83459-27-8

Author

Dr. Dr. Manoj Sinha
Associate Professor,
Department of Political Science,
RamLal Anand College (Eve.)
University of Delhi

Published by

Bonfring
292/2, 5th Street Extension, Gandhipuram,
Coimbatore-641 012.
Tamilnadu, India.
E-mail: info@bonfring.org
Website: www.bonfring.org
Contact: 0422 3928700

About Author

Dr. Manoj Sinha
Associate Professor
Department of Political Science,
RamLal Anand College (Eve.)
University of Delhi

Dr. Manoj Sinha (b. 1965) obtained his M.A., M.Phil. and Ph.D. degrees in Political Science from the University of Delhi. He has been teaching Political Science and Public Administration at the undergraduate level at Ram Lal Anand (Eve.) College, University of Delhi since 1991 and has taught at the postgraduate level at Annamalai, Himachal and Delhi Universities since 1996.

His areas of specialization include Gandhian Thought, Political Theory and Environmental issues. He has also worked on Federalism in the Department of Political Science, University of California, Berkeley, U.S.A. He has presented a number of papers on Gandhian perspectives, Environmental issues, Public Administration and Public policy at various National and International Seminars and Conferences.

He is an active member of the Indian Society for Gandhian Studies and is associated with a number of academic organizations. Dr. Sinha has been a member of the Academic Council of the Delhi University and an Executive member of the Indian Institute of Public Administration (IIPA), New Delhi.

His academic work includes authorship of widely appreciated books like "Public Policy and Democracy, Bonfring, Coimbatore, 2014", "Modernisation and Ecology: A Gandhian Perspective, National Book Organisation, New Delhi, 2004" and "Cooperative Federalism in India and the USA, National Book Organisation, New Delhi, 1998". Apart from these he has also edited a number of books like "Contemporary India, Orient Blackswan, New Delhi, 2012", "Gandhi Adhyayan, Orient Blackswan, New Delhi, 2010", "Prashashan Awam Lok Neeti, Orient Blackswan, New Delhi, 2010" and "Gandhi Adhyayan, Orient Longman, New Delhi, 2008". Besides he has also published a number of Chapters in various Edited and Curricula Books.

ACKNOWLEDGEMENT

I am overwhelmed with joy, and avail this opportunity, to express my deepest gratitude and sincere regards to people who in one way or the other have helped me throughout the year 2013 to complete my work successfully. The present work would not have come into existence without their sincere contributions and efforts.

I express my heartfelt thanks to Professor Ujjwal Kumar Singh, Head, Department of Political Science, University of Delhi, and Dr. Rekha Saxena, Associate Prof., Department of Political Science, University of Delhi,and my Guru Prof M. P. Singh, Retired from Dept. of Political Science, University of Delhi for their constant motivation for all the Academic endeavours I choose to undertake and especially for the completion of this book.

Every project like this a lot of Academic support from Libraries and I would in my duty if I don"t acknowledge the help of Shri Dharam Kumar the librarian of my college, for giving me a 'no complaints' look whenever his help was needed. The staff of Teen Murti Library have also been more than supportive in their dealings.

It gives me immense pleasure to express my deep sense of gratitude to my wife, Dr. Rosy Sinha for her timely advice and perennial encouragement throughout the course of my work.

I am also thankful to my children Piyush and Parag who were incessant pillars of support for me and created an atmosphere and gave me this golden opportunity to complete this book "Indian Government and Politics".

Dr. Manoj Sinha
Associate Professor
Department of Political Science
Ram Lal Anand College (Evening)
University of Delhi

The Constitution of India provides the overall framework for the operation of democracy in the country, the functions and authority of the State in India, and the Government and its limitations with regard to the rights of the people. Arguably, the Constitution set forth the task of re-engineering a society based on predominantly caste, regional, linguistic, religious and other localized identities towards a society based on the modern identity of a citizen with legally defined rights and duties, irrespective of our caste, religion, language, region and other identities. This is the basis of the constitutional principle of equality as well as nation building. However, the quintessential compulsion of unity in diversity has not been compromised. The Constitution protects equally the rights of various cultural, religious and linguistic groups. The Constitution provides protection of rights of rights of citizens as individuals and as member of communities, including all types of minorities, both against the State as well as against the Society. This Constitution of ours is uniquely framed charter of rights and a contract of social transformation and nation- building.

Constitutional developments, the political training of leaders during the colonial period and political exigencies at the time of independence greatly influenced the framing of the Constitution. Further, the task of reforming the socio economic distortions of the time weighed heavily on the minds of the framers of the Constitution. Arguably, the institutional setup of our democracy and its principles, the organization and structure of governments in a federal setup, the rights of the people both as individuals and as a community are by and large are drawn on liberal values. What makes the Constitution predominantly liberal are the charter of fundamental rights of the individual citizens; limited and responsible majority government based on popular elections, and which is periodically replaceable; and separation of powers with checks and balance between organs of the government. Various other value systems, such as Marxian, Socialist and Gandhian, do find a place in the form of Directive Principles, which are to be followed by the State in the formulation and implementation of its policies, but are not compulsorily enforceable. However, institutions and policies regarding Panchayti Raj (local self government), abolition of the right to private property, constitutional protection to land reforms and nationalization initiatives do reflect the effort by the State to follow such directives.

We have tried to explore the expectations of the Constitution for its people and whether we have lived up to them. Most writings on the Indian Constitution have focused either on legal provisions, institutional mechanisms and their interpretations, or examination and analysis of the Indian polity from the perspective of socio-economic demand-support dynamics affecting the political process. We have endeavored to focus on the dynamics of the interaction between the constitutional provisions and the socioeconomic demand support requirements. The constitutional provisions are drawn on various historical and socio-economic compulsions, including the legacy of the nationalist movement, the requirement of social and economic reforms. In post Independent India, the operation of democracy and the enjoyment of fundamental rights have resulted in the rising expectations of the people- a source of demand and pressure as well as support for political institutions. The constitutional provisions have introduced and facilitated reforms and transformation in society, and, by extension, have put pressure on the political institutions for further distributive justice and political participation. Interaction between the constitutional provisions and their implementation, and demand and support from society is a dynamic process that has resulted in various amendments to the Constitution.

The Parliament, Executive and Judiciary have played a critical role in this interaction. We have tried to explore the dynamics of these interactions.. this has required combining the legal-institutional approach with structural- functional approach for understanding the dynamics. We hope that this help in providing a more comprehensive view of the Constitution and polity to the readers.

Dr. Manoj Sinha
Associate Professor
Department of Political Science,
RamLal Anand College (Eve.)
University of Delhi

<table>
<tr><th>Unit</th><th>Contents</th><th>Page No</th></tr>
</table>

Unit I

INDIAN CONSTITUTION

1.1 SOURCES OF INDIAN CONSTITUTION

The Constitution refers to the fundamental laws and principles which prescribe the nature, functions and the limits of a government. It reflects the aspirations of the people it belongs to.

In India, the Constituent Assembly was constituted in November 1946, under the scheme formulated by the Cabinet Mission Plan. The Constituent Assembly was to be a partly elected and partly nominated body. The members were to be indirectly elected by the members of the provincial assemblies, who themselves were elected on a limited franchise. It comprised of representatives of all sections of Indian society.

The Constitution framers adopted from several sources, features which are present in the Indian Constitution. The main sources may be identified as

(I) GOVERNMENT OF INDIA ACT, 1935 (26 GEO. 5 & 1 EDW. 8 C. 2)

OVERVIEW

The most significant aspects of the Act were:

- the grant of a large measure of autonomy to the provinces of British India (ending the system of dyarchy introduced by the Government of India Act 1919)
- provision for the establishment of a "Federation of India", to be made up of both British India and some or all of the "princely states"

- the introduction of direct elections, thus increasing the franchise from seven million to thirty-five million people
- a partial reorganization of the provinces:
    o Sindh was separated from Bombay
    o Bihar and Orissa was split into separate provinces of Bihar and Orissa
    o Burma was completely separated from India
    o Aden was also detached from India, and established as a separate Crown colony
- membership of the provincial assemblies was altered so as to include more elected Indian representatives, who were now able to form majorities and be appointed to form governments
- the establishment of a Federal Court

However, the degree of autonomy introduced at the provincial level was subject to important limitations: the provincial Governors retained important reserve powers, and the British authorities also retained a right to suspend responsible government.

The parts of the Act intended to establish the Federation of India never came into operation, due to opposition from rulers of the princely states. The remaining parts of the Act came into force in 1937, when the first elections under the Act were also held.

THE ACT

BACKGROUND TO THE ACT

Indians had increasingly been demanding a greater role in the government of their country since the late 19th century. The Indian contribution to the British war effort during the First World War meant that even the more conservative elements in the British political establishment felt the necessity of constitutional change, resulting in the Government of India Act 1919. That Act introduced a novel system of government known as provincial "dyarchy", i.e., certain areas of government (such as education) were placed in the hands of ministers responsible to the provincial even for those areas over which they had gained nominal control, the "purse strings" were still in the hands of British officialdom.

The intention had been that a review of India's constitutional arrangements and those princely states that were willing to accede to it. However, division between Congress and Muslim representatives proved to be a major factor in preventing agreement as to much of the important detail of how federation would work in practice.

Against this practice, the new Conservative-dominated National Government in London decided to go ahead with drafting its own proposals (the white paper). A joint parliamentary select committee, chaired by Lord Linlithgow, reviewed the white paper proposals at great length. On the basis of this white paper, the Government of India Bill was framed. At the committee stage and later, to appease the diehards, the "safeguards" were strengthened, and indirect elections were reinstated for the Central Legislative Assembly (the central legislature's lower house). The bill duly passed into law in August 1935.

As a result of this process, although the Government of India Act 1935 was intended to go some way towards meeting Indian demands, both the detail of the bill and the lack of Indian involvement in drafting its contents meant that the Act met with a lukewarm response at best in India, while still proving too radical for a significant element in Britain.

SOME FEATURES OF THE ACT

NO PREAMBLE: THE AMBIGUITY OF BRITISH COMMITMENT TO DOMINION STATUS

While it had become uncommon for British Acts of Parliament to contain a preamble, the absence of one from the Government of India Act 1935 contrasts sharply with the 1919 Act, which set out the broad philosophy of that Act's aims in relation to Indian political development.

The 1919 Act's preamble quoted, and centered on, the statement of the Secretary of State for India, Edwin Montagu (17 July 1917 – 19 March 1922) to the House of Commons on 20 August 1917, which pledged:

...the gradual development of self-governing institutions, with a view to the progressive realization of responsible government in India as an integral Part of the British Empire.

Indian demands were by now centering on British India achieving constitutional parity with the existing Dominions such as Canada and Australia, which would have meant complete autonomy within the British Commonwealth. A significant element in British political circles doubted that Indians were capable of running their country on this basis, and saw Dominion status as something that might, perhaps, be aimed for after a long period of gradual constitutional development, with sufficient "safeguards".

This tension between and within Indian and British views resulted in the clumsy compromise of the 1935 Act having no preamble of its own, but keeping in place the 1919 Act's preamble even while repealing the remainder of that Act. Unsurprisingly, this was seen in India as yet more mixed messages from the British, suggesting at best a lukewarm attitude and at worst suggesting a "minimum necessary" approach towards satisfying Indian desires.

NO BILL OF RIGHTS

In contrast with most modern constitutions, but in common with Commonwealth constitutional legislation of the time, the Act does not include a "bill of rights" within the new system that it aimed to establish. However, in the case of the proposed Federation of India there was a further complication in incorporating such a set of rights, as the new entity would have included nominally sovereign (and generally autocratic) princely states.

A different approach was considered by some, though, as the draft outline constitution in the Nehru Report included such a bill of rights.

RELATIONSHIP TO A DOMINION CONSTITUTION

In 1947, a relatively few amendments in the Act made it the functioning interim constitutions of India and Pakistan.

SAFEGUARDS

The Act was not only extremely detailed, but it was riddled with 'safeguards' designed to enable the British Government to intervene whenever it saw the need in order to maintain British responsibilities and interests. To achieve this, in the face of a gradually increasing Indianization of the institutions of the Government of India, the Act concentrated the decision for the use and the actual administration of the safeguards in the hands of the British-appointed Viceroy and provincial governors who were subject to the control of the Secretary of State for India.

'In view of the enormous powers and responsibilities which the Governor-General must exercise in his discretion or according to his individual judgment, it is obvious that he (the Viceroy) is expected to be a kind of superman. He must have tact, courage, and ability and be endowed with an infinite capacity for hard work. "We have put into this Bill many safeguards," said Sir Robert Horne… "but all of those safeguards revolve about a single individual, and that is the Viceroy. He is the linch-pin of the whole system…. If the Viceroy fails, nothing can save the system you have set up." This speech reflected the point of view of the die-hard Tories who were horrified by the prospect that someday there might be a Viceroy appointed by a Labour government.'[1]

REALITY OF RESPONSIBLE GOVERNMENT UNDER THE ACT – IS THE CUP HALF-FULL OR HALF-EMPTY?

A close reading of the Act[2] reveals that the British Government equipped itself with the legal instruments to take back total control at any time they considered this to be desirable. However, doing so without good reason would totally sink their credibility with groups in India whose support the act was aimed at securing. Some contrasting views:

"In the federal government... the semblance of responsible government is presented. But the reality is lacking, for the powers in defense and external affairs necessarily, as matters stand, given to the governor-general limit vitally the scope of ministerial activity, and the measure of representation given to the rulers of the Indian States negatives any possibility of even the beginnings of democratic control. It will be a matter of the utmost interest to watch the development of a form of government so unique; certainly, if it operates successfully, the highest credit will be due to the political capacity of Indian leaders, who have infinitely more serious difficulties to face than had the colonial statesmen who evolved the system of self-government which has now culminated in Dominion status."[3]

Lord Lothian "I agree with the diehards that it has been surrender. You who are not used to any constitution cannot realize what great power you are going to wield. If you look at the constitution it looks as if all the powers are vested in the Governor-General and the Governor. But is not every power here vested in the King? Everything is done in the name of the King but does the King ever interfere? Once the power passes into the hands of the legislature, the Governor or the Governor-General is never going to interfere. ...The Civil Service will be helpful. You too will realize this. Once a policy is laid down they will carry it out loyally and faithfully...

We could not help it. We had to fight the diehards here. You could not realize what great courage has been shown by Mr. Baldwin and Sir Samuel Hoare. We did not want to spare the diehards as we had to talk in a different language...

These various meetings — and in due course G.D. (Birla), before his return in September, met virtually everyone of importance in Anglo-Indian affairs — confirmed G.D.'s original opinion that the differences between the two countries were largely psychological, the same proposals open to diametrically opposed interpretations. He had not, probably, taken in before his visit how considerable, in the eyes of British conservatives, the concessions had been... If nothing else, successive conversations made clear to G.D. that the agents of the Bill had at least as heavy odds against them at home as they had in India.[4]

FALSE EQUIVALENCES

"The law, in its majestic equality, forbids the rich as well as the poor to sleep under bridges, to beg in the streets, and to steal bread."[5]

Under the Act, British citizens resident in the UK and British companies registered in the UK must be treated on the same basis as Indian citizens and Indian registered companies unless UK law denies reciprocal treatment. The unfairness of this arrangement is clear when one considers the dominant position of British capital in much of the Indian modern sector and the complete dominance, maintained through unfair commercial practices, of UK shipping interests in India's international and coastal shipping traffic and the utter insignificance of Indian capital in Britain and the non-existence of Indian involvement in shipping to or within the UK. There are very detailed provisions requiring the Viceroy to intervene if, in his unappealable view, any India law or regulation is intended to, or will in fact, discriminate against UK resident British subjects, British registered companies and, particularly, British shipping interests.

"The Joint Committee considered a suggestion that trade with foreign countries should be made by the Minister of Commerce, but it decided that all negotiations with foreign countries should be conducted by the Foreign Office or Department of External Affairs as they are in the United Kingdom. In concluding agreements of this character, the Foreign Secretary always consults the Board of Trade and it was assumed that the Governor-General would in like manner consult the Minister of Commerce in India. This may be true, but the analogy itself is false. In the United Kingdom, both departments are subject to the same legislative control, whereas in India one is responsible to the federal legislature and the other to the Imperial Parliament."[1]

BRITISH POLITICAL NEEDS VS. INDIAN CONSTITUTIONAL NEEDS – THE ONGOING DYSFUNCTION

From the moment of the Montagu statement of 1917, it was vital that the reform process stay ahead of the curve if the British were to hold the strategic initiative. However, imperialist sentiment, and a lack of realism, in British political circles made this impossible. Thus the grudging conditional concessions of power in the Acts of 1919 and 1935 caused more resentment and signally failed to win the Raj the backing of influential groups in India which it desperately needed. In 1919 the Act of 1935, or even the Simon Commission plan would have been well received. There is evidence that Montagu would have backed something of this sort but his cabinet colleagues would not have considered it. By 1935, a constitution establishing a Dominion of India, comprising the British Indian provinces might have been acceptable in India though it would not have passed the British Parliament.

'Considering the balance of power in the Conservative party at the time, the passing of a Bill more liberal than that which was enacted in 1935 is inconceivable.'[6]

PROVINCIAL PART OF THE ACT

The provincial part of the Act, which went into effect automatically, basically followed the recommendations of the Simon Commission. Provincial dyarchy was abolished; that is, all provincial portfolios were to be placed in charge of ministers enjoying the support of the provincial legislatures. The British-appointed provincial governors, who were responsible to the British Government via the Viceroy and Secretary of State for India, were to accept the recommendations of the ministers unless, in their view, they negatively affected his areas of statutory "special responsibilities" such as the prevention of any grave menace to the peace or tranquility of a province and the safeguarding of the legitimate interests of minorities. In the event of political breakdown, the governor, under the supervision of the Viceroy, could take over total control of the provincial government. This, in fact, allowed the governors a more untrammeled control than any British official had enjoyed in the history of the Raj. After the resignation of the congress provincial ministries in 1939, the governors did directly rule the ex-Congress provinces throughout the war.

It was generally recognized, that the provincial part of the Act, conferred a great deal of power and patronage on provincial politicians as long as both British officials and Indian politicians played by the rules. However, the paternalistic threat of the intervention by the British governor rankled.

FEDERAL PART OF THE ACT

Unlike the provincial portion of the Act, the Federal portion was to go into effect only when half the States by weight agreed to federate. This never happened and the establishment of the Federation was indefinitely postponed after the outbreak of the Second World War.

TERMS OF THE ACT

The Act provided for Dyarchy at the Centre. The British Government, in the person of the Secretary of State for India, through the Governor-General of India – Viceroy of India, would continue to control India's financial obligations, defense, foreign affairs and the British Indian Army and would make the key appointments to the Reserve Bank of India (exchange rates) and Railway Board and the Act stipulated that no finance bill could be placed in the Central Legislature without the consent of the Governor General. The funding for the British responsibilities and foreign obligations (e.g. loan repayments, pensions), at least 80 percent of the federal expenditures, would be non-votable and be taken off the top before any claims could be considered for (for example) social or economic development programs. The Viceroy, under the supervision of the Secretary of State for India, was provided with overriding and certifying powers that could, theoretically, have allowed him to rule autocratically.[7]

OBJECTIVES OF THE BRITISH GOVERNMENT

The federal part of the Act was designed to meet the aims of the Conservative Party. Over the very long term, the Conservative leadership expected the Act to lead to a nominally dominion status India, conservative in outlook, dominated by an alliance of Hindu princes and right-wing Hindus which would be well disposed to place itself under the guidance and protection of the United Kingdom. In the medium term, the Act was expected to (in rough order of importance):

- **win the support of moderate nationalists** since its formal aim was to lead eventually to a Dominion of India which, as defined under the Statute of Westminster 1931 virtually equaled independence;

- **retain British of control of the Indian Army, Indian finances, and India's foreign relations** for another generation;

- **win Muslim support** by conceding most of Jinnah's Fourteen Points;[8]

- **convince the Princes to join the Federation** by giving the Princes conditions for entry never likely to be equaled. It was expected that enough would join to allow the establishment of the Federation. The terms offered to the Princes included:
    - Each Prince would select his state's representative in the Federal Legislature. There would be no pressure for Princes to democratize their administrations or allow elections for state representatives in the Federal Legislature.
    - The Princes would enjoy heavy weight age. The Princely States represented about a quarter of the population of India and produced well under a quarter of its wealth. Under the Act:
        - The Upper House of the Federal Legislature, the Council of State, would consist of 260 members: 156 (60%) elected from the British India and 104 (40%) nominated by the rulers of the princely states.
        - The Lower House, the Federal Assembly, would consist of 375 members: 250 (67%) elected by the Legislative Assemblies of the British Indian provinces; 125 (33%) nominated by the rulers of the princely states.

- **ensuring that the Congress could never rule alone or gain enough seats to bring down the government**

This was done by over-representing the Princes, by giving every possible minority the right to separately vote for candidates belonging to their respective communities (see separate electorate), and by making the executive theoretically, but not practically, removable by the legislature.

GAMBLES TAKEN BY THE BRITISH GOVERNMENT

- **Viability of the proposed Federation**. It was hoped that the gerrymandered federation, encompassing units of such hugely different sizes, sophistication and varying in forms of government from autocratic Princely States to democratic provinces, could provide the basis for a viable state. However, this was not a realistic possibility (see e.g. The Making of India's Paper Federation, 1927-35 in Moore 1988). In reality, the Federation, as planned in the Act, almost certainly was not viable and would have rapidly broken down with the British left to pick up the pieces without any viable alternative.

- **Princes Seeing and Acting in Their Own Long-Range Best Interests** - That the Princes would see that their best hope for a future would lie in rapidly joining and becoming a united block without which no group could hope, mathematically, to wield power. However, the princes did not join, and thus exercising the veto provided by the Act prevented the Federation from coming into existence. Among the reasons for the Princes staying out were the following:
  - They did not have the foresight to realize that this was their only chance for a future.
  - Congress had begun, and would continue, agitating for democratic reforms within the Princely States. Since the one common concern of the 600 or so Princes was their desire to continue to rule their states without interference, this was indeed a mortal threat. It was on the cards that this would lead eventually to more democratic state regimes and the election of states' representatives in the Federal Legislature. In all likelihood, these representatives would be largely Congressmen. Had the Federation been established, the election of states' representatives in the Federal Legislature would amount to a Congress coup from the inside. Thus, contrary to their official position that the British would look favorably on the democratization of the Princely States, their plan required that the States remain autocratic. This reflects a deep contradiction on British views of India and its future.

'At a banquet in the princely state of Benares Hailey observed that although the new federal constitution would protect their position in the central government, the internal evolution of the states themselves remained uncertain. Most people seemed to expect them to develop representative institutions. Whether those alien grafts from Westminster would succeed in British India, however, itself remained in doubt. Autocracy was "a principle which is firmly seated in the Indian States," he pointed out; "round it burn the sacred fires of an age-long tradition," and it should be given a fair chance first. Autocratic rule, "informed by wisdom, exercised in moderation, and vitalized by a spirit of service to the interests of the subject, may well prove that it can make an appeal in India as strong as that of representative and responsible institutions." This spirited defense brings to mind Nehru's classic paradox of how the representatives of the advanced, dynamic West allied themselves with the most reactionary forces of the backward, stagnant East.'[9]

Under the Act,

'There are a number of restrictions on the freedom of discussion in the federal legislature. For example the act forbids ... any discussion of, or the asking of questions about, a matter connected with an Indian State, other than a matter with respect to which the federal legislature has power to make laws for that state, unless the Governor-General in his discretion is satisfied that the matter affects federal interests or affects a British subject, and has given his consent to the matter being discussed or the question being asked.'[1]

- o They were not a cohesive group and probably realized that they would never act as one.
- o Each Prince seemed consumed by the desire to gain the best deal for himself were his state to join the Federation: the most money, the most autonomy.
- **That enough was being offered at the Centre to win the support of moderate nationalist Hindu and Muslim support.** In fact, so little was offered that all significant groups in British India rejected and denounced the proposed Federation. A major contributing factor was the continuing distrust of British intentions for which there was considerable basis in fact. In this vital area the Act failed Irwin's test:

'I don't believe that... it is impossible to present the problem in such a form as would make the shop window look respectable from an Indian point of view, which is really what they care about, while keeping your hand pretty firmly on the things that matter.' (Irwin to Stonehaven, 12 November 1928)

- **That the wider electorate would turn against the Congress**. In fact, the 1937 elections showed overwhelming support for Congress among the Hindu electorate.

That by giving Indian politicians a great deal of power at the provincial level, while denying them responsibility at the Centre, it was hoped that Congress, the only national party, would disintegrate into a series of provincial fiefdoms. In fact, the congress High Command was able to control the provincial ministries and to force their resignation in 1939. The Act showed the strength and cohesion of Congress and probably strengthened it. This does not imply that Congress was not made up of and found its support in various sometimes competing interests and groups. Rather, it recognizes the ability of Congress, unlike the British Raj, to maintain the cooperation and support of most of these groups even if, for example in the forced resignation of Congress provincial ministries in 1939 and the rejection of the Cripps Offer in 1942, this required a negative policy that was harmful, in the long run, to the prospects for an independent India that would be both united and democratic.

INDIAN REACTION TO THE PROPOSED FEDERATION

No significant group in India accepted the Federal portion of the Act. A typical response was:

'After all, there are five aspects of every Government worth the name: (a) The right of external and internal defence and all measures for that purpose; (b) The right to control our external relations; (c) The right to control our currency and exchange; (d) The right to control our fiscal policy; (e) the day-to-day administration of the land.... (Under the Act) You shall have nothing to do with external affairs. You shall have nothing to do with defence. You shall have nothing to do, or, for all practical purposes in future, you shall have nothing to do with your currency and exchange, for indeed the Reserve Bank Bill just passed has a further reservation in the Constitution that no legislation may be undertaken with a view to substantially alter the provisions of that Act except with the consent of the Governor-General.... there is no real power conferred in the Centre.' (Speech by Mr Bhulabhai DESAI on the Report of the Joint Parliamentary Committee on Indian Constitutional Reform, 4 February 1935.[10]

However, the Liberals, and even elements in the Congress were tepidly willing to give it a go:

"Linlithgow asked Sapru whether he thought there was a satisfactory alternative to the scheme of the 1935 Act. Sapru replied that they should stand fast on the Act and the federal plan embodied in it. It was not ideal but at this stage it was the only thing.... A few days after Sapru's visit Birla came to see the Viceroy. He thought that Congress was moving towards acceptance of Federation. Gandhi was not over-worried, said Birla, by the reservation of defence and external affairs to the centre, but was concentrating on the method of choosing the States' representatives. Birla wanted the Viceroy to help Gandhi by persuading a number of Princes to move towards democratic election of representatives. ...Birla then said that the only chance for Federation lay in agreement between Government and Congress and the best hope of this lay in discussion between the Viceroy and Gandhi."[11][12]

THE WORKING OF THE ACT

The British government sent out Lord Linlithgow as the new viceroy with the remit of bringing the Act into effect. Linlithgow was intelligent, extremely hard working, honest, serious and determined to make a success out of the Act. However, he was also unimaginative, stolid, legalistic and found it very difficult to "get on terms" with people outside his immediate circle.

In 1937, after the holding of provincial elections, Provincial Autonomy commenced. From that point until the declaration of war in 1939, Linlithgow tirelessly tried to get enough of the Princes to accede to launch the Federation. In this he received only the weakest backing from the Home Government and in the end the Princes rejected the Federation en masse. In September 1939, Linlithgow simply declared that India was at war with Germany. Though Linlithgow's behaviour was constitutionally correct it was also offensive to much of Indian opinion that the Viceroy had not consulted the elected representatives of the Indian people before taking such a momentous decision. This led directly to the resignation of the Congress provincial ministries.

From 1939, Linlithgow concentrated on supporting the war effort.

(II) BRITISH CONSTITUTION:

The **Constitution of the United Kingdom** is the set of laws and principles under which the United Kingdom is governed.[13]

Unlike many other nations, the UK has no single constitutional document. This is sometimes expressed by stating that it has an uncodified or "unwritten" constitution.[14] Much of the British constitution is embodied in written documents, within statutes, court judgments and treaties. The constitution has other unwritten sources, including parliamentary constitutional conventions (as laid out in Erskine May) and royal prerogatives.

Historically, "No Act of Parliament can be unconstitutional, for the law of the land knows not the word or the idea."[15]

Since the Glorious Revolution in 1688, the bedrock of the British constitution has traditionally been the doctrine of parliamentary sovereignty, according to which the statutes passed by Parliament are the UK's supreme and final source of law.[16] It follows that Parliament can change the constitution simply by passing new Acts of Parliament. There is some debate about whether this principle remains valid,[17] particularly in light of the UK's membership in the European Union.[18]

ACTS OF PARLIAMENT

One of several shelves full of books about the UK constitution at a law library

Acts of Parliament are laws (statutes) that have received the approval of Parliament – that is, the Monarch, the House of Lords and the House of Commons. On rare occasions, the House of Commons uses the "Parliament Acts" (the Parliament Act 1911 and the Parliament Act 1949) to pass legislation without the approval of the House of Lords. It is unheard of in modern times for the Monarch to refuse to assent to a bill, though the possibility was contemplated by George V in relation to the fiercely controversial Government of Ireland Act 1914.[19]

Acts of Parliament are among the most important sources of the constitution. According to the traditional view, Parliament has the ability to legislate however it wishes on any subject it wishes. For example, most of the iconic mediaeval statute known as Magna Carta has been repealed since 1828, despite previously being regarded as sacrosanct. It has traditionally been the case that the courts are barred from questioning any Act of Parliament, a principle that can be traced back to the mediaeval period.[20] On the other hand, this principle has not been without its dissidents and critics over the centuries, and attitudes among the judiciary in this area may be changing.[21]

One consequence of the principle of parliamentary sovereignty is that there is no hierarchy among Acts of Parliament: all parliamentary legislation is, in principle, of equal validity and effectiveness. However, the judgment of Lord Justice Laws in the Thoburn case in 2002 indicated that there may be a special class of "constitutional statutes" such as Magna Carta, the Human Rights Act 1998, the European Communities Act 1972, the Act of Union and Bill of Rights which have a higher status than other legislation. This part of his judgment was "obiter" (i.e. not binding) – and, indeed, was controversial. It remains to be seen whether the doctrine will be accepted by other judges.

TREATIES

Treaties do not, on ratification, automatically become incorporated into UK law. Important treaties have been incorporated into domestic law by means of Acts of Parliament. The European

Convention on Human Rights, for example, was given "further effect" into domestic law through the preamble of the Human Rights Act 1998.

Also, the Treaty of Union of 1707 was important in creating the unitary state which exists today. The treaty was between the governments of England and Scotland and was put into effect by two Acts of Union which were passed by the Parliaments of England and Scotland, respectively. The Treaty, along with the subsequent Acts, brought into existence the Kingdom of Great Britain, uniting the Kingdom of England and the Kingdom of Scotland.

EUROPEAN UNION LAW

Under European Law, as developed by the ECJ, the EC Treaty created a "new legal order" under which the validity of European Union law cannot be impeded by national law; though the UK, like a number of other EU members, does not share the ECJ's monist interpretation unconditionally, it accepts the supremacy of EU law in practice.[22]:344 Because, in the UK, international law is treated as a separate body of law, EU law is enforceable only on the basis of an Act of Parliament, such as the European Communities Act 1972, which provides for the supremacy of EU law.[23][22]:344 The supremacy of EU law has been confirmed by the House of Lords, as in the Factor tame litigation. Replying to comments on the decision to override national legislation on the basis of EU law, Lord Bridge wrote "Under the terms of the 1972 Act it has always been clear that it was the duty of a United Kingdom court, when delivering final judgment, to override any rule of national law found to be in conflict with any directly enforceable rule of Union law."[23]:367–368

On one analysis, EU law is simply a subcategory of international law that depends for its effect on a series of international treaties (notably the Treaty of Rome and the Maastricht Treaty). It therefore has effect in the UK only to the extent that Parliament permits it to have effect, by means of statutes such as the European Communities Act 1972, and Parliament could, as a matter of British law, unilaterally bar the application of EU law in the UK simply by legislating to that effect.[23][24] However, at least in the views of some British authorities, the doctrine of implied repeal, which applies to normal statutes, does not apply to "constitutional statutes", meaning that any statute that was to have precedence over EU law (thus disapplying the 1972 European Communities Act) would have to provide for this expressly or in such a way as to make the inference "irresistible".[23]:369 The actual legal effect of a statute enacted with the express intention of taking precedence over EU law is as yet unclear.[25] However, it has been stated that if Parliament were to expressly repudiate its treaty obligations the courts would be obliged to give effect to a corresponding statute:

"If the time should come when our Parliament deliberately passes an Act – with the intention of repudiating the Treaty or any provision of it – or intentionally of acting inconsistently with it –

and says so in express terms – then . . . it would be the duty of our courts to follow the statute of our Parliament" (per Lord Denning in Macartys Ltd v Smith [1979] ICR at p. 789)"[26]

In 2011 parliament passed the European Union Act which states in clause 18: **"Status of EU law dependent on continuing statutory basis** Directly applicable or directly effective EU law (that is, the rights, powers, liabilities, obligations, restrictions, remedies and procedures referred to in section 2(1) of the European Communities Act 1972) falls to be recognised and available in law in the United Kingdom only by virtue of that Act or where it is required to be recognised and available in law by virtue of any other Act."[27]

COMMON LAW

Common law Northern Ireland and in England and Wales but not in ScotlandScots law) which involves a great deal of Common Law. Court judgments also commonly form a source of the constitution: generally speaking in English Law, judgments of the higher courts form precedents or case law that binds lower courts and judges; Scots Law does not accord the same status to precedent and judgments in one legal system do not have a direct effect in the other legal systems.[28]

Historically important court judgments include those in the Case of Proclamations, the Ship money case and Entick v. Carrington, all of which imposed limits on the power of the executive.

A constitutional precedent applicable to British colonies is Campbell v. Hall, which effectively extended those same constitutional limitations to any territory which has been granted a representative assembly.

CONVENTIONS

Many British constitutional conventions are ancient in origin, though others (like the Salisbury Convention) date from within living memory. Such conventions, which include the duty of the Monarch to act on the advice of his or her ministers, are not formally enforceable in a court of law; rather, they are primarily observed "because of the political difficulties which arise if they are not."[29]

WORKS OF AUTHORITY

Works of authority is the formal name for works that are sometimes cited as interpretations of aspects of the UK constitution. Most are works written by nineteenth- or early-twentieth-century constitutionalists, in particular A. V. Dicey, Walter Bagehot and Erskine May.

(III) US Constitution:

The **Constitution of the United States** is the supreme law of the United States of America.[30] The Constitution originally consisted of seven Articles. The first three Articles embody the doctrine of the separation of powers, whereby the federal government is divided into three branches: the legislature, consisting of the bicameral Congress; the executive, consisting of the President; and the judiciary, consisting of the Supreme Court and other federal courts. The fourth and sixth Articles frame the doctrine of federalism, describing the relationship between State and State, and between the several States and the federal government. The fifth Article provides the procedure for amending the Constitution. The seventh Article provides the procedure for ratifying the Constitution.

The Constitution was adopted on September 17, 1787, by the Constitutional Convention in Philadelphia, Pennsylvania, and ratified by conventions in eleven States. It went into effect on March 4, 1789.[31]

Since the Constitution was adopted, it has been amended twenty-seven times. The first ten amendments (along with two others that were not ratified at the time) were proposed by Congress on September 25, 1789, and were ratified by the necessary three-fourths of the States on December 15, 1791.[32] These first ten amendments are known as the Bill of Rights.

The Constitution is interpreted, supplemented, and implemented by a large body of constitutional law. The Constitution of the United States was the first constitution of its kind, and has influenced the constitutions of other nations. Research has shown that this influence may be on the wane, however.[33][34]

Fundamental Law

Several ideas in the Constitution were new. These were associated with the combination of consolidated government along with federal relationships with constituent states.

The due process clause of the Constitution was partly based on common law and on Magna Carta (1215), which had become a foundation of English liberty against arbitrary power wielded by a tyrant.

Both the influence of Edward Coke and William Blackstone were evident at the Convention. In his Institutes of the Laws of England, Edward Coke interpreted Magna Carta protections and rights to apply not just to nobles, but to all British subjects. In writing the Virginia Charter of 1606, he enabled the King in Parliament to give those to be born in the colonies all rights and liberties as though they were born in England. William Blackstone's Commentaries on the Laws of England were the most influential books on law in the new republic.

British political philosopher John Locke following the Glorious Revolution was a major influence expanding on the contract theory of government advanced by Thomas Hobbes. Locke advanced the principle of consent of the governed in his Two Treatises of Government. Government's duty under a social contract among the sovereign people was to serve them by protecting their rights. These basic rights were life, liberty and property.

Montesquieu emphasized the need for balanced forces pushing against each other to prevent tyranny (reflecting the influence of Polybius's 2nd century BC treatise on the checks and balances of the Roman Republic). In his The Spirit of the Laws, Montesquieu argues that the separation of state powers should be by its service to the people's liberty: legislative, executive and judicial.

Division of power in a republic was informed by the British experience with mixed government, as well as the study of republics ancient and modern. A substantial body of thought had been developed from the literature of republicanism in the United States, including work by John Adams and applied to the creation of state constitutions.

NATIVE AMERICANS

The Iroquois nations' political confederacy and democratic government under the Great Law of Peace have been credited as influences on the Articles of Confederation and the United States Constitution.[35] Relations had long been close, as from the beginning, the colonial English needed allies against New France. Prominent figures, such as Thomas Jefferson in colonial Virginia and Benjamin Franklin in colonial Pennsylvania, two colonies whose territorial claims extended into Iroquois territory, were involved with leaders of the New York-based Iroquois Confederacy.[36]

In the 1750s, at the Albany Congress, Franklin called for "some kind of union" of English colonies to effectively deal with Amerindian tribes.[37] John Rutledge (SC) quoted Iroquoian law to the Constitutional Convention, "We, the people, to form a union, to establish peace, equity, and order..." [38]

The Iroquois experience with confederacy was both a model and a cautionary tale. Their "Grand Council" had no coercive control over the constituent members, and decentralization of authority and power had frequently plagued the Six Nations since the coming of the Europeans. The governance adopted by the Iroquois suffered from "too much democracy" and the long term independence of the Iroquois confederation suffered from intrigues within each Iroquois nation.[39]

The 1787 United States had similar problems, with individual states making separate agreements with European and Amerindian nations apart from the Continental Congress. Without the Convention's proposed central government, the framers feared that the fate of the confederated Articles' United States would be the same as the Iroquois Confederacy.

OTHER BILLS OF RIGHTS

The United States Bill of Rights consists of the 10 amendments added to the Constitution in 1791, as supporters of the Constitution had promised critics during the debates of 1788.[40] The English Bill of Rights (1689) was an inspiration for the American Bill of Rights. Both require jury trials, contain a right to keep and bear arms, prohibit excessive bail and forbid "cruel and unusual punishments." Many liberties protected by state constitutions and the Virginia Declaration of Rights were incorporated into the Bill of Rights.

(IV) IRISH CONSTITUTION:

The **Constitution of Ireland** (Irish: Bunreacht na hÉireann, is the fundamental law of Ireland. The constitution falls broadly within the tradition of liberal democracy. It establishes an independent state based on a system of representative democracy. It guarantees certain fundamental rights, along with a popularly elected non-executive president, a bicameral parliament based on the Westminster system, a separation of powers and judicial review.

It is the second constitution of the state since independence, replacing the 1922 Constitution of the Irish Free State.[41] It came into force on 29 December 1937 following national plebiscite held on 1 July 1937. The Constitution may be amended solely by a national referendum.

BACKGROUND

The Constitution of Ireland replaced the Constitution of the Irish Free State which had been in effect since the independence of the Irish state from the United Kingdom on 6 December 1922. There were two main motivations for replacing the constitution in 1937. Firstly, the Statute of Westminster 1931 granted parliamentary autonomy to the six British Dominions (now known as Commonwealth realms) within a Commonwealth of Nations. The Irish Free State constitution of 1922 was, in the eyes of many, associated with the controversial Anglo-Irish Treaty. The largest political group in the anti-treaty faction, who opposed the treaty initially by force of arms, had boycotted the institutions of the new Irish Free State until 1926. In 1932 they were elected into power as the Fianna Fáil party.

After 1932, under the provisions of the Statute, some of the articles of the original Constitution which were required by the Anglo-Irish Treaty were dismantled by acts of the Oireachtas of the Irish Free State. Such amendments removed references to the Oath of Allegiance, appeals to the United Kingdom's Judicial Committee of the Privy Council, the British Crown and the Governor General. The sudden abdication of Edward VIII in December 1936 was quickly used to redefine the royal connection.[42] Nevertheless, the Fianna Fáil government, led by Éamon de Valera, still desired to replace the constitutional document they saw as having been imposed by the UK government in 1922.

The second motive for replacing the original constitution was primarily symbolic. De Valera wanted to put an Irish stamp on the institutions of government, and chose to do this in particular through the use of Irish Gaelic nomenclature.

DRAFTING PROCESS

De Valera personally supervised the writing of the Constitution. It was drafted initially by John Hearne, legal adviser to the Department of External Affairs (now called the Department of Foreign Affairs). It was translated into Irish over a number of drafts by a group headed by Micheál Ó Gríobhtha (assisted by Risteárd Ó Foghludha), who worked in the Irish Department of Education. De Valera served as his own External Affairs Minister, hence the use of the Department's Legal Advisor, with whom he had previously worked closely, as opposed to the Attorney General or someone from the Department of the President of the Executive Council. He also received significant input from John Charles McQuaid, the Archbishop of Dublin, on religious, educational, family and social welfare issues.

There are a number of instances where the texts in English and Irish clash, a potential dilemma which the Constitution resolves by favoring the Irish text even though English is more commonly used in the official sphere.

A draft of the constitution was presented personally to the Vatican for review and comment on two occasions by the Department Head at External Relations, Joseph P. Walsh. Prior to its tabling in Dáil Éireann and presentation to the Irish electorate in a plebiscite, Vatican Secretary of State Eugenio Cardinal Pacelli, the future Pope Pius XII, said about the final amended draft "We do not approve, neither do we disapprove; We shall maintain silence."[43] The quid pro quo for this indulgence of the Catholic Church's interests in Ireland was the degree of respectability which it conferred on De Valera's formerly denounced republican faction and its reputation as the 'semi-constitutional' political wing of the 'irregular' anti-treaty forces.

ENACTMENT

The text of the draft constitution, with minor amendments, was approved on 14 June by Dáil Éireann (then the sole house of parliament, the Senate having been abolished the previous year).

The draft constitution was then put to a plebiscite on 1 July 1937 (the same day as the 1937 general election), when it was passed by a plurality. 56% of voters were in favour, comprising 38.6% of the whole electorate. The constitution formally came into force on 29 December 1937.

Among the groups who opposed the constitution were supporters of Fine Gael and the Labour Party, Unionists, and some independents and feminists. The question put to voters was simply "Do you approve of the Draft Constitution which is the subject of this plebiscite?".

Plebiscite on the Constitution of Ireland[44]		
Choice	**Votes**	**Percentage**
✓ **Yes**	**685,105**	**56.52%**
No	526,945	43.48%
Valid votes	1,212,050	90.03%
Invalid or blank votes	134,157	9.97%
Total votes	**1,346,207**	**100.00%**
Voter turnout	75.84%	
Electorate	1,775,055	

INTERNATIONAL RESPONSE

When the new constitution was enacted, the British government, according to the New York Times "contented itself with a legalistic protest".[45] Its protest took the form of a communiqué on 30 December 1937 in which the British stated:[46][47][48]

His Majesty's Government in the United Kingdom has considered the position created by the new Constitution ... of the Irish Free State, in future to be described under the Constitution as 'Eire' or 'Ireland' ... [and] cannot recognize that the adoption of the name 'Eire' or 'Ireland', or any other provision of those articles [of the Irish constitution], involves any right to territory ... forming part of the United Kingdom of Great Britain and Northern Ireland ... They therefore regard the use of the name 'Eire' or 'Ireland' in this connection as relating only to that area which has hitherto been known as the Irish Free State.

The Irish Government received a message of goodwill from 268 United States congressmen including eight senators. The signatories expressed "their ardent congratulations on the birth of the State of Ireland and the consequent coming into effect of the new constitution", adding that

"We regard the adoption of the new constitution and the emergence of the State of Ireland as events of the utmost importance."[49]

MAIN PROVISIONS

The official text of the Constitution consists of a Preamble and fifty Articles arranged under sixteen headings. Its overall length is approximately 16,000 words. The headings are:

1. The Nation (Arts. 1–3)
2. The State (Arts. 4–11)
3. The President (Arts. 12–14)
4. The National Parliament (Arts. 15–27)
5. The Government (Art. 28)
6. Local Government (Art. 28A)
7. International Relations (Art. 29)
8. The Attorney General (Art. 30)
9. The Council of State (Arts. 31–32)
10. The Comptroller and Auditor General (Art. 33)
11. The Courts (Arts. 34–37)
12. Trial of Offences (Arts. 38–39)
13. Fundamental Rights (Arts. 40–44)
14. Directive Principles of Social Policy (Art. 45)
15. Amendment of the Constitution (Art. 46)
16. The Referendum (Art. 47)
17. Repeal of Constitution of Saorstát Éireann and Continuance of Laws (Arts. 48–50)

The Constitution also includes a number of "Transitory Provisions" (Arts. 51–63) which have, in accordance with their terms, been omitted from all official texts since 1941. These provisions are still in force but are now mostly spent.

CHARACTERISTICS OF THE NATION AND STATE

- **National sovereignty**: The constitution asserts the "inalienable, indefeasible, and sovereign right" of the Irish people to self-determination (Article 1). The state is declared to be "sovereign, independent, [and] democratic" (Article 5).

- **Popular sovereignty**: It is stated that all powers of government "derive, under God, from the people" (Article 6.1). However, it is also stated that those powers "are exercisable only by or on the authority of the organs of State" established by the Constitution (Article 6.2).

- **Name of the state**: The Constitution declares that "[the] name of the State is Éire, or, in the English language, Ireland" (Article 4). Under the Republic of Ireland Act 1948 the term "Republic of Ireland" is the official "description" of the state; the Oireachtas, however, has left unaltered "Ireland" as the formal name of the state as defined by the Constitution.

- **United Ireland**: Article 2, as substituted after the Good Friday Agreement, asserts that "every person born in the island of Ireland" has the right "to be part of the Irish Nation"; however, Article 9.2 now limits this to persons having at least one parent as an Irish citizen. Article 3 declares that it is the "firm will of the Irish Nation" to bring about a united Ireland, provided that this occurs "only by peaceful means", and only with the express consent of the majority of the people in Northern Ireland.

- **National flag**: The national flag is defined as "the tricolour of green, white and orange" (Article 7).

- **Capital city**: The Houses of the Oireachtas (parliament) must usually meet in or near Dublin (Article 15.1.3°) ("or in such other place as they may from time to time determine"), and the President's official residence must be in or near the city (Article 12.11.1°).

LANGUAGES

Article 8 of the Constitution states:

1. The Irish language as the national language is the first official language.
2. The English language is recognized as a second official language.
3. Provision may, however, be made by law for the exclusive use of either of the said languages for any one or more official purposes, either throughout the State or in any part thereof.

Interpretation of these provisions has been contentious. The Constitution itself is enrolled in both languages, and in case of conflict the Irish language version takes precedence, even though in practice the Irish text is a translation of the English rather than vice versa. The 1937 Constitution introduced some Irish-language terms into English, such as Taoiseach and Tánaiste, while others, such as Oireachtas, had been used in the Free State Constitution. The use in English of Éire, the Irish-language name of the state, is deprecated.

ORGANS OF GOVERNMENT

The Constitution establishes a government under a parliamentary system. It provides for a directly elected, largely ceremonial President of Ireland (Article 12), a head of government called the Taoiseach (Article 28), and a national parliament called the Oireachtas (Article 15). The Oireachtas has a dominant directly elected lower house known as Dáil Éireann (Article 16) and an upper house Seanad Éireann (Article 18), which is partly appointed, partly indirectly elected and partly elected by a limited electorate. There is also an independent judiciary headed by the Supreme Court (Article 34).

NATIONAL EMERGENCY

Under Article 28.3.3° the Constitution grants the state sweeping powers "in time of war or armed rebellion", which may (if so resolved by both Houses of the Oireachtas) include an armed conflict in which the state is not a direct participant. During a national emergency the Oireachtas may pass laws that would otherwise be unconstitutional, and the actions of the executive cannot be found to be ultra vires or unconstitutional provided they at least "purport" to be in pursuance of such a law. However, the constitutional prohibition on the death penalty (Article 15.5.2°), introduced by an amendment made in 2001, is an absolute exception to these powers.

There have been two national emergencies since 1937: an emergency declared in 1939 to cover the threat to national security posed as a consequence of World War II (although the state remained formally neutral throughout that conflict), and an emergency declared in 1976 to deal with the threat to the security of the state posed by the Provisional IRA.

INTERNATIONAL RELATIONS

- **European Union**: Under Article 29.4.6° EU law takes precedence over the Constitution if there is a conflict between the two, but only to the extent that such EU law is "necessitated" by Ireland's membership. The Supreme Court has ruled that any EU Treaty that substantially alters the character of the Union must be approved by a constitutional amendment. For this reason separate provisions of Article 29 have permitted the state to ratify the Single European Act, Maastricht Treaty, Amsterdam Treaty, Nice Treaty and Treaty of Lisbon.

- **International law**: Under Article 29.6 international treaties to which the state is a party are not to be considered part of Ireland's domestic law unless the Oireachtas has so provided. Under Article 29.3 it is declared that the state "accepts the generally recognised principles of international law as its rule of conduct in its relations with other States", but the High Court has ruled that this provision is merely aspirational, and not enforceable.

INDIVIDUAL RIGHTS

AS ENUMERATED UNDER THE HEADING "FUNDAMENTAL RIGHTS"

- **Equality before the law**: Equality of all citizens before the law is guaranteed by Article 40.1.

- **Prohibition on titles of nobility**: The state may not confer titles of nobility, and no citizen may accept such a title without the permission of the Government (Article 40.2). In practice, governmental approval is usually a formality.

- **Personal rights**: The state is bound to protect "the personal rights of the citizen", and in particular to defend "the life, person, good name, and property rights of every citizen" (Article 40.3).

- **Unremunerated rights**: The language used in Article 40.3.1° has been interpreted by the courts as implying the existence of unremunerated rights afforded to Irish citizens under natural law. Such rights upheld by the courts have included the right to marital privacy and the right of the unmarried mother to custody of her child.

- **Prohibition of abortion**: Abortion is prohibited by Article 40.3.3°, except in cases in which there is a threat to the life of the mother. However, this prohibition may be lawfully circumvented as it is expressly stated not to interfere with the right to travel abroad; there also exists a qualified right to obtain and distribute information of "services lawfully available in another state" (such as abortion).

- **Habeas corpus**: The citizen's right to personal liberty is guaranteed by Article 40.4, which section also sets out in detail the procedure for obtaining habeas corpus. However, these rights are specifically excepted from applying to the actions of the Defence Forces during a "state of war or armed rebellion" (Article 40.4.5°). Since the Sixteenth Amendment it has also been constitutional for a court to deny bail to someone charged with a crime where "it is reasonably considered necessary", to prevent that person from committing a "serious offence" (Article 40.4.6°).

- **Inviolability of the home**: A citizen's home may not be forcibly entered, except as permitted by law (Article 40.5).

- **Freedom of speech**: Subject to "public order and morality", a qualified right of freedom of speech is guaranteed by Article 40.6.1°. However, "the State shall endeavor to ensure that organs of public opinion" (such as the news media) "shall not be used to undermine public order or morality or the authority of the State". Furthermore, "the publication or utterance of blasphemous, seditious, or indecent matter" is specifically stated to be a criminal offence. In Corway v. Independent Newspapers (1999), the Supreme Court dismissed an attempt to bring a prosecution for blasphemy on the basis that, amongst other things, no coherent definition of the offence was provided by law. Such a definition is now provided by the Defamation Act 2009 which defines it as the publication of matter "grossly abusive or insulting in relation to matters held sacred by any religion, thereby [intentionally] causing outrage among a substantial number of the adherents of that religion".

- **Freedom of peaceful assembly**: Subject to "public order and morality", the right of citizens to peaceful assembly "without arms" is guaranteed by Article 40.6.1°. However, the Oireachtas is empowered to limit this right by law when a meeting may be "calculated to cause a breach of the peace or to be a danger or nuisance to the general public"; the Oireachtas is similarly empowered to limit this right in relation to meetings held "in the vicinity" of either House.

- **Freedom of association**: Subject to "public order and morality", the right of citizens "to form associations and unions" is also guaranteed by Article 40.6.1°; however, the exercise of this right may be regulated by law "in the public interest".

- **Family and home life**: Under Article 41.1 the state promises to "protect the Family", and recognizes the family as having "inalienable and imprescriptibly rights, antecedent and superior to all positive law". Under Article 41.2 the state is required to ensure that "economic necessity" does not oblige a mother "to engage in labour to the neglect of [her] duties in the home". Article 41.3 sets out conditions that must be fulfilled before a court may grant a divorce, including that adequate financial provision has been made for both spouses and any of their children.

- **Education**: Article 42 guarantees parents the right to determine where their children shall be educated (including at home), provided a minimum standard is met. Under the same article the state must provide for free primary level education. Currently Irish law also guarantees free second and third level education.

- **Private property**: The right to own and transfer private property is guaranteed by Article 43, subject to "the principles of social justice", and in accordance with laws passed reconciling the right "with the exigencies of the common good" (Article 43).

- **Religious freedom**: A citizen's freedom of religious conscience, practice, and worship is guaranteed, "subject to public order and morality", by Article 44.2.1°. The state may not "endow" any religion (Article 44.2.2°), nor discriminate on religious grounds (Article 44.2.3°).

(v) CANADIAN CONSTITUTION:

The **Constitution of Canada** is the supreme law in Canada; the country's constitution is an amalgamation of codified acts and uncodified traditions and conventions. It is one of the oldest working constitutions in the world, with a basis in the Magna Carta.[50] The constitution outlines Canada's system of government, as well as the civil rights of all Canadian citizens and those in Canada. Interpretation of the Constitution is called Canadian constitutional law.

The composition of the Constitution of Canada is defined in subsection 52(2) of the Constitution Act, 1982 as consisting of the Canada Act 1982 (including the Constitution Act, 1982), all acts and orders referred to in the schedule (including the Constitution Act, 1867, formerly The British North America Act, 1867), and any amendments to these documents. The Supreme Court of Canada held that the list is not exhaustive and includes a number of pre-confederation acts and unwritten components as well.[51] See list of Canadian constitutional documents for details.

HISTORY

The first semblance of a constitution for Canada was the Royal Proclamation of 1763. The act renamed the northeasterly portion of the former French province of New France as Province of Quebec, roughly coextensive with the southern third of contemporary Quebec. The proclamation, which established an appointed colonial government, was the de facto constitution of Quebec until 1774, when the British parliament passed the Quebec Act, which expanded the province's boundaries to the Ohio and Mississippi Rivers, which was one of the grievances listed in the United States Declaration of Independence. Significantly, the Quebec Act also replaced the French criminal law presumption of guilty until proven innocent with the English criminal law presumption of innocent until proven guilty; but the French code or civil law system was retained for non-criminal matters.

The Treaty of Paris of 1783 ended the American War of Independence and sent a wave of British loyalist refugees northward to Quebec and Nova Scotia. In 1784, the two provinces were divided; Nova Scotia was split into Nova Scotia, Cape Breton Island (rejoined to Nova Scotia in 1820), Prince Edward Island, and New Brunswick, while Quebec was split into Lower Canada (southern Quebec) and Upper Canada (southern through lower northern Ontario). The winter of 1837–38 saw rebellion in both of the Canadas, with the result they were rejoined as the Province of Canada in 1841. This was reversed by the British North America Act in 1867 which established the Dominion of Canada.

Initially, on 1 July 1867, there were four provinces in confederation as "One dominion under the name of Canada": Canada West (former Upper Canada, now Ontario), Canada East (former

Lower Canada, now Quebec), Nova Scotia, and New Brunswick. Title to the Northwest Territories was transferred by the Hudson's Bay Company in 1870 and the province of Manitoba (the first to be established by the Parliament of Canada) was in the same year the first created out of it. British Columbia joined confederation in 1871, followed by Prince Edward Island in 1873. The Yukon Territory was created by Parliament in 1898, followed by Alberta and Saskatchewan in 1905. The Dominion of Newfoundland, Britain's oldest colony in the Americas, joined Canada as a province in 1949. Nunavut was created in 1999.

An Imperial Conference in 1926 that included the leaders of all Dominions and representatives from India (which then included Burma, Bangladesh, and Pakistan), led to the eventual creation of the Statute of Westminster in 1931. The statute, an essential transitory step from the British Empire to the Commonwealth of Nations, provided that all existing Dominions became fully independent of the United Kingdom (upon its ratification by the federal legislature for Canada) and all new Dominions would be fully independent upon the grant of Dominion status. Newfoundland never ratified the statute, so it was still subject to imperial authority when its entire system of government and economy collapsed in the mid-1930s. Canada did ratify the statute, but had requested an exception because the Canadian federal and provincial governments could not agree on an amending formula for the Canadian constitution. It would be another 50 years before this was achieved. In the interim, the British parliament periodically passed enabling acts with respect to amendments to Canada's constitution; this was never anything but a rubber stamp.[52]

The patriation of the Canadian constitution was achieved in 1982 when the British and Canadian parliaments passed parallel acts: the Canada Act, 1982 ([UK] 1982, c.11), in London, and the Constitution Act, 1982, in Ottawa. Thereafter, the United Kingdom was formally absolved of any remaining responsibility for, or jurisdiction over, Canada and Canada became responsible for her own destiny. In a formal ceremony on Parliament Hill in Ottawa, Queen Elizabeth II signed both acts into law on 17 April 1982. The Canada Act/Constitution Act included the Canadian Charter of Rights and Freedoms. Prior to the charter, there were various statutes which protected an assortment of civil rights and obligations, but nothing was enshrined in the constitution until 1982. The charter has thus placed a strong focus upon individual and collective rights of the people of Canada.

Enactment of the Charter of Rights and Freedoms has also fundamentally changed much of Canadian constitutional law. The Magna Carta, which has constitutional status in Canada, was occasionally called into service in legal argument. Since 1982, however, the arguments have been easier to make, because lawyers have been able to cite the relevant sections of the constitution rather than rely upon legal abstraction. The act also codified many previously oral constitutional conventions and has made amendment of the constitution significantly more difficult. Previously, the Canadian federal constitution could be amended by solitary act of the Canadian or British parliaments, by formal or informal agreement between the federal and provincial governments, or even simply by adoption as ordinary custom of an oral convention or unwritten tradition that was perceived to be the best way to do something. Since the act, amendments must now conform to certain specified provisions in the written portion of the Canadian constitution.

CONSTITUTION ACT, 1867

This was an Act of the British parliament, originally called the British North America Act 1867. It outlined Canada's system of government, which combines Britain's Westminster model of parliamentary government with division of sovereignty (federalism). Although it is the first of 20 British North America Acts, it is still the most famous of these and is understood to be the document of Canadian Confederation. With the patriation of the Constitution in 1982, this Act was renamed Constitution Act, 1867. In recent years, the 1867 document has mainly served as the basis on which the division of powers between the provinces and federal government has been analyzed.

CONSTITUTION ACT, 1982

Endorsed by all provincial governments except that of Quebec (led by René Lévesque), this was the formal Canadian Act of Parliament that achieved full and final political independence from the United Kingdom. Part V of this act established an amending formula for the Canadian constitution, the lack of which (due to more than 50 years of disagreement between the federal and provincial governments) was the only reason Canada's constitutional amendments still required approval by the British parliament after ratification of the Statute of Westminster in 1931.

In UK, the parallel act passed simultaneously by the British parliament was called the Canada Act 1982. As a bilingual act of parliament, the Canada Act 1982 has the distinction of being the only legislation in French that has been passed by an English or British parliament since Norman French (Law French) ceased to be the language of government in England.

SOURCES OF THE CONSTITUTION

There are three general methods of constitutional entrenchment:

1. Specific mention as a constitutional document in section 52(2) of the Constitution Act, 1982, such as the Constitution Act, 1867.
2. Constitutional entrenchment of an otherwise statutory English, British, or Canadian document because of subject matter provisions in the amending formula of the

Constitution Act, 1982, such as provisions with regard to the monarchy in the English Bill of Rights 1689[53][54] or the Act of Settlement 1701. English and British statutes are part of Canadian law because of the Colonial Laws Validity Act, 1865, section 129 of the Constitution Act, 1867, and the Statute of Westminster 1931. Those laws then became entrenched when the amending formula was made part of the constitution.

3. Reference by an entrenched document, such as the Preamble of the Constitution Act, 1867's entrenchment of written and unwritten principles from the constitution of the United Kingdom or the Constitution Act, 1982's reference of the Proclamation of 1763.

UNWRITTEN SOURCES

The existence of an unwritten constitution was reaffirmed by the Supreme Court in Reference re Secession of Quebec.

"The Constitution is more than a written text. It embraces the entire global system of rules and principles which govern the exercise of constitutional authority. A superficial reading of selected provisions of the written constitutional enactment, without more, may be misleading."

In practice, there have been three sources of unwritten constitutional law:

CONVENTIONS

Constitutional conventions form part of the constitution, but they are not legally enforceable. They include the existence of a prime minister and Cabinet, the fact that the governor general in most circumstances is required to grant Royal Assent to bills adopted by both houses of parliament, and the requirement that the prime minister either resign or request a dissolution and general election upon losing a vote of confidence in the House of Commons.

ROYAL PREROGATIVE

Reserve powers of the Canadian Crown, being remnants of the powers once held by the British Crown, reduced over time by the parliamentary system. Primarily, these are the Orders in Council, which give the government the authority to declare war, conclude treaties, issue passports, make appointments, make regulations, incorporate, and receive lands that escheat to the Crown.

UNWRITTEN PRINCIPLES

Principles that are incorporated into the Canadian constitution by reference from the preamble of the Constitution Act, 1867, including a statement that the constitution is "similar in Principle to that of the United Kingdom", much of which is unwritten. Unlike conventions, they are legally binding. Amongst the recognized constitutional principles are federalism, liberal democracy, constitutionalism, the rule of law, and respect for minorities.[55] Other principles include responsible government, representation by population,[56] judicial independence, parliamentary supremacy,[57] and an implied bill of rights. In one case, the Provincial Judges Reference (1997), it was found a law can be held invalid for contradicting unwritten principles, in this case judicial independence.

(VI) SOVIET CONSTITUTION:

There were three versions of the constitution of the Soviet Union, modeled after the 1918 Constitution established by the Russian Socialist Federative Soviet Republic (RSFSR), the immediate predecessor of the Union of Soviet Socialist Republics.

CHRONOLOGY OF SOVIET CONSTITUTIONS

These three constitutions were:

- 1924 Soviet Constitution
- 1936 Soviet Constitution
- 1977 Soviet Constitution

These constitutions had most provisions in common. These provisions declared the leadership of the working class and, in the latter two, the leading role of the CPSU in government and society. All the constitutions upheld the forms of social property. Each of the constitutions called for a system of soviets, or councils, to exercise governmental authority.

1924 SOVIET CONSTITUTION

The **1924 Soviet Constitution** legitimated the December 1922 Treaty on the Creation of the USSR between the Russian SFSR, the Ukrainian SSR, the Belarusian SSR, and the Transcaucasian SFSR to form the Union of Soviet Socialist Republics.

In essence, it was but an expansion of the Treaty, as most of the key points were already outlined there. The Constitution contained the identical to the Treaty Declaration, reflecting the current world order, and the common good causes of such a Union, allowing for a potential expansion.

Whereas the original Treaty contained only 26 articles, the Constitution now encompassed 72, divided into eleven chapters. Ratified by the Second Congress of Soviets of the Soviet Union 31 January 1924, it survived six editions, before being superseded by the 1936 Soviet Constitution.

It established the Congress of Soviets to be the supreme body of state authority, with the Central Executive Committee holding this authority in the interim. The Central Executive

Committee is divided into the Soviet of the Union, which would represent the constituent republics, and the Soviet of Nationalities, which would represent the interests of nationality groups. The Presidium of the Central Executive Committee served as the collective presidency. Between sessions of the Central Executive Committee, the Presidium supervised the government administration. The Central Executive Committee also elected the Sovnarkom, which served as the executive arm of the government.

1936 SOVIET CONSTITUTION

The 1936 Soviet constitution, adopted on December 5, 1936, and also known as the Stalin constitution, redesigned the government of the Soviet Union.

Beginning in 1936, December 5 was celebrated as Soviet Constitution day in the USSR until the 1977 Soviet Constitution moved the day to October 7. Before 1936, there was no Soviet Constitution day.[58]

BASIC PROVISIONS

The constitution repealed restrictions on voting and added universal direct suffrage and the right to work to rights guaranteed by the previous constitution. In addition, the Constitution recognized collective social and economic rights including the rights to work, rest and leisure, health protection, care in old age and sickness, housing, education, and cultural benefits. The constitution also provided for the direct election of all government bodies and their reorganization into a single, uniform system. It was written by a special commission of 31 members which Joseph Stalin chaired. Those who participated included (among others) Andrei Vyshinsky, Andrei Zhdanov, Maksim Litvinov, Kliment Voroshilov, Vyacheslav Molotov, Lazar Kaganovich, Nikolai Bukharin and Karl Radek, though the latter two had less active input.[59]

NOMENCLATURE CHANGES

The 1936 constitution replaced the Congress of Soviets of the Soviet Union and its Central Executive Committee by the Supreme Soviet of the Union of Soviet Socialist Republics. Like its predecessor, the Supreme Soviet contained two chambers: the Soviet of the Union and the Soviet of Nationalities. The constitution empowered the Supreme Soviet to elect commissions, which performed most of the Supreme Soviet's work. As under the former constitution, the Presidium of the Supreme Soviet exercised the full powers of the Supreme Soviet between sessions and had the right to interpret laws. The Chairman of the Presidium of the Supreme Soviet became the titular head of state. The Sovnarkom (after 1946 known as the Council of Ministers) continued to act as the executive arm of the government.

Of the four Soviet constitutions, the 1936 constitution survived longest. It was amended in 1944 but replaced in 1977. (See 1977 Soviet Constitution.)

LEADING ROLE OF COMMUNIST PARTY

For the first time, the role of the Communist Party was clearly defined. Article 126 stated that the party was "vanguard of the working people in their struggle to strengthen and develop the socialist system and is the leading core of all organizations of the working people, both public and state." This provision was used to justify banning all other parties from functioning in the Soviet Union.

SOVIET PORTRAYAL AND LIBERAL CRITICISM

The constitution provided economic rights not included in constitutions in the western democracies. The constitution was presented as a personal triumph for Stalin, who on this occasion was described by Pravda as "genius of the new world, the wisest man of the epoch, the great leader of communism." Western historians and historians from former Soviet countries have seen the constitution as a propaganda document. Leonard Schapiro, for example, writes that "The decision to alter the electoral system from indirect to direct election, from a limited to a universal franchise, and from open to secret voting, was a measure of the confidence of the party in its ability to ensure the return of candidates of its own choice without the restrictions formerly considered necessary," and that "...a careful scrutiny of the draft of the new constitution showed that it left the party's supreme position unimpaired, and was therefore worthless as a guarantee of individual rights."[60]

FREEDOM OF RELIGION

Article 124 of the constitution guaranteed freedom of religion, the inclusion of which was opposed by large segments of the Communist Party. The article resulted in members of the Russian Orthodox Church petitioning to reopen closed churches, gain access to jobs that had been closed to them as religious figures, and the attempt to run religious candidates in the 1937 elections.[61]

REORGANIZATION OF THE ARMED FORCES AND THE REPUBLICS

The 1944 amendments to the 1936 Constitution established separate branches of the Red Army for each Soviet Republic. They also established Republic-level commissariats for foreign affairs and defense, allowing them to be recognized as sovereign states in international law. This allowed for two Soviet Republics, Ukraine and Byelorussia, to join the United Nations General Assembly as founding members in 1945.[62][63]

1977 SOVIET CONSTITUTION

At the Seventh (Special) Session of the Supreme Soviet of the USSR Ninth Convocation on October 7, 1977, the third and last Soviet Constitution, also known as the Brezhnev Constitution, was unanimously adopted. The official name of the Constitution was "Constitution (Fundamental Law) of the Union of Soviet Socialist Republics" (Russian: Конститу́ция (Основно́й Зако́н) Сою́за Сове́тских Социалисти́ческих Респу́блик).

The preamble stated that "the aims of the dictatorship of the proletariat having been fulfilled, the Soviet state has become the state of the whole people." Compared with previous constitutions, the Brezhnev Constitution extended the bounds of constitutional regulation of society. The first chapter defined the leading role of the Communist Party of the Soviet Union (CPSU) and established principles for the management of the state and the government. Article 1 defined the USSR as a socialist state, as did all previous constitutions:

> "The Union of Soviet Socialist Republics is a socialist state of the whole people, expressing the will and interests of the workers, peasants, and intelligentsia, the working people of all the nations and nationalities of the country".

The difference is that, according to the new Constitution, the government no longer represented the workers and peasants alone. Later chapters established principles for economic management and cultural relations.

The 1977 Constitution was long and detailed. It included twenty-eight more articles than the 1936 Soviet Constitution. The Constitution explicitly defined the division of responsibilities between the central and republic governments. For example, the Constitution placed the regulation of boundaries and administrative divisions within the jurisdiction of the republics. However, provisions established the rules under which the republics could make such changes. Thus, the Constitution concentrated on the operation of the government system as a whole.

Just like all preceding versions of the Soviet Constitution, the 1977 Constitution preserved the right of constituent Soviet republics to secede from the Union; this provision would later play an important role in the dissolution of the Soviet Union.

Since 1977 7 October was celebrated as Soviet Constitution day in the USSR.[64] It was never observed in the Ukrainian SSR.[65] The previous date for Soviet Constitution day had been 5 December from 1936 after the day the 1936 Soviet Constitution had been adopted.[66]

CONSTITUTIONAL RIGHTS

The Soviet Constitution included a series of civil and political rights. Among these were the rights to freedom of speech, freedom of press, and freedom of assembly and the right to religious belief and worship. In addition, the Constitution provided for freedom of artistic work, protection of the family, inviolability of the person and home, and the right to privacy. In line with the Marxist-Leninist ideology of the government, the Constitution also granted social and economic rights not provided by constitutions in some capitalist nations. Among these were the rights to work, rest and leisure, health protection, care in old age and sickness, housing, education, and cultural benefits.

Unlike Western constitutions, the Soviet Constitution outlined limitations on political rights, whereas in democratic countries these limitations are usually left up to the legislative and/or judicial institutions. Article 6 effectively eliminated partisan opposition and division within government by granting to the CPSU the power to lead and guide society. Article 39 enabled the government to prohibit any activities it considered detrimental by stating that "Enjoyment of the rights and freedoms of citizens must not be to the detriment of the interests of society or the state." Article 59 obliged citizens to obey the laws and comply with the standards of socialist society as determined by the party. The government did not treat as inalienable those political and socioeconomic rights the Constitution granted to the people. Citizens enjoyed rights only when the exercise of those rights did not interfere with the interests of the state, and the CPSU alone had the power and authority to determine policies for the government and society. For example, the right to freedom of expression contained in Article 52 could be suspended if the exercise of that freedom failed to be in accord with party policies. Until the era of glasnost, freedom of expression did not entail the right to criticize the government. The constitution did provide a "freedom of conscience, that is, the right to profess or not to profess any religion, and to conduct religious worship or atheistic propaganda." It prohibited incitement of hatred or hostility on religious grounds.

The Constitution also failed to provide political and judicial mechanisms for the protection of rights. Thus, the Constitution lacked explicit guarantees protecting the rights of the people. In fact, the Supreme Soviet has never introduced amendments specifically designed to protect individual rights. Neither did the people have a higher authority within the government to which to appeal when they believed their rights had been violated. The Supreme Court had no power to ensure that constitutional rights were observed by legislation or were respected by the rest of the government. The Soviet Union also signed the Final Act of the Conference on Security and Cooperation in Europe (Helsinki Accords), which mandated that internationally recognized human rights be respected in the signatory countries. In the late 1980s, however, realigning constitutional and domestic law with international commitments on human rights was publicly debated.

ROLE OF THE CITIZEN

Article 59 of the Constitution stated that citizens' exercise of their rights was inseparable from performance of their duties. Articles 60 through 69 defined these duties. Citizens were required to work and to observe labor discipline. The legal code labeled evasion of work as "parasitism" and provided punishment for this crime. The Constitution also obliged citizens to protect socialist property and oppose corruption. All citizens performed military service as a duty to safeguard and "enhance the power and prestige of the Soviet state." Violation of this duty was considered "a betrayal of the motherland and the gravest of crimes". Finally, the Constitution required parents to train their children for socially useful work and to raise them as worthy members of socialist society.

The Constitution and other legislation protected and enforced Soviet citizenship. Legislation on citizenship granted equal rights of citizenship to naturalized citizens as well as to the native born. Laws also specified that citizens could not freely renounce their citizenship. Citizens were required to apply for permission to do so from the Presidium of the Supreme Soviet, which could reject the application if the applicant had not completed military service, had judicial duties, or was responsible for family dependants. In addition, the Presidium could refuse the application to protect national security, or revoke citizenship for defamation of the Soviet Union or for acts damaging to national prestige or security.

CRITICS OF SOVIET CONSTITUTION

Several Soviet professionals criticized the project of the Constitution of 1977,[67] but such critiques were not taken into account and were not published in time; during the Brezhnev stagnation, only publications in favor were allowed.

(VII) FRENCH CONSTITUTION:

The current Constitution of France was adopted on 4 October 1958. It is typically called the Constitution of the Fifth Republic, and replaced that of the Fourth Republic dating from 1946. Charles de Gaulle was the main driving force in introducing the new constitution and inaugurating the Fifth Republic, while the text was drafted by Michel Debré. Since then the constitution has been amended eighteen times, most recently in 2008

SUMMARY

The preamble of the constitution recalls the Declaration of the Rights of Man and of the Citizen from 1789 and establishes France as a secular and democratic country, deriving its sovereignty from the people.

It provides for the election of the President and the Parliament, the selection of the Government, and the powers of each and the relations between them. It ensures judicial authority and creates a High Court (a never convened court for judging the President), a Constitutional Council, and an Economic and Social Council. It was designed to create a politically strong President.

It enables the ratification of international treaties and those associated with the European Union. It is unclear whether the wording (especially the reserves of reciprocity) is compatible with European Union law.

The Constitution also sets out methods for its own amendment either by referendum or through a Parliamentary process with Presidential consent. The normal procedure of constitutional amendment is as follows: the amendment must be adopted in identical terms by both houses of Parliament, then must be either adopted by a simple majority in a referendum, or by 3/5 of a joint session of both houses of Parliament (the French Congress) (article 89). However, president Charles de Gaulle bypassed the legislative procedure in 1962 and directly sent a constitutional amendment to a referendum (article 11), which was adopted. This was highly controversial at the time; however, the Constitutional Council ruled that since a referendum expressed the will of the sovereign people, the amendment was adopted.

On 21 July 2008, Parliament passed constitutional reforms championed by President Nicolas Sarkozy by a margin of two votes. These changes, if finalized, introduce a consecutive two-term limit for the presidency, give parliament a veto over some presidential appointments, end government control over parliament's committee system, allow parliament to set its own agenda, allow the president to address parliament in-session, and end the president's right of collective pardon. (See French constitutional law of 23 July 2008)[68]

IMPACT ON PERSONAL FREEDOMS

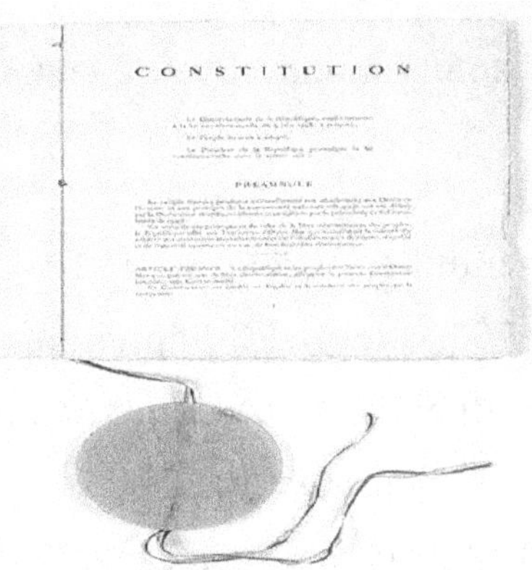

CONSTITUTION OF FRANCE (1958)

Prior to 1971, though executive, administrative and judicial decisions had to comply with the general principles of law (jurisprudence derived from law and the practice of law in general), there were no such restrictions on legislation. It was assumed that unelected judges and other appointees should not be able to overrule laws voted for by the directly elected French parliament.

In 1971, a landmark decision by the Constitutional Council (71-44DC[69]) cited the preamble of the Constitution and its references to the principles laid in the Declaration of the Rights of Man and of the Citizen as a reason for rejecting a law that, according to the Council, violated one of these principles. Since then, it is assumed that the "constitutional block" includes not only the Constitution, but also the other texts referred to in its preamble: the Declaration, but also the preamble of the 1946 Constitution (which adds a number of "social rights", as well as the equality of males and females) and the Environment Charter of 2004.

Since then, the possibility of sending laws before the Council has been extended. In practice, the political opposition sends all controversial laws before it.

AMENDMENTS

The Constitution defines in Article 89 the rules for amending itself. First, a constitutional bill must be approved by both houses of Parliament. Then, the bill must be approved by the Congress, a special joint session of both houses; alternatively, the bill can be submitted to a referendum.

In 1962, president Charles de Gaulle controversially submitted a bill to a referendum through another procedure defined at article 11 of the Constitution – see French presidential election referendum, 1962. This procedure has never been used since then for constitutional changes.

PAST CONSTITUTIONS

France has had numerous past constitutions.

- The ancien régime was an absolute monarchy and lacked a formal constitution; the régime essentially relied on custom.

- The Revolutionary Era saw a number of constitutions:
  - The Constitution of 1791, adopted 3 September 1791, established the Kingdom of the French, a constitutional monarchy, and the Legislative Assembly
  - The Girondin constitutional project in process of being adopted before the coup that lead to the Montagnard faction being in control
  - The Constitution of 1793, ratified 24 June 1793, was ratified but never applied due to the suspension of all ordinary legality 10 October 1793 (under the French First Republic)
  - The Constitution of 1795, adopted 22 August 1795, established the Directory
  - The Constitution of the Year VIII, adopted 24 December 1799, established the Consulate
  - The Constitution of the Year X, adopted 1 August 1802, established the Consulate for Life
  - The Constitution of the Year XII, adopted 18 May 1804, established the First French Empire
- Following the restoration of the Monarchy
  - The Charter of 1814, adopted 4 June 1814, established the Bourbon Restoration
  - The Charter of 1815, adopted 22 April 1815, was used during the Hundred Days
  - The Charter of 1830, adopted 14 August 1830, established the July Monarchy
- 19th century
  - The French Constitution of 1848, adopted 4 November 1848, established the French Second Republic
  - The French Constitution of 1852, adopted 14 January 1852, established the French Second Empire
  - The French Constitutional Laws of 1875 of the French Third Republic, 24 and 25 February, and 16 July 1875

- 20th Century
    - The French Constitutional Law of 1940, adopted 10 July 1940, established Vichy France
    - The French Constitutional Law of 1945, adopted 1945, established the Provisional Government of the French Republic
    - The French Constitution of 1946, adopted 27 October 1946, established the French Fourth Republic
    - The French Constitution of 1958, adopted 4 October 1958, established the French Fifth Republic, current Constitution in force

(VIII) SOUTH AFRICAN CONSTITUTION:

The **Constitution of South Africa** is the supreme law of the country of South Africa. It provides the legal foundation for the existence of the republic, sets out the rights and duties of its citizens, and defines the structure of the government. The current constitution, the country's fifth, was drawn up by the Parliament elected in 1994 in the first non-racial elections. It was promulgated by President Nelson Mandela on 10 December 1996 and came into effect on 4 February 1997, replacing the Interim Constitution of 1993.[70]

Since 1996, the Constitution has been amended by seventeen amendment acts. The Constitution is formally entitled the **"Constitution of the Republic of South Africa, 1996."** It was previously also numbered as if it were an Act of Parliament—Act No. 108 of 1996—but, since the passage of the Citation of Constitutional Laws Act, neither it nor the acts amending it are allocated act numbers.

HISTORY

NEGOTIATIONS

An integral part of the negotiations to end apartheid in South Africa was the creation of a new, non-discriminatory constitution for the country. One of the major disputed issues was the process by which such a constitution would be adopted. The African National Congress (ANC) insisted that it should be drawn up by a democratically-elected constituent assembly, while the governing National Party (NP) feared that the rights of minorities would not be protected in such a process, and proposed instead that the constitution be negotiated by consensus between the parties and then put to a referendum.[71][72]

Formal negotiations began in December 1991 at the Convention for a Democratic South Africa (CODESA). The parties agreed on a process whereby a negotiated transitional constitution would provide for an elected constitutional assembly to draw up a permanent constitution.[71] The CODESA negotiations broke down, however, after the second plenary session in May 1992. One of the major points of dispute was the size of the supermajority that would be required for the assembly to adopt the constitution: The NP wanted a 75 per cent requirement,[72] which would effectively have given it a veto.[71]

In April 1993, the parties returned to negotiations, in what was known as the Multi-Party Negotiating Process (MPNP). A committee of the MPNP proposed the development of a collection of "constitutional principles" with which the final constitution would have to comply, so that basic freedoms would be ensured and minority rights protected, without overly limiting the role of the elected constitutional assembly.[72] The parties to the MPNP adopted this idea and proceeded to draft the Interim Constitution of 1993, which was formally enacted by Parliament and came into force on 27 April 1994.

INTERIM CONSTITUTION

The Interim Constitution provided for a Parliament made up of two houses: a 400-member National Assembly, directly elected by party-list proportional representation, and a ninety-member senate, in which each of the nine provinces was represented by ten senators, elected by the provincial legislature. The Constitutional Assembly consisted of both houses sitting together, and was responsible for drawing up a final constitution within two years. The adoption of a new constitutional text required a two-thirds supermajority in the Constitutional Assembly, as well as the support of two-thirds of senators on matters relating to provincial government. If a two-thirds majority could not be obtained, a constitutional text could be adopted by a simple majority and then put to a national referendum in which sixty per cent support would be required for it to pass.

The Interim Constitution contained 34 constitutional principles with which the new constitution was required to comply. These included multi-party democracy with regular elections and universal adult suffrage, supremacy of the constitution over all other law, a quasi-federal system in place of centralised government, non-racism and non-sexism, the protection of "all universally accepted fundamental rights, freedoms and civil liberties," equality before the law, the separation of powers with an impartial judiciary, provincial and local levels of government with democratic representation, and protection of the diversity of languages and cultures. The Bill of Rights, now in Chapter Two of the Constitution of South Africa, was largely written by Kader Asmal and Albie Sachs. The new constitutional text was to be tested against these principles by the newly established Constitutional Court. If the text complied with the principles, it would become the new constitution; if it did not, it would be referred back to the Constitutional Assembly.

FINAL TEXT

The Constitutional Assembly engaged in a massive public participation programme to solicit views and suggestions from the public. As the deadline for the adoption of a constitutional text approached, however, many issues were hashed out in private meetings between the parties' representatives.[71] On 8 May 1996, a new text was adopted with the support of 86 per cent of the members of the assembly,[72] but in the First Certification judgment, delivered on 6 September 1996, the Constitutional Court refused to certify this text, identifying a number of provisions that did not comply with the constitutional principles.[73]

The Constitutional Assembly reconvened and, on 11 October, adopted an amended constitutional text containing many changes relative to the previous text. Some dealt with the court's reasons for non-certification, while others tightened up the text. The amended text was returned to the Constitutional Court to be certified, which the court duly did in its Second Certification judgment, delivered on 4 December.[74] The Constitution was signed by President Mandela on 10 December and officially published in the Government Gazette on 18 December. It did not come into force immediately; it was brought into operation on 4 February 1997, by a presidential proclamation, except for some financial provisions which were delayed until 1 January 1998.

AMENDMENTS

Section 74 of the Constitution provides that a bill to amend the Constitution can only be passed if at least two-thirds of the members of the National Assembly (that is, at least 267 of the 400 members) vote in favour of it. If the amendment affects provincial powers or boundaries, or if it amends the Bill of Rights, at least six of the nine provinces in the National Council of Provinces must also vote for it. To amend section 1 of the Constitution, which establishes the existence of South Africa as a sovereign, democratic state, and lays out the country's founding values, would require the support of three-quarters of the members of the National Assembly. There have been seventeen amendments since 1996, although one of them is not yet in force.

Amendment	Date of assent	Date of commencement	Brief description
First	28 August 1997	4 February 1997 (retroactive)	Provided that an Acting President need not swear the oath of office again if they had previously served as Acting President. Allowed the President of the Constitutional Court to designate another judge to administer the oath

			of office to the President or Acting President. Extended the cut-off date for deeds which could be considered for amnesty by the Truth and Reconciliation Commission from 6 December 1993 to 11 May 1994.
Second	28 September 1998	7 October 1998	Extended the term of office of municipal councils from four to five years, and modified the schedule for the transformation of local government. Allowed the nomination of alternate members of the Judicial Service Commission to replace unavailable members. Allowed Parliament to assign additional powers to the Public Service Commission. Renamed the Human Rights Commission the South African Human Rights Commission.
Third	20 October 1998	30 October 1998	Allowed the demarcation of municipalities partly in one province and partly in another. Effectively repealed by the 12th Amendment.
Fourth Fifth	17 March 1999	19 March 1999	Clarified that elections to the National Assembly and the provincial legislatures may be called either before or after the term of office of the previous Assembly or legislature has expired. Modified the formula for the allocation to parties of seats in the National Council of Provinces. Allowed the chairperson and deputy chairperson of the Financial and Fiscal Commission to be part-time members. Passed as two separate acts because of the special procedures for provincial matters which applied to some of the changes.
Sixth	20 November 2001	21 November 2001	Renamed Chief Justice to President of the Supreme Court of Appeal, and renamed President of the Constitutional Court to Chief Justice. Allowed an Act of Parliament to extend

			the term of office of a Constitutional Court judge. Permitted the President to appoint two Deputy Ministers from outside the National Assembly. Extended the powers of municipal councils to raise loans.
Seventh	7 December 2001	26 April 2002 / 1 December 2003	Various amendments relating to the passage of financial legislation and the financial relationship between the provincial and national governments.
Eighth	19 June 2002	20 June 2002	Allowed members of municipal councils to cross the floor, that is, to move from one political party to another without losing their seats. Effectively repealed by the 14th and 15th Amendments.
Ninth	19 June 2002	20 June 2002	Provided for the re-allocation of seats in the National Council of Provinces after floor-crossing in provincial legislatures. The Loss or Retention of Membership of National and Provincial Legislatures Act, 2002, which would have allowed floor-crossing in the National Assembly and provincial legislatures, was declared unconstitutional by the Constitutional Court. Effectively repealed by the 14th and 15th Amendments.
Tenth	19 March 2003	20 March 2003	Allowed floor-crossing in the National Assembly and provincial legislatures. Effectively repealed by the 14th and 15th Amendments.
Eleventh	9 April 2003	11 July 2003	Renamed the Northern Province to Limpopo Province. Modified the procedure for national

			government intervention in dysfunctional provincial governments. Expanded the powers of provincial governments to intervene in dysfunctional municipalities.
Twelfth	22 December 2005	1 March 2006	Redefined the boundaries of the provinces in terms of the district and metropolitan municipalities, and repealed the provisions inserted by the 3rd amendment which allowed for cross-boundary municipalities. The community of Matatiele, which had been transferred from KwaZulu-Natal to the Eastern Cape, challenged the amendment before the Constitutional Court, which ruled that the KwaZulu-Natal Legislature had not allowed for the necessary public participation before approving the amendment. The court's order was suspended for eighteen months and Parliament re-enacted the changes in the 13th Amendment.
Thirteenth	13 December 2007	14 December 2007	Re-enacted the transfer of Matatiele from KwaZulu-Natal to the Eastern Cape.
Fourteenth Fifteenth	6 January 2009	17 April 2009	Repealed the floor-crossing provisions added by the 8th, 9th and 10th Amendments, making it impossible for a legislator to cross the floor without losing his or her seat. Passed as two separate acts because of the special procedures for provincial matters which applied to some of the changes.
Sixteenth	25 March 2009	3 April 2009	Transferred the Merafong City Local Municipality from North West province to Gauteng, reversing a change made by the 12th Amendment.
Seventeenth	1 February	23 August 2013	Declared the Chief Justice to be head of the

	2013		judiciary. Allowed the appointment of an acting Deputy Chief Justice. Extended the jurisdiction of the Constitutional Court over non-constitutional matters. Removed the jurisdiction of the Supreme Court of Appeal over appeals from the Labour and Competition Appeal Courts. Restructured the High Courts as divisions of a single High Court of South Africa

PREVIOUS CONSTITUTIONS

The South Africa Act 1909, an act of the Parliament of the United Kingdom, unified four British colonies – Cape Colony, Transvaal Colony, Orange River Colony and Natal Colony – into the Union of South Africa, a self-governing Dominion.

The Republic of South Africa Constitution Act, 1961 transformed the Union into a Republic, replacing the Queen with a State President, but otherwise leaving the system of government unchanged.

The Republic of South Africa Constitution Act, 1983 created the Tricameral Parliament, with separate houses representing white, coloured and Indian people but without representation for black people. The figurehead State President and executive Prime Minister were replaced by an executive State President.

The Constitution of the Republic of South Africa, 1993 or Interim Constitution was introduced at the end of apartheid to govern the period of transition. It introduced universal adult suffrage, constitutional supremacy and a bill of rights.

(IX) JAPANESE CONSTITUTION:

The Constitution of Japan (Shinjitai: 日本国憲法 Kyūjitai: 日本國憲法 Nihon-Koku Kenpō?) is the constitution of Japan. It was enacted on 3 May 1947 as a new constitution for postwar Japan.

PROVISIONS

The constitution has a length of approximately 5,000 words and consists of a preamble and 103 articles grouped into eleven chapters. These are:

- I. The Emperor (Articles 1–8)
- II. Renunciation of War (Article 9)
- III. Rights and Duties of the People (Articles 10–40)

- IV. The Diet (Articles 41–64)
- V. The Cabinet (Articles 65–75)
- VI. Judiciary (Articles 76–82)
- VII. Finance (Articles 83–91)
- VIII. Local Self–Government (Articles 92–95)
- IX. Amendments (Article 96)
- X. Supreme Law (Articles 97–99)
- XI. Supplementary Provisions (Articles 100–103)

PREAMBLE

The constitution contains a firm declaration of the principle of popular sovereignty in the preamble. This is proclaimed in the name of the "Japanese people" and declares that "sovereign power resides with the people" and government is a sacred trust of the people, the authority for which is derived from the people, the powers of which are exercised by the representatives of the people, and the benefits of which are enjoyed by the people.

Part of the purpose of this language is to refute the previous constitutional theory that sovereignty resided in the Emperor. The constitution asserts that the Emperor is merely a symbol and that he derives "his position from the will of the people with whom resides sovereign power" (Article 1). The text of the constitution also asserts the liberal doctrine of fundamental human rights. In particular Article 97 states that the fundamental human rights by this Constitution guaranteed to the people of Japan are fruits of the age-old struggle of man to be free; they have survived the many exacting tests for durability and are conferred upon this and future generations in trust, to be held for all time inviolate.

THE EMPEROR (ARTICLES 1-8)

Under the Constitution, the Emperor carries out most of the functions of a head of state; he formally appoints the Prime Minister and Chief Justice of the Supreme Court, promulgates statutes and treaties and has other enumerated functions. His role is merely ceremonial and, unlike the forms of constitutional monarchy found in some other nations, he possesses no reserve powers. The budget for the maintenance of the imperial household is controlled by resolution of the Diet.

RENUNCIATION OF WAR (ARTICLE 9)

Under Article 9, the "Japanese people forever renounce war as a sovereign right of the nation and the threat or use of force as means of settling international disputes". To this end the article provides that "land, sea, and air forces, as well as other war potential, will never be maintained." The necessity and practical extent of Article 9 has been debated in Japan since its enactment, particularly following the establishment of the Japan Self-Defense Forces, a de facto military force, in 1954. Various political groups have called for either revising or abolishing the restrictions of Article 9 in order to permit collective defense efforts and strengthen Japan's military capabilities.

INDIVIDUAL RIGHTS (ARTICLES 10-40)

"The rights and duties of the people" are prominently featured in the postwar constitution. Altogether, thirty-one of its 103 articles are devoted to describing them in considerable detail, reflecting the commitment to "respect for the fundamental human rights" of the Potsdam Declaration. Although the Meiji Constitution had a section devoted to the "rights and duties of subjects", which guaranteed "liberty of speech, writing, publication, public meetings, and associations", these rights were granted "within the limits of law". Freedom of religious belief was allowed "insofar as it does not interfere with the duties of subjects" (all Japanese were required to acknowledge the Emperor's divinity, and those, such as Christians, who refused to do so out of religious conviction were accused of lèse-majesté). Such freedoms are delineated in the postwar constitution without qualification.

Individual rights under the Japanese constitution are rooted in Article 13 where the constitution asserts the right of the people "to be respected as individuals" and, subject to "the public welfare", to "life, liberty, and the pursuit of happiness." This article's core notion is jinkaku, which represents "the elements of character and personality that come together to define each person as an individual," and which represents the aspects of each individual's life that the government is obligated to respect in the exercise of its power.[75] Article 13 has been used as the basis to establish constitutional rights to privacy, self-determination and the control of one's own image, which rights are not explicitly stated in the constitution.

Subsequent provisions provide for:

- Equality: The constitution guarantees equality before the law and outlaws discrimination against Japanese citizens based on "political, economic or social relations" or "race, creed, sex, social status or family origin" (Article 14). The right to vote cannot be denied on the grounds of "race, creed, sex, social status, family origin, education, property or income" (Article 44). Equality between the sexes is explicitly guaranteed in relation to marriage (Article 24) and childhood education (Article 26).
- Prohibition of peerage: Article 14 forbids the state from recognising peerage. Honours may be conferred but they must not be hereditary or grant special privileges.

- Democratic elections: Article 15 provides that "the people have the inalienable right to choose their public officials and to dismiss them". It guarantees universal adult (in Japan, persons age 20 and older) suffrage and the secret ballot.

- Prohibition of slavery: Guaranteed by Article 18. Involuntary servitude is only permitted as punishment for a crime.

- Separation of Religion and State: The state is prohibited from granting privileges or political authority to a religion, or conducting religious education (Article 20).

- Freedom of assembly, association, speech, and secrecy of communications: All guaranteed without qualification by Article 21, which forbids censorship.

- Workers' rights: Work is declared both a right and obligation by Article 27 which also states that "standards for wages, hours, rest and other working conditions shall be fixed by law" and that children shall not be exploited. Workers have the right to participate in a trade union (Article 28).

- Right to property: Guaranteed subject to the "public welfare". The state may take property for public use if it pays just compensation (Article 29). The state also has the right to levy taxes (Article 30).

- Right to due process: Article 31 provides that no one may be punished "except according to procedure established by law". Article 32, which provides that "No person shall be denied the right of access to the courts," originally drafted to recognize criminal due process rights, is now understood as source of due process rights for civil and administrative law cases.[76]

- Protection against unlawful detention: Article 33 provides that no one may be apprehended without an arrest warrant, save where caught in flagrante delicto. Article 34 guarantees habeas corpus, right to counsel, and right to be informed of charges. Article 40 enshrines the right to sue the state for wrongful detention.

- Right to a fair trial: Article 37 guarantees the right to a public trial before an impartial tribunal with counsel for one's defence and compulsory access to witnesses.

- Protection against self-incrimination: Article 38 provides that no one may be compelled to testify against themselves, that confessions obtained under duress are not admissible and that no one may be convicted solely on the basis of their own confession.

- Other guarantees:
    - Right to petition government (Article 16)
    - Right to sue the state (Article 17)
    - Freedom of thought and conscience (Article 19)

- o   Freedom of expression (Article 19)
- o   Freedom of religion (Article 20)
- o   Rights to change residence, choose employment, move abroad and relinquish nationality (Article 22)
- o   Academic freedom (Article 23)
- o   Prohibition of forced marriage (Article 24)
- o   Compulsory education (Article 26)
- o   Protection against entries, search and seizures (Article 35)
- o   Prohibition of torture and cruel punishments (Article 36)
- o   Prohibition of ex post facto laws (Article 39)
- o   Prohibition of double jeopardy (Article 39)

Under Japanese case law, constitutional human rights apply to corporations to the extent possible given their corporate nature. Constitutional human rights also apply to foreign nationals to the extent that such rights are not by their nature only applicable to citizens (for example, foreigners have no right to enter Japan under Article 22 and no right to vote under Article 15, and their other political rights may be restricted to the extent that they interfere with the state's decision making).

International bodies such as the United Nations Human Rights Committee, which monitors compliance with the International Covenant on Civil and Political Rights, and Amnesty International have argued that many of the guarantees for individual rights contained in the Japanese constitution have not been effective in practice. Such critics have also argued that, contrary to Article 98, and its requirement that international law be treated as part of the domestic law of the state, human rights treaties to which Japan is a party are seldom enforced in Japanese courts.[citation needed] In one study, the conviction rate in contested Japanese trials in 1994 was found to be 98.8%, while the comparable conviction rate in contested United States federal trials in 1994 was 30.9%. The study concluded that this was due to the limited budgets for prosecutors in Japan compared to the United States, leading them to prosecute only the most solid cases, rather than due to bias by judges.[77]

ORGANS OF GOVERNMENT (ARTICLES 41-95)

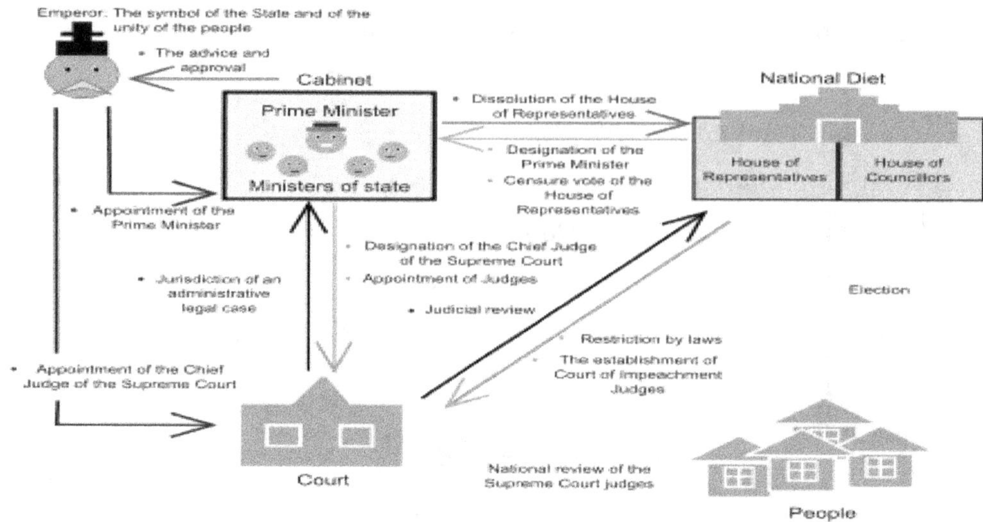

Politics under the Postwar Constitution

The constitution establishes a parliamentary system of government in which legislative authority is vested in a bicameral National Diet. Although a bicameral Diet existed under the existing constitution, the new constitution abolished the upper House of Peers, which consisted of members of the nobility (similar to the British House of Lords). The new constitution provided that both chambers be directly elected, with a lower House of Representatives and an upper House of Councillors. The House of Representatives has the sole ability to pass a vote of no confidence in the Cabinet, can override the House of Councillors' veto on any bill, and has priority in determining the national budget, approving treaties and nominating the Prime Minister when the two houses disagree.

Executive authority is vested in a cabinet headed by a Prime Minister. The Prime Minister and a majority of the Cabinet members must be members of the Diet, and have the right and obligation to attend sessions of the Diet. The Cabinet may also dissolve the House of Representatives and call for a general election to be held.

The judiciary consists of several lower courts headed by a Supreme Court. The Chief Justice of the Supreme Court is nominated by the Cabinet and appointed by the Emperor, while other justices are nominated and appointed by the Cabinet and approved by the Emperor. Lower court judges are nominated by the Supreme Court, appointed by the Cabinet and approved by the Emperor. As in the United States, all courts have the power of judicial review and may interpret the Constitution to overrule statutes and other government acts, but only in the event that such interpretation is relevant to an actual dispute.

The Constitution also provides a framework for local government, requiring that local entities have elected heads and assemblies, and providing that government acts applicable to particular local areas must be approved by the residents of those areas. These provisions formed the framework of the Local Autonomy Law of 1947, which established the modern system of prefectures, municipalities and other local government entities.

AMENDMENTS (ARTICLE 96)

Under Article 96, amendments to the Constitution "shall be initiated by the Diet, through a concurring vote of two-thirds or more of all the members of each House and shall thereupon be submitted to the people for ratification, which shall require the affirmative vote of a majority of all votes cast thereon, at a special referendum or at such election as the Diet shall specify." The Constitution has not been amended since its implementation in 1947, although there have been movements led by the Liberal Democratic Party to make various amendments to it.

OTHER PROVISIONS (ARTICLES 97 - 103)

Article 97 provides for the inviolability of fundamental human rights. Article 98 provides that the constitution takes precedence over any "law, ordinance, imperial rescript or other act of government" that offends against its provisions, and that "the treaties concluded by Japan and established laws of nations shall be faithfully observed". In most nations it is for the legislature to determine to what extent, if at all, treaties concluded by the state will be reflected in its domestic law; under Article 98, however, international law and the treaties Japan has ratified automatically form a part of domestic law. Article 99 binds the Emperor and public officials to observe the Constitution.

The final four articles set forth a six-month transitional period between adoption and implementation of the Constitution. This transitional period took place from November 3, 1946 to May 3, 1947. Pursuant to Article 100, the first House of Councillors election was held during this period in April 1947, and pursuant to Article 102, half of the elected Councillors were given three-year terms. A general election was also held during this period, as a result of which several former House of Peers members moved to the House of Representatives. Article 103 provided that public officials currently in office would not be removed as a direct result of the adoption or implementation of the new Constitution.

AMENDMENTS AND REVISIONS

The constitution has not been amended since its 1947 enactment. Article 96 provides that amendments can be made to any part of the constitution. However, a proposed amendment must first be approved by both houses of the Diet, by at least a super majority of two-thirds of each house (rather than just a simple majority). It must then be submitted to a referendum in which it is sufficient for it to be endorsed by a simple majority of votes cast. A successful amendment is finally promulgated by the Emperor, but the monarch cannot veto an amendment.

Some commentators have suggested that the difficulty of the amendment process was favoured by the constitution's American authors from a desire that the fundamentals of the regime they had imposed would be resistant to change. However, among Japanese themselves, any change to the document and to the post-war settlement it embodies is highly controversial. From the 1960s to the 1980s, constitutional revision was rarely debated. In the 1990s, right-leaning and conservative voices broke some taboos, for example, when the Yomiuri Shimbun published a suggestion for constitutional revision in 1994. This period saw a number of right-leaning groups forming to aggressively push for constitutional revision, but also a significant number of organizations and individuals speaking out against revision and in support of "the peace constitution."

The debate has been highly polarized. The most controversial issues are proposed changes to Article 9, the "peace article" and provisions relating to the role of the Emperor. Progressive, left, center-left and peace movement related individuals and organizations, as well as the opposition parties labor and youth groups advocate keeping (and even strengthening) the existing constitution in these areas, while right-leaning, nationalist and/or conservative groups and individuals advocate changes to increase the prestige of the Emperor (though not granting him political powers) and to allow a more aggressive stance of the self-defense force, e.g. by turning it officially into a military. Others areas of the constitution and connected laws discussed for potential revision relate to the status of women, the education system and the system of public corporations (including social welfare, non-profit and religious organizations as well as foundations), and structural reform of the election process, e.g. to allow for direct election of the prime minister. There are countless grassroots groups, associations, NGOs, think tanks, scholars, and politicians speaking out in favor of one or the other side of the issue.

1.2 CONSTITUENT ASSEMBLY OF INDIA

The Constituent Assembly of India was elected to write the Constitution of India. Following India's independence from Great Britain, its members served as the nation's first Parliament.

NATURE OF THE ASSEMBLY

The Constituent Assembly, consisting of indirectly elected representatives, was set up for the purpose of drafting a constitution for India (including what are now the separate countries of Pakistan and Bangladesh). In the event, it remained in being for almost three years, acting as the first parliament of India after independence in 1947. The Assembly was not elected on the basis of universal adult franchise; plus only Muslims and Sikhs were given special representation as "minorities". The influential Muslim League initially boycotted the Assembly after having failed to prevent its gathering. While a large number of the Constituent Assembly was drawn from the Congress party in a one-party political ecosphere, it is also important to note that at that point in history, the Congress party included wide diversity within itself, from conservative industrialists and radical Marxists, to Hindu revivalists, all of whom drove the process.

The Assembly met for the first time in New Delhi on 9 December 1946. The last session of the Assembly was held on 24 January 1950.[1] Over the course of this period (two years, eleven months and eighteen days), the Assembly held eleven sessions, sitting on a total of 166 days.[2] The hope behind the Assembly was expressed by Jawaharlal Nehru: "The first task of this Assembly is to free India through a new constitution, to feed the starving people, and to cloth the naked masses, and to give every Indian the fullest opportunity to develop himself according to his capacity."

BACKGROUND AND ELECTION

The Constituent Assembly was set up while India was still under British rule, following negotiations between Indian leaders and members of the 1946 Cabinet Mission to India from the United Kingdom. The provincial assembly elections had been conducted early in 1946. The Constituent Assembly members were elected to it indirectly by the members of these newly elected provincial assemblies, and initially included representatives for those provinces which came to form part of Pakistan, some of which are now within Bangladesh. The Constituent Assembly had 299 representatives, including nine women.

The Interim Government of India was formed on 2 September 1946 from the newly elected Constituent Assembly.

The Congress held a large majority in the Assembly, with 69 percent of all of the seats, while the Muslim League held almost all of the seats reserved in the Assembly for Muslims. There were also some members from smaller parties, such as the Scheduled Caste Federation, the Communist Party of India, and the Unionist Party.

In June 1947, the delegations from the provinces of Sindh, East Bengal, Baluchistan, West Punjab, and the North West Frontier Province withdrew, to form the Constituent Assembly of Pakistan, meeting in Karachi.

On 15 August 1947, the Dominion of India and Dominion of Pakistan became independent nations, and the members of the Constituent Assembly who had not withdrawn to Karachi became India's Parliament. Only 28 members of the Muslim League finally joined the Indian Assembly. Later, 93 members were nominated from the princely states. The Congress thus secured a majority of 82%.

CONSTITUTION AND ELECTIONS

At 11AM on 9 December 1946, the Assembly began its first session, with 207 members attending. By early 1947, representatives of the Muslim League and princely states joined. The Assembly formally approved the draft Constitution on 26 November 1949. On 26 January 1950, the Constitution took effect, a day now commemorated in India as Republic Day. At this point, the Constituent Assembly became the **Provisional Parliament** of India, which continued in existence until after the first elections under the new Constitution took place in 1952.

ORGANIZATION

Dr. Sachchidananda Sinha was the first president (temporary chairman) of the Constituent Assembly when it met on 9 December 1946. Dr. Rajendra Prasad then became the President of the Constituent Assembly, and would later become the first President of India. The Vice-President of the Constituent Assembly was Professor Harendra Coomar Mookerjee, a former Vice-Chancellor of Calcutta University and a prominent Christian from Bengal, who also served as the Chairman of the Constituent Assembly's Minorities Committee; he was appointed Governor of West Bengal after India became a republic. Eminent bureaucrat & jurist Sir Benegal Narsing Rau was appointed as the Constitutional Adviser to the Constituent Assembly. He prepared the original draft of the constitution and was later appointed a judge in the Permanent Court of International Justice, The Hague.

The Assembly's work was organised into five stages: (1) committees were asked to present reports on basic issues; (2) the constitutional adviser, B.N. Rau, prepared an initial draft on the basis of these committees and his own research into the constitutions of other countries; (3) the drafting committee, chaired by B.R. Ambedkar, presented a detailed draft constitution that was published for public discussion and comments; (4) the draft constitution was discussed and amendments were proposed and enacted; (5) the constitution was adopted. A committee of experts led by the Congress Party, called the Congress Assembly Party, played a critical role.[3]

9 December 1946 : The first meeting of Constituent Assembly was held in the constitution hall(now 'Central Hall of Parliament House'). Demanding a separate state,the Muslim League boycotted the meeting. Dr.Sanchidanand Sinha was elected as temporary President of Assembly following the French practice.

11 December 1946: Elected Dr.Rajendra Prasad and H.C.Mukherjee as the President and Vice-President of the Assembly respectively.Appointed Sir B.N.Rau as Constitutional advisor to the Assembly.

13 December 1946: 'Objective Resolution' was introduced by Jawaharlal Nehru.Underlying principles of Constitution were laid by Objective Resolution.

22 January 1947: Unanimously adopted the Objective Resolution.

May 1949: It ratified India's membership of the Commonwealth

22 July 1947: Adopted the national flag

24 January 1950: Adopted the national anthem,national song.Elected Dr. Rajendra Prasad as the first president of India

Assembly was chaired by Dr. Rajendra Prasad whenever it met as Constituent body and by G.V.Mavlankar when it met as the legislative body. Constituent Assembly completed the task of drafting Constitution in 2 years, 11 months and 18 days. The total expenditure incurred was Rs. 6.4 million.

MEMBERS OF THE INDIAN CONSTITUENT ASSEMBLY

Indian National Congress

- Pandit Jawaharlal Nehru, 1st Prime Minister
- Sardar Vallabhbhai Patel, Deputy Prime Minister cum Home Minister
- Bhimrao Ramji Ambedkar, Minister for Law, Chairman of Drafting committee
- Maulana Azad, Minister for Education,
- Dr. Rajendra Prasad, Chairman of the Assembly
- C. Rajagopalachari, Governor General
- Sarat Chandra Bose
- Sri Krishna Sinha, Chief Minister, Bihar
- Shyam Nandan Prasad Mishra
- Anugrah Narayan Sinha, Deputy Chief Minister cum Finance Minister, Bihar
- Rafi Ahmed Kidwai,
- Asaf Ali,
- Sri Sheik Galib Sahib,

- Syama Prasad Mookerjee, President, Hindu Mahasabha
- Moturi Satyanarayana, Freedom Fighter
- Rajkumari Amrit Kaur, Minister for Health
- Hansa Mehta, President, All India Women's Conference
- Prof. N.G. Ranga
- Deep Narayan Singh
- P. Subbarayan
- Kailashnath Katju
- N. G Ayyangar
- T. T. Krishnamachari
- Rameshwar Prasad Sinha
- Durgabai Deshmukh
- K. M. Munshi
- Krishana Ballabh Sahay
- Frank Anthony, Anglo-Indian representative
- Sarvepalli Radhakrishnan
- Dr. John Mathai
- Pratap Singh Kairon

MEMBERS OF THE INDIAN CONSTITUENT ASSEMBLY (PROVINCE/STATE WISE)

Madras O. V. Alagesan, Mrs. Amma Swaminathan, M. Ananthasayanam Ayyangar, Moturi Satyanarayana, Mrs. Dakshayani Velayudhan, Mrs. G. Durgabai, Kala Venkatarao, N. Gopalaswamy Ayyangar, D. Govinda Das, Revd. Jerome D'Souza, P. Kakkan, T.M.Kaliyannan Gounder, K. Kamaraj, V. C. Kesava Rao, T. T. Krishnamachari, Alladi Krishnaswamy Iyer L. Krishnaswami Bharathi, P. Kunhiraman, Mosalikanti Thirumala Rao, V. I. Munuswamy Pillai, M. A. Muthiah Chettiar, V. Nadimuthu Pillai, S. Nagappa, P. L. Narasimha Raju, B. Pattabhi Sitaramayya, C. Perumalswamy Reddy, T. Prakasam, S. H. Prater, Raja Swetachalapati Ramakrishna Renga Roa of Bobbili, R. K. Shanmukham Chetty, T. A. Ramalingam Chettiar, Ramnath Goenka, O. P. Ramaswamy Reddiar, N. G. Ranga, Neelam Sanjeeva Reddy, Sri Sheik Galib Sahib, K. Santhanam, B. Shiva Rao, Kallur Subba Rao, U. Srinivasa Mallya, P. Subbarayan, C. Subramaniam, V Subramaniam, M. C. Veerabahu, P. M. Velayudapani, A. K. Menon, T. J. M. Wilson, Mohamed Ismail Sahib, K. T. M. Ahmed Ibrahim, Mahboob Ali Baig Sahib Bahadur, B. Pocker Sahib Bahadur

Bombay Balchandra Maheshwar Gupte, Hansa Mehta, Hari Vinayak Pataskar, B. R. Ambedkar, Joseph Alban D'Souza, Kanayalal Nanabhai Desai, Keshavrao Marutirao Jedhe, Khandubhai Kasanji Desai, Bal Gangadhar Kher, M.R. Masani, K.M. Munshi, Narahar Vishnu Gadgil, S. Nijalingappa, S. K.

Patil, Ramchandra Manohar Nalavade, R. R. Diwakar, Shankarrao Deo, G. V. Mavalankar, Vallabhbhai Patel, Abdul Kadar Mohammad Shaikh, A. A. Khan

West Bengal Monomohan Das, Arun Chandra Guha, Lakshmi Kanta Maitra, Mihir Lal Chattopadhyay, Satis Chandra Samanta, Suresh Chandra Majumdar, Upendranath Barman, Prabhudayal Himatsingka, Basanta Kumar Das, Mrs. Renuka Ray, H. C. Mukherjee, Surendra Mohan Ghose, Syama Prasad Mookerjee, Ari Bahadur Gurung, R. E. Platel, K. C. Neogy, Raghib Ahsan, Somnath Lahiri, Jasimuddin Ahmad, Naziruddin Ahmad, Abdul Hamid[disambiguation needed], Abdul Halim Ghuznavi

United Provinces Ajit Prasad Jain, Algu Rai Shastri, Balkrishna Sharma, Banshi Dhar Misra, Bhagwan Din, Damodar Swarup Seth, Dayal Das Bhagat, Dharam Prakash, A. Dharam Dass, R. V. Dhulekar, Feroz Gandhi, Gopal Narain, Krishna Chandra Sharma, Govind Ballabh Pant, Govind Malaviya, Har Govind Pant, Harihar Nath Shastri, Hriday Nath Kunzru, Jaspat Roy Kapoor, Jagannath Baksh Singh, Jawaharlal Nehru, Jogendra Singh, Jugal Kishore, Jwala Prasad Srivastava, B. V. Keskar, Mrs. Kamala Chaudhri, Kamalapati Tiwari, J. B. Kripalani, Mahavir Tyagi, Khurshed Lal, Masurya Din, Mohan Lal Saksena, Padampat Singhania, Phool Singh, Paragi Lal, Mrs. Purnima Banerjee, Prurshottam Das Tandon, Hira Vallabha Tripathi, Ram Chandra Gupta, Shibban Lal Saxena, Satish Chandra, John Matthai, Mrs. Sucheta Kripalani, Sunder Lall, Venkatesh Narayan Tivary, Mohanlal Gautam, Vishwambhar Dayal Tripathi, Vishnu Sharan Dublish, Begum Aizaz Rasul, Hyder Hussain, Hasrat Mohani, Abul Kalam Azad, Muhammad Ismail Khan, Rafi Ahmad Kidwai, Mohd. Hifzur Rahman

East Punjab Bakshi Tek Chand, Jairamdas Daulatram, Thakurdas Bhargava, Bikramlal Sondhi, Yashwant Rai, Ranbir Singh, Achint Ram, Nand Lal, Sardar Baldev Singh, Giani Gurmukh Singh Musafir, Sardar Hukam Singh, Sardar Bhopinder Singh Mann, Sardar Rattan Singh Lohgarh Chaudhry Suraj Mal

Bihar Amiyo Kumar Ghosh, Anugrah Narayan Sinha, Banarsi Prasad Jhunjhunwala, Bhagwat Prasad, Boniface Lakra, Brajeshwar Prasad, Chandika Ram, K. T. Shah, Devendra Nath Samanta, Dip Narain Sinha, Guptanath Singh, Jadubans Sahay, Jagat Narain Lal, Jagjivan Ram, Jaipal Singh, Kameshwara Singh of Darbhanga, Kamaleshwari Prasad Yadav, Mahesh Prasad Sinha, Krishna Ballabh Sahay, Raghunandan Prasad, Rajendra Prasad, Rameshwar Prasad Sinha, Ramnarayan Singh, Sachchidananda Sinha, Sarangdhar Sinha, Satyanarayan Sinha, Binodanand Jha, P. K. Sen, Sri Krishna Sinha, Sri Narayan Mahtha, Syamanandan Sahaya, Hussain Imam, Syed Jafar Imam, Latifur Rahman, Mohammad Tahir, Tajamul Hussain, Choudhry Abid Hussain. Pt Hargovind Mishra.

Central Provinces and Berar Raghu Vira, Rajkumari Amrit Kaur, B.A. Mandloi, Brijlal Nandlal Biyani, Thakur Cheedilal, Seth Govind Das, Hari Singh Gour, Hari Vishnu Kamath, Hemchandra

Jagobaji Khandekar, Ghanshyam Singh Gupta, Lakshman Shrawan Bhatkar, Panjabrao Shamrao Deshmukh, Ravi Shankar Shukla, R. K. Sidhva, Shankar Trimbak Dharmadhikari, Frank Anthony, Kazi Syed Karimuddin, Ganpatrao Dani

Assam Nibaran Chandra Laskar, Dharanidhar Basu-Matari, Gopinath Bardoloi, J. J. M. Nichols-Roy, Kuladhar Chaliha, Rohini Kumar Chaudhury, Muhammad Saadulla, Abdur Rouf

Orissa Biswanath Das, Krishna Chandra Gajapati Narayana Dev, Harekrushna Mahatab, Laxminarayan Sahu Lokanath Mishra, Nandkishore Das, Rajkrishna Bose, Santanu Kumar Das, Yudhishir Mishra

Delhi Deshbhandhu Gupta

Ajmer-Merwara Mukut Bihari Lal Bhargava

Coorg C. M. Poonacha

Mysore K.C. Reddy, T. Siddalingaiya, H. R. Guruv Reddy, S. V. Krishnamurthy Rao, K. Hanumanthaiya, H. Siddaveerappa, T. Channiah

Jammu and Kashmir Sheikh Muhammad Abdullah, Motiram Baigra, Mirza Mohmmad Afzal Beg, Maulana Mohammad Sayeed Masoodi

Travancore-Cochin Pattom A. Thanu Pillai, R. Sankar, P. T. Chacko, Panampilly Govinda Menon, Annie Mascarene, P.S.Nataraja Pillai, K.A.Mohamed

Madhya Bharat Vinayak Sitaram Sarwate, Brijraj Narain, Gopikrishna Vijayavargiya, Ram Sahai, Kusum Kant Jain, Radhavallabh Vijayavargiya, Sitaram S. Jajoo

Saurashtra Balwant Rai Gopalji Mehta, Jaisukhlal Hathi, Amritlal Vithaldas Thakkar, Chimanlal Chakubhai Shah, Samaldas Laxmidas Gandhi

Rajasthan V. T. Krishnamachari, Hiralal Shastri, Sardar Singhjhi of Khetri, Jaswant Singhji, Raj Bhadur, Manikya Lal Varma, Gokul Lal Asava, Ramchandra Upadhyaya, Balwant Sinha Mehta, Dalel Singh, Jainarain Vyas

Patiala and East Punjab States Union Ranjit Singh, Sochet Singh, Bhagwant Roy

Bombay States Vinayakrao Balshankar Vaidya, B. N. Munavalli, Gokulbhai Daulatram Bhatt, Jivraj Narayan Mehta, Gopaldas A. Desai, Paranlal Thakurlal Munshi, B. H. Khardekar, Ratnappa Bharamappa Kumbhar

Orissa States Lal Mohan Pati, N. Madhava Rau, Raj Kunwar, Sarangadhar Das, Yudhishthir Mishra

Central Provinces States R. L. Malaviya, Kishorimohan Tripathi, Ramprasad Potai

United Provinces States B. H. Zaidi, Krishna Singh

Madras States V. Ramaiah, Ramakrishna Ranga Rao

Vindhya Pradesh Avdesh Pratap Singh, Shambu Nath Shukla, Ram Sahai Tiwari, Mannulalji Dwidedi

Cooch Behar Himmat Singh K. Maheshwari

Tripura and Manipur Girja Shankar Guha

Bhopal Lal Singh

Kutch Bhawani Arjun Khimji

Himachal Pradesh Yashwant Singh Parmar

SESSIONS

The Constituent Assembly of India met for 12 sessions on the following dates.[4]

Session	Dates
I	9–23 December 1946
II	20–25 January 1947
III	28 April to 2 May 1947
IV	14–31 July 1947
V	14–30 August 1947
VI	27 January 1948
VII	4 November 1948 to 8 January 1949
VIII	16 May to 16 June 1949
IX	30 July to 18 September 1949
X	6–17 October 1949
XI	14–26 November 1949
XII	24 January 1950

DEBATES

Constituent Assembly Debates were the discussions, arguments etc. that took place in order to write the Constitution of India. These discussions happened between the elected members of the assembly who later served as the nation's First Parliament.

It is said that only 28% people of the total population were eligible to vote at that time, so only this percentage of people participated in the elections for the assembly.

1.3 CONSTITUTIONAL VALUES

The Constitution of any country serves several purposes. It lays down certain ideals that form the basis of the kind of country that we as citizens aspire to live in. A country is usually made up of different communities of people who share certain beliefs, but may not necessarily agree on all issues. A Constitution helps serve as a set of principles, rules and procedures on which there is a consensus. These form the basis according to which the people want the country to be governed and the society to move on. This includes not only an agreement on the type of government but also on certain ideals that the country should uphold. The Indian Constitution has certain core constitutional values that constitute its spirit and are expressed in various articles and provisions. But do you know what is the meaning of the word, 'value'? You may immediately say that truth, non-violence, peace, cooperation, honesty, respect and kindness are values, and you may continue to count many such values. In fact, in a layman's understanding, value is that which is very essential or 'worth having and observing' for the existence of human society as an entity. The Indian Constitution contains all such values, the values that are the universal, human and democratic of the modern age.

CONSTITUTIONAL VALUES AND THE PREAMBLE OF THE CONSTITUTION

1. Sovereignty: You may have read the Preamble. It declares India "a sovereign socialist secular democratic republic". Being sovereign means having complete political freedom and being the supreme authority. It implies that India is internally all powerful and externally free. It is free to determine for itself without any external interference (either by any country or individual) and nobody is there within to challenge its authority. This feature of sovereignty gives us the dignity of existence as a nation in the international community. Though the Constitution does not specify where the sovereign authority lies but a mention of 'We the People of India' in the Preamble clearly indicates that sovereignty rests with the people of India. This means that the constitutional authorities and organs of government derive their power only from the people.

2. Socialism: You may be aware that social and economic inequalities have been inherent in the Indian traditional society. Which is why, socialism has been made a constitutional value aimed at promoting social change and transformation to end all forms of inequalities. Our Constitution directs the governments and the people to ensure a planned and coordinated social development in all fields. It directs to prevent concentration of wealth and power in a few hands. The Constitution has specific provisions that deal with inequalities in the Chapters on Fundamental Rights and Directive Principles of State Policy.

(DO U KNOW)

[The following provisions under the Directive Principles of State Policy promote the value of socialism:

"The State shall, in particular, strive to minimise the inequalities in income, and Endeavour to eliminate inequalities in status, facilities and opportunities, not only amongst individuals but also amongst groups of people residing in different areas or engaged in different vocations. " (Article 38(2) "The State shall, in particular, direct its policy towards securing- (a) that the citizens, men and women equally, have the right to an adequate means of livelihood; (b) that the ownership and control of the material resources of the community are so distributed as best to sub serve the common good; (c) that the operation of the economic system does not result in the concentration of wealth and means of production to the common detriment; (d) that there is equal pay for equal work for both men and women…"]

3. Secularism: We all are pleased when anyone says that India is a home to almost all major religions in the world. In the context of this plurality (means more than one or two; many), secularism is seen as a great constitutional value. Secularism implies that our country is not guided by any one religion or any religious considerations. However, the Indian state is not against religions. It allows all its citizens to profess, preach and practise any religion they follow. At the same time, it ensures that the state does not have any religion of its own. Constitution strictly prohibits any discrimination on the ground of religion.

4. Democracy: The Preamble reflects democracy as a value. As a form of government it derives its authority from the will of the people. The people elect the rulers of the country and the elected representatives remain accountable to the people. The people of India elect them to be part of the government at different levels by a system of universal adult franchise, popularly known as 'one man one vote'. Democracy contributes to stability, continuous progress in the society and it secures peaceful political change. It allows dissent and encourages tolerance. And more importantly, it is based on the principles of rule of law,inalienable rights of citizens, independence of judiciary, free and fair elections and freedom of the press.

5. Republic: India is not only a democratic nation but it is also a republic. The most important symbol of being a republic is the office of the Head of the State, i.e. the President who is elected and who is not selected on the basis of heredity, as is found in a system with monarchy. This value strengthens and substantiates democracy where every citizen of India is equally eligible to be elected as the Head of the State. Political equality is the chief message of this provision.

6. Justice: At times you may also realise that living in a democratic system alone does not ensure justice to citizens in all its totality. Even now we find a number of cases where not only the social and economic justice but also the political justice is denied. Which is why, the constitution-makers have included social, economic and political justice as constitutional values. By doing so, they have stressed that the political freedom granted to Indian citizens has to be instrumental in the creation of a new social order, based on socio-economic justice. Justice must be availed to every citizen. This ideal of a just and egalitarian society remains as one of the foremost values of the Indian Constitution.

7. Liberty: The Preamble prescribes liberty of thought, expression, belief, faith and worship as one of the core values. These have to be assured to every member of all the communities. It has been done so, because the ideals of democracy can not be attained without the presence of certain minimal rights which are essential for a free and civilized existence of individuals.

8. Equality: Equality is as significant constitutional value as any other. The Constitution ensures equality of status and opportunity to every citizen for the development of the best in him/her. As a human being everybody has a dignified self and to ensure its full enjoyment, inequality in any form present in our country and society has been prohibited. Equality reflected specifically in the Preamble is therefore held as an important value.

9. Fraternity: There is also a commitment made in the Preamble to promote the value of fraternity that stands for the spirit of common brotherhood among all the people of India. In the absence of fraternity, a plural society like India stands divided. Therefore, to give meaning to all the ideals like justice, liberty and equality, the Preamble lays great emphasis on fraternity. In fact, fraternity can be realized not only by abolishing untouchability amongst different sects of the community, but also by abolishing all communal or sectarian or even local discriminatory feelings which stand in the way of unity of India.

10. Dignity of the individual: Promotion of fraternity is essential to realize the dignity of the individual. It is essential to secure the dignity of every individual without which democracy can not function. It ensures equal participation of every individual in all the processes of democratic governance.

11. Unity and integrity of the Nation: As we have seen above, fraternity also promotes one of the critical values, i.e. unity and integrity of the nation. To maintain the independence of the country intact, the unity and integrity of the nation is very essential. Therefore, the stress has been given on fostering unity amongst all the inhabitants of the country. Our Constitution expects from all the citizens of India to uphold and protect the unity and integrity of India as a matter of duty.

12. International peace and a just international order: The value of international peace and a just international order, though not included in the Preamble is reflected in other provisions of the Constitution. The Indian Constitution directs the state (a) to promote international peace and security, (b) maintain just and honourable relations between nations, (c) foster respect for international law and treaty obligations, and (d) encourage settlement of international disputes by arbitration. To uphold and observe these values is in the interest of India. The peace and just international order will definitely contribute to the development of India.

13. Fundamental Duties: Our Constitution prescribes some duties to be performed by the citizens. It is true that these duties are not enforceable in the court of law like the fundamental rights are, but these duties are to be performed by citizens. Fundamental duties have still greater importance because these reflect certain basic values like patriotism, nationalism, humanism, environmentalism, harmonious living, gender equality, scientific temper and inquiry, and individual and collective excellence.

VALUES AND THE SALIENT FEATURES OF THE CONSTITUTION

The discussion on the Preamble embodying constitutional values clearly demonstrates that these are important for the successful functioning of Indian democracy. Your understanding of these values will be further reinforced, when you will find in the following discussion that constitutional values permeate all the salient features of Indian Constitution. The main features of the Constitution as shown in the illustration are as follows:

1. Written Constitution: As has been stated earlier, the Constitution of India is the longest written constitution. It contains a Preamble, 395 Articles in 22 Parts, 12 Schedules and 5 Appendices. It is a document of fundamental laws that define the nature of the political system and the structure and functioning of organs of the government. It expresses the vision of India as a democratic nation. It also identifies the fundamental rights and fundamental duties of citizens. While doing so, it also reflects core constitutional values.

2. A Unique Blend of Rigidity and Flexibility: In our day-to-day life, we find that it is not easy to bring about changes in a written document. As regards Constitutions, generally written constitutions are rigid. It is not easy to bring about changes in them frequently. The Constitution lays down special procedure for constitutional amendments. In the unwritten constitution like the British Constitution, amendments are made through ordinary law-making procedure. The British Constitution is a flexible constitution. In the written constitution like the US Constitution, it is very difficult to make amendments. The US Constitution, therefore, is a rigid constitution. However, the Indian Constitution is neither as flexible as the British Constitution nor as rigid as the US Constitution. It reflects the value of continuity and change. There are three ways of amending the Constitution of India. Some of its provisions can be amended by the simple majority in the Parliament, and some by special majority, while some amendments require special majority in the parliament and approval of States as well.

3. Fundamental Rights and Duties: You must be familiar with the term fundamental rights. We quite often find it in newspapers or while watching television. The Constitution of India includes these rights in a separate Chapter which has often been referred to as the 'conscience' of the Constitution. Fundamental Rights protect citizens against the arbitrary and absolute exercise of power by the State. The Constitution guarantees the rights to individuals against the State as well as against other individuals. The Constitution also guarantees the rights of minorities against the majority. Besides these rights, the Constitution has provisions identifying fundamental duties, though these are not enforceable as the fundamental rights are. These duties reflect some of the basic values embodied in the Constitution.

4. Directive Principles of State Policy: In addition to Fundamental Rights, the Constitution also has a section called Directive Principles of State Policy. It is a unique feature of the Constitution. It is aimed at ensuring greater social and economic reforms and serving as a guide to the State to institute laws and policies that help reduce the poverty of the masses and eliminate social discrimination. In fact, as you will study in the lesson on "India-A Welfare State", these provisions are directed towards establishment of a welfare state.

5. Integrated Judicial System: Unlike the judicial systems of federal countries like the United States of America, the Indian Constitution has established an integrated judicial system. Although the Supreme Court is at the national level, High Courts at the state level and Subordinate Courts at the district and lower level, there is a single hierarchy of Courts. At the top of the hierarchy is the Supreme Court. This unified judicial system is aimed at promoting and ensuring justice to all the citizens in uniform manner. Moreover, the constitutional provisions ensure the independence of Indian judiciary which is free from the influence of the executive and the legislature.

6. Single Citizenship: Indian Constitution has provision for single citizenship. Do you know what does it mean? It means that every Indian is a citizen of India, irrespective of the place of his/her residence or birth in the country. This is unlike the United States of America where there is the system of double citizenship.A person is a citizen of a State where he/she lives as well as he/she is a citizen of U.S.A. This provision in the Indian Constitution definitely reinforces the values of equality, unity and integrity.

7. Universal Adult Franchise: The values of equality and justice are reflected in yet another salient feature of the Constitution. Every Indian after attaining certain age (at present 18 years) has a right to vote. No discrimination can be made on the basis of religion, race, caste, sex, descent, and place of birth or residence. This right is known as universal adult franchise.

8. Federal System and Parliamentary Form of Government: Another salient feature of the Indian Constitution is that it provides for a federal system of state and parliamentary form of government. We shall discuss these below in detail. But it is necessary to note here that the federal system reflects the constitutional value of unity and integrity of the nation, and more importantly the value of decentralization of power. The parliamentary form of government reflects the values of responsibility and sovereignty vested in the people. The core principle of a parliamentary government is the responsibility of the executive to the legislature consisting of the representatives of the people.

1.4 NATURE OF INDIAN CONSTITUTION

The Constitution of India is not an end but a means to an end, not mere democracy as a political project but a socio-juridical process which opens up through a humanist, radical social order, the opportunity to unfold the full personhood of every citizen. The Indian Federalism is unique in nature and is tailored according to the specific needs of the country. Federalism is a basic feature of the Constitution of India in which the Union of India is permanent and indestructible. Both the Centre and the States are co-operating and coordinating institutions having independence and ought to exercise their respective powers with mutual adjustment, respect, understanding and accommodation. Tension and conflict of the interests of the Centre and the respective units is an integral part of federalism. Prevention as well as amelioration of conflicts is necessary. Thus, the Indian federalism was devised with a strong Centre. Federalism with a strong Centre was inevitable as the framers of the Indian Constitution were aware that there were economic disparities as several areas of India were economically as well as industrially far behind in comparison to others. The nation was committed to a socio economic revolution not only to secure the basic needs of the common man and economic unity of the country but also to bring about a fundamental change in the structure of Indian society in accordance with the egalitarian principles. With these considerations in mind the Constitution makers devised the Indian federation with a strong Union.

DEFINITION OF FEDERALISM:

Federalism constitutes a complex governmental mechanism for the governance of a country. It seeks to draw a balance between the forces working in favor of concentration of power in the Centre and those urging a dispersal of it in a number of units. A federal Constitution envisages a demarcation of governmental functions and powers between the Centre and the regions by the sanction of the Constitution, which is a written document. From this follows two necessary consequences-

 (i) That the invasion by one level of government on the area assigned to the other level of the government is a breach of the Constitution.

(ii) That any breach of the Constitution is a justifiable issue to be determined by the Courts as each level of government functions within the area assigned to it by the Constitution.

INDIAN CONSTITUTION IS A FEDERAL CONSTITUTION:

K.C. Where defines federal government as an association of states, which has been formed for certain common purposes, but in which the member states retain a large measure of their original independence. A federal government exists when the powers of the government for a community are divided substantially according to a principle that there is a single independent authority for the whole area in respect of some matters and there are independent regional authorities for other matters, each set of authorities being co-ordinate to and subordinate to the others within its own sphere. The framers of the Indian Constitution attempted to avoid the difficulties faced by the federal Constitutions of U.S.A, Canada and Australia and incorporate certain unique features in the working of the Indian Constitution. Thus, our Constitution contains certain novel provisions suited to the Indian conditions. The doubt which emerges about the federal nature of the Indian Constitution is the powers of intervention in the affairs of the states given to the Central Government by the Constitution According to Wheare, in practice the Constitution of India is quasi-federal in nature and not strictly federal. Sir Ivor Jennings was of the view that India has a federation with a strong centralizing policy. In the words of D.D.Basu The Constitution of India is neither purely federal nor unitary, but is a combination of both. It is a union or a composite of a novel type.

The Indian Constitution is not only regarded as Federal or Unitary in the strict sense of the terms. It is often defined to be quasi-federal in nature also. Throughout the Constitution, emphasis is laid on the fact that India is a single united nation. India is described as a Union of States and is constituted into a sovereign, secular, socialist, democratic republic.

As opposed to this is the opinion of some scholars who regard the Indian Constitution to be unitary in nature. It has been argued that the Indian Constitution does not satisfy certain essential tests of federalism, namely- the right of the units to make their own Constitution and provision of double citizenship. Further, in the three-fold distribution of powers, the most important subjects have been included in the Union list, which is the longest of the three lists containing 97 items. Even regarding the Concurrent list, Parliament enjoys an overriding authority over the State Legislatures. Article 253 empowers the Union Parliament to make laws implementing any treaty, agreement or convention with another country or any decision made at any international conference, association, or other body.

Some of the other Constitutional provisions, which are often quoted in favor of the Unitary status of the Indian Constitution are- emergency powers of the president to declare national emergency or declaring emergency in a state in the event of failure of Constitutional machinery, the appointment of governors, unification of judiciary and the dependence of the States on the Centre for finance. The power of the Union to alter the names and territory of the states, to carry out Constitutional amendments and to affect co-ordination among the States and settle their mutual disputes is also regarded as an indicator of the unitary character of the Indian Constitution.

It should be remembered that the aforementioned provisions in the Constitution are aimed at establishing a working balance between the requirements of national unity and autonomy of the States.

CONSTITUTIONAL INTENT:

Being aware that notwithstanding a common cultural heritage, without political unity, the country would disintegrate under the pressure of fissiparous forces, the Constituent Assembly addressed itself to the immensely complex task of devising a Union with a strong Centre. In devising the pattern of the Centre State relations they were influenced by the Constitutions of Canada and Australia which have a Parliamentary form of government and America which has a Presidential form of government. The Government of India Act, 1935 was also relied upon with significant changes. The Constitution cannot be called "federal" or "unitary" in the ideal sense of the terms.

It is stipulated in the Constitution that India will be a Union of States (Art.1). The Constitution, thus postulated India as a Union of States and consequently, the existence of federal structure of governance for this Union of States becomes a basic structure of the Union of India. Dr. Ambedkar, the principal architect of the Constitution observed- The use of the word Union is deliberate. The Drafting Committee wanted to make it clear that though India was to be a federation, the federation was not a result of an agreement by the States to join in the federation and that the federation not being the result of an agreement no state has a right to secede from it. Though the country and the people may be divided into different states for convenience of administration the whole country is one integral whole, its people a single people living under a single imperium derived from a single source.

The Constitution makes a distribution of powers between the Union and the States, the jurisdiction of each being demarcated by the Union, State and Concurrent lists. In case of a conflict between the two legislatures over a matter in the Concurrent list the will of the Parliament prevails. The supremacy of the Constitution- the hallmark of a federation- is an important feature of the Indian polity. Neither the Central government nor the State Governments can override or contravene the provisions of the Constitution. Another pre-requisite of a federation, namely, an independent judiciary - an interpreter and guardian of the Constitution - is also present in the Indian Federation. The Supreme Court can declare any law passed by the Union Parliament or a State legislature ultra vires if it contravenes any of the provisions of the Constitution.

JUDICIAL INTERPRETATION:

The debate whether India has a 'Federal Constitution' and 'Federal Government' has been grappling the Apex court in India because of the theoretical label given to the Constitution of India, namely, federal, quasi-federal, unitary. The first significant case where this issue was discussed at length by the apex Court was State of West Bengal V. Union of India. The main issue involved in this case was the exercise of sovereign powers by the Indian states. The legislative competence of the Parliament to enact a law for compulsory acquisition by the Union of land and other properties vested in or owned by the state and the sovereign authority of states as distinct entities was also examined. The apex court held that the Indian Constitution did not propound a principle of absolute federalism. Though the authority was decentralized this was mainly due to the arduous task of governing the large territory. The court outlined the characteristics, which highlight the fact that the Indian Constitution is not a "traditional federal Constitution". Firstly, there is no separate Constitution for each State as is required in a federal state. The Constitution is the supreme document, which governs all the states. Secondly, the Constitution is liable to be altered by the Union Parliament alone and the units of the country i.e. the States have no power to alter it. Thirdly, the distribution of powers is to facilitate local governance by the states and national policies to be decided by the Centre. Lastly, as against a federal Constitution, which contains internal checks and balances, the Indian Constitution renders supreme power upon the courts to invalidate any action violative of the Constitution. The Supreme Court further held that both the legislative and executive power of the States are subject to the respective supreme powers of the Union. Legal sovereignty of the Indian nation is vested in the people of India. The political sovereignty is distributed between the Union and the States with greater weight age in favor of the Union. Another reason which militates against the theory of the supremacy of States is that there is no dual citizenship in India. Thus, the learned judges concluded that the structure of the Indian Union as provided by the Constitution one is centralized, with the States occupying a secondary position vis-à-vis the Centre, hence the Centre possessed the requisite powers to acquire properties belonging to States.

As against this opinion, was the judgment rendered by Justice Subba Rao, the great champion of State rights. Justice Subba Rao was of the opinion that under the scheme of the Indian Constitution, sovereign powers are distributed between the Union and the States within their respective spheres. As the legislative field of the union is much wider than that of the State legislative assemblies, the laws passed by the Parliament prevail over the State laws in case of any conflict. In a few cases of legislation where inter-State disputes are involved, sanction of the President is made mandatory for the validity of those laws. Further, every State has its judiciary with the State High Court at the apex. This, in the opinion of the learned judge does not affect the federal principle. He gives the parallel of Australia, where appeals against certain decisions of the High Courts of the Commonwealth of Australia lie with the Privy Council. Thus the Indian federation cannot be negated on this account. In financial matters the Union has more resources at its disposal as compared to the states. Thus, the Union being in charge of the purse strings, can always, persuade the States to abide by its advice. The powers vested in the union in case of national emergencies, internal disturbance or external aggression, financial crisis, and failure of the Constitutional machinery of the State are all extraordinary powers in the nature of safety valves to protect the country's future. The power granted to the Union to alter the boundaries of the States is also an extraordinary power to meet future contingencies. In their respective spheres, both executive and legislative, the States are supreme. The minority view expressed by Justice Subba Rao has consistency with the federal scheme under the Indian Constitution. The Indian Constitution accepts the federal concept and distributes the sovereign powers between the coordinate Constitutional entities, namely, the Union and the States.

The next landmark case where the nature of the Indian Constitution was discussed at length was State of Rajasthan V. Union of India. The learned judges embarked upon a discussion of the abstract principles of federalism in the face of the express provisions of the Constitution. It was stated that even if it is possible to see a federal structure behind the establishment of separate executive, legislative and judicial organs in the States, it is apparent from the provision illustrated in Article 356 that the Union Government is entitled to enforce its own views regarding the administration and granting of power in the States. The extent of federalism of the Indian Union is largely watered down by the needs of progress, development and making the nation integrated, politically and economically co-ordinated, and socially and spiritually uplifted. The Court then proceeded to list out some of the Constitutional provisions which establish the supremacy of the Parliament over the State legislatures. In conclusion the apex Court held that it was the 'prerogative' of the Union Parliament to issue directives if they were for the benefit of the people of the State and were aimed at achieving the objectives set out in the Preamble.

The issue of federalism was carried forward in S.R.Bommai V. Union of India. Four opinions were rendered, expressing varying views. Justice Ahmadi opined that in order to understand the true nature of the Indian Constitution, it is essential to comprehend the concept of federalism. The essence of the federation is the existence of the Union and the States and the distribution of powers between them. The significant absence of expressions like 'federal' or 'federation' in the Constitution, the powers of the Parliament under Articles 2 and 3, the extraordinary powers conferred to meet emergency situations, residuary powers, powers to issue directions to the States, concept of single citizenship and the system of integrated judiciary create doubts about the federal nature of the Indian Constitution. Thus, it would be more appropriate to describe the

Constitution of India as quasi- federal or unitary rather than a federal Constitution in the true nature of the term. As opposed to this, Justice Sawant and Justice Kuldip Singh regarded democracy and federalism as essential features of the Indian Constitution. The overriding powers of the Centre in the event of emergency do not destroy the federal character of the Indian Constitution. The learned judges elaborated upon the scope and justified use of the power conferred on the president by Article 356 which will not restrict the scope of the independent powers of the respective States for "......every State is constituent political unit and has to have an exclusive Executive and Legislature elected and constituted by the same process as the Union Government."

In the opinion of Justice Ramaswamy, the units of the federation had no roots in the past and hence the Constitution does not provide mechanisms to uphold the territorial integrity of the States above the powers of the Parliament. The end sought to be achieved by the Constitution makers was to place the whole country under the control of a unified Central Government, while the States were allowed to exercise their sovereign powers within their legislative, executive and administrative powers. The essence of federalism lies in the distribution of powers between the Centre and the State. Justice Ramawamy declared the Indian structure as organic federalism, designed to suit the parliamentary form of Government and the diverse conditions prevailing in India. Justice Jeevan Reddy and Justice Agarwal opined that the expression federal or federal form of government has no fixed meaning. The Constitution is also distinct in character, a federation with a bias in favour of the Centre. But this factor does not reduce the States to mere appendages of the Centre. Within the sphere allotted to them the states are supreme.

If we concluded that we can hence forth see that the Indian judiciary had interpreted the Constitution to declare India a unitary nation. This view of the apex court has lately undergone a change. The Court has recognized the fact that the framers of the Indian Constitution intended to provide a federal structure with a strong Centre, which would prevent the nation from disintegration.

In a subsequent case Chief Justice P.B.Gajendragadkar, emphasized upon the federal nature of the Constitution and the Judiciary as the sole interpreter of the Constitution which could not be changed by the process of ordinary legislation. In the basic structure thesis case Keshavananda Bharti V. State of Kerala some of the judges in the full Constitutional Bench expressed federalism as one of the basic features of the Indian Constitution. In another case Justice Bhagwati, described Indian Constitution as a federal or quasi- federal Constitution. In Sat Pal V. State of Punjab, the Supreme Court again held that Ours is a Constitution where there is a combination of federal structure with unitary features....... In Pradeep Jain V. Union of India, the Apex Court expressed a non-traditionalistic yet pragmatic opinion while explaining the federal concept in the context of the unified legal system in India- India is not a federal State in the traditional sense of that term. It is not a compact of sovereign State which have come together to form a federation by ceding undoubtedly federal features. In Ganga Ram Moolchandani v. State of Rajasthan the Supreme Court reiterated: Indian Constitution is basically federal in form and is marked by the traditional characteristics of a federal system, namely supremacy of the Constitution, division of power between the Union and States and existence independent judiciary. The apex Court in ITC LTD v Agricultural Produce Market Committee expressed a similar opinion.

The finer federal facet has often been misinterpreted by the central operators. So the battle for federal affirmation and restoration of democratic decentralization has gained momentum over the decade. Important Commissions like Rajamannar and Sarkaria Commission have stressed on the federal soul of the Constitution. In the opinion of Amal Ray, the Indian Constitution is a product of two conflicting cultures one representing the national leader's normative concern for India's unique personality and the other over-emphasizing the concern for national unity, security, etc. And as a result, the founding fathers opted for a semi-hegemonic federal structure where the balance is in favour of the Centre. This concept is aptly described in the insight offered by Dr. Ambedkar: the Indian Constitution would work as a federal system in 'normal times' but in times of 'emergency' it could be worked as though it were a unitary system. The critics of the Indian Federal system must not ignore the fact that not only the Federal Government in India has been made deliberately strong, there is also a centralizing tendency in the other federal states of the world such as Switzerland, Australia, Canada and the United States.

In an attempt to assert their independence the States have, at various points of time tried to flout the Centre's orders. An example was the disobedience of Karnataka to confirm to the Centre's directives regarding release of water to Tamil Nadu. Such actions have generated wide spread opposition from interested parties. A similar situation arose when Punjab Termination of Agreements Bill, 2004, was flouted by the State of Punjab recently. The unilateral termination of a tripartite agreement raised a controversy in which the authority of the State to commit such an act is being questioned. Annulling the very basis on which the Supreme Court had pressured the State to implement the river water-sharing agreement of 1981, the Bill has created an unprecedented Constitutional crisis.

In a response to the increasing number of water disputes the United Progressive Alliance Government has proposed to set up two Commissions to look into the Centre- State relations, including river water- sharing, and to examine administrative reforms.

In the light of the past experiences of misuse of power certain amendments should be effected which will strengthen the federal nature of our Constitution. Firstly, there should be devolution of more financial resources and powers on the States so that they do not have to depend on the

Centre for financial assistance. Secondly number of statutory grants to which the States are entitled should increase. Thirdly, the States should also be given greater autonomy to undertake developmental programmes. Lastly, there should be some inbuilt safeguards against the blatant misuse of Article 356 by successive central Governments. It is time to undertake a study of Indian Federalism with a view to valuate the trends, frictions and difficulties which have developed in the area of inter-governmental relations and to seek to evolve ways and means to meet the challenging task of making the Indian federation a more robust, strong and workable system so that the country may meet the tasks of self-improvement and development.

The responsibility lies on not only the jurists and policy framers, but also the citizens of the country to work in a harmonious manner for the development of the country.

Unit II

Union Executive and Judiciary

2.1 PRESIDENT OF INDIA

The **President of India** is the head of state of the Republic of India. The President is the formal head of the executive, legislature and judiciary of India and is the commander-in-chief of the Indian Armed Forces.

The President is indirectly elected by the people through elected members of the Parliament of India (Lok Sabha and Rajya Sabha) as well as of the state legislatures (Vidhan Sabhas and Vidhan Parishads) and serves for a term of five years. Historically, ruling party (majority in the Lok Sabha) nominees (for example, United Progressive Alliance nominee Shri Pranab Mukherjee) have been elected or largely elected unanimously. Incumbent presidents are permitted to stand for re-election. A formula is used to allocate votes so there is a balance between the population of each state and the number of votes assembly members from a state can cast, and to give an equal balance between State Assembly members and the members of the Parliament of India. If no candidate receives a majority of votes, then there is a system by which losing candidates are eliminated from the contest and their votes are transferred to other candidates, until one gains a majority.

Although Article 53 of the Constitution of India states that the President can exercise his or her powers directly or by subordinate authority,[78] with few exceptions, all of the executive authority vested in the President are, in practice, exercised by the popularly elected Government of India, headed by the Prime Minister. This Executive power is exercised by the Prime Minister with the help of the Council of Ministers.

The President of India resides in an estate in New Delhi known as the Rashtrapati Bhavan[79] (which roughly translates as President's Palace). The presidential retreat is The Retreat in Chharabra, Shimla and Rashtrapati Nilayam (President's Place) in Hyderabad.

The 13th and current President is Pranab Mukherjee, who was elected on 22 July 2012, and sworn-in on 25 July 2012. He is also the first Bengali to be elected as President.[80] He took over the position from Pratibha Patil, who was the first woman to serve in the office.[81]

ORIGIN

India achieved independence from the British Rule on 15 August 1947, initially as a Dominion within the Commonwealth of Nations with George VI as the king of India, represented in the country by a governor-general.[82] Still, following this, the Constituent Assembly of India, under the leadership of Dr. B. R. Ambedkar, undertook the process of drafting a completely new constitution for the country. The Constitution of India was eventually enacted on 26 November 1949 and came into force on 26 January 1950,[83] making India a republic.[84] The offices of monarch and governor-general were replaced by the new office of President of India, with Rajendra Prasad as the first incumbent.[84]

POWERS AND DUTIES

LEGISLATIVE

Legislative power is constitutionally vested in the Parliament of India of which the president is the titular head. The President summons both the Houses (the Lok Sabha and the Rajya Sabha) of the Parliament and prorogues them. He can dissolve the Lok Sabha.[83] These powers are formal and by convention, the President uses these powers according to the advice of the Council of Ministers headed by the Prime Minister.[85]

The President inaugurates the Parliament by addressing it after the general elections and also at the beginning of the first session each year. Presidential address on these occasions is generally meant to outline the new policies of the government.[86]

All bills passed by the Parliament can become laws only after receiving the assent of the President. The President can return a bill to the Parliament, if it is not a money bill or a constitutional amendment bill, for reconsideration. When, after reconsideration, the bill is passed and presented to the President, with or without amendments, the President is obliged to assent it. The President can also withhold his assent to a bill when it is initially presented to him (rather than return it to the Parliament) thereby exercising a pocket veto.[87]

When either of the two Houses of the Parliament of India is not in session, and if government feels the need for immediate procedure, the President can promulgate ordinances which have the same force and effect as laws passed by Parliament. These are in the nature of interim or temporary legislation and their continuance is subject to parliamentary approval. Ordinances remain valid for no more than six weeks from the date the Parliament is convened unless approved by it earlier.[88]

APPOINTMENT POWERS

The President appoints, as Prime Minister, the person most likely to command the support of the majority in the Lok Sabha (usually the leader of the majority party or coalition). The President then appoints the other members of the Council of Ministers, distributing portfolios to them on the advice of the Prime Minister.[89]

The Council of Ministers remains in power during the 'pleasure' of the President. In practice, however, the Council of Ministers must retain the support of the Lok Sabha. If a President were to dismiss the Council of Ministers on his or her own initiative, it might trigger a constitutional crisis. Thus, in practice, the Council of Ministers cannot be dismissed as long as it commands the support of a majority in the Lok Sabha.

The President is responsible for making a wide variety of appointments. These include:[89]

- Governors of States
- The Chief Justice, other judges of the Supreme Court and High Courts of India
- The Attorney General
- The Comptroller and Auditor General
- The Chief Election Commissioner and other Election Commissioners
- The Chairman and other Members of the Union Public Service Commission
- Vice Chancellor of central university and academic staff of central university through his nominee
- Directors of IITs and NITs
- Ambassadors and High Commissioners to other countries[85][90]

FINANCIAL POWERS

All money bills originate in Parliament, but only if the President recommends them. He or she presents the Annual Budget and supplementary Budget before Parliament. No money bill can be introduced in Parliament without his or her assent. The President appoints a finance commission every five years. Withdrawal from the contingency fund of India is done after the permission of the President.[91][92] The Contingency Fund of India is at the disposal of the President.

JUDICIAL POWERS

The President appoints the Chief Justice of the Union Judiciary and other judges on the advice of the Chief Justice. He or she dismisses the judges if and only if the two Houses of the Parliament pass resolutions to that effect by a two-thirds majority of the members present.[93]

According to Article 143 of Indian Constitution, if the President considers a question of law or a matter of public importance has arisen, he or she can ask for the advisory opinion of the Supreme Court.

DIPLOMATIC POWERS

All international treaties and agreements are negotiated and concluded on behalf of the President.[94] However, in practice, such negotiations are usually carried out by the Prime Minister along with his Cabinet (especially the Foreign Minister). Also, such treaties are subject to the approval of the Parliament. The President represents India in international forums and affairs where such a function is chiefly ceremonial. The President may also send and receive diplomats, i.e. the officers from the Indian Foreign Service.[86] The President is the first citizen of the country.[85]

MILITARY POWERS

The President is the supreme commander of the defence forces of India. The President can declare war or conclude peace,[85] subject to the approval of parliament only under the decision of the Council of the Armed Forces Chief staffs, Military Secretary and President's Officer (Deputy Military Secretary). All important treaties and contracts are made in the President's name.[95] He also appoints the heads of the armed forces.

PARDONING POWERS

As mentioned in Article 72 of Indian Constitution, the President is empowered with the powers to grant pardons in the following situations:[85]

- Punishment is for offence against Union Law
- Punishment is by a Military Court
- Sentence is a death sentence[95]

The decisions involving pardoning and other rights by the President are independent of the opinion of the Prime Minister or the Lok Sabha majority. In most cases, however, the President exercises his or her executive powers on the advice of the Prime Minister and the cabinet[89][96]

EMERGENCY POWERS

The President can declare three types of emergencies: national, state, financial.[94]

NATIONAL EMERGENCY

National emergency can be declared in the whole of India or a part of its territory on causes of war or armed rebellion or an external aggression. Such an emergency was declared in India in 1962 (Indo-China war), 1971 (Indo-Pakistan war),[97] 1975 to 1977 (declared by Indira Gandhi on account of "internal disturbance").

Under Article 352 of the India Constitution, the President can declare such an emergency only on the basis of a written request by the Cabinet Ministers headed by the Prime Minister. Such a proclamation must be approved by the Parliament within one month. Such an emergency can be imposed for six months. It can be extended by six months by repeated parliamentary approval, there's no maximum duration.

In such an emergency, Fundamental Rights of Indian citizens can be suspended. The six freedoms under Right to Freedom are automatically suspended. However, the Right to Life and Personal Liberty cannot be suspended.(Article 21)[98]

The President can make laws on the 66 subjects of the State List (which contains subjects on which the state governments can make laws).[99] Also, all money bills are referred to the President for its approval. The term of the Lok Sabha can be extended by a period of up to one year, but not so as to extend the term of Parliament beyond six months after the end of the declared emergency.

STATE EMERGENCY

If the President is satisfied, on the basis of the report of the Governor of the concerned state or from other sources that the governance in a state cannot be carried out according to the provisions in the Constitution, he/she can declare a state of emergency in the state. Such an emergency must be approved by the Parliament within a period of 2 months.

Under Article 356 of the Indian Constitution, it can be imposed from six months to a maximum period of three years with repeated parliamentary approval every six months. If the emergency needs to be extended for more than three years, this can be achieved by a constitutional amendment, as has happened in Punjab and Jammu and Kashmir.

During such an emergency, the President can take over the entire work of the executive, and the Governor administers the state in the name of the President. The Legislative Assembly can be dissolved or may remain in suspended animation. The Parliament makes laws on the 66 subjects of the state list [100] (see National emergency for explanation).

A State Emergency can be imposed via the following:

1. By Article 356 – If that state failed to run constitutionally i.e. constitutional machinery has failed[101]
2. By Article 365 – If that state is not working according to the given direction of the Union Government.[102]

This type of emergency needs the approval of the parliament within 2 months. It can last up to a maximum of three years via extensions after each 6-month period. However, after one year it can be extended only if

1. A state of National Emergency has been declared in the country or in the particular state.
2. The Election Commission finds it difficult to organise an election in that state.

On 19 January 2013, President's rule was imposed on the Indian State of Jharkhand, making it the latest state where this kind of emergency has been imposed.[103]

FINANCIAL EMERGENCY

If the President is satisfied that there is an economic situation in which the financial stability or credit of India is threatened,[104] he/she can then proclaim a financial emergency, as per the Article 360. Such an emergency must be approved by the Parliament within two months. It has never been declared.[105]

A state of financial emergency remains in force indefinitely until revoked by the President.

The President can reduce the salaries of all government officials, including judges of the Supreme Court and High Courts, in case of a financial emergency. All money bills passed by the State legislatures are submitted to the President for approval. He can direct the state to observe certain principles (economy measures) relating to financial matters.[106]

SELECTION PROCESS

ELIGIBILITY

Article 58 of the Constitution sets the principle qualifications one must meet to be eligible to the office of the President. A President must be:

- A citizen of India
- Of 35 years of age or above
- Qualified to become a member of the Lok Sabha

A person shall not be eligible for election as President if he holds any office of profit under the Government of India or the Government of any State or under any local or other authority subject to the control of any of the said Governments.

Certain office-holders, however, are permitted to stand as Presidential candidates. These are:

- The current Vice President.
- The Governor of any State.
- A Minister of the Union or of any State (Including Prime Minister and Chief Ministers).[89]

In the event that the Vice President, a State Governor or a Minister is elected President, they are considered to have vacated their previous office on the date they begin serving as President.

Under The Presidential and Vice-Presidential Elections Act, 1952,[107] a candidate, to be nominated for the office of president needs 50 electors as proposers and 50 electors as seconders for his or her name to appear on ballot.[108]

CONDITIONS FOR PRESIDENCY

Certain conditions, as per Article 59 of the Constitution, debar any eligible citizen from contesting the presidential elections. The conditions are:

- The President shall not be a member of either House of Parliament or of a House of the Legislature of any State, and if a member of either House of Parliament or of a House of the Legislature of any State be elected President, he shall be deemed to have vacated his seat in that House on the date on which he enters upon his office as President.
- The President shall not hold any other office of profit.
- The President shall be entitled without payment of rent to the use of his official residences and shall be also entitled to such emoluments, allowances and privileges as may be determined by Parliament by law and until provision in that behalf is so made, such emoluments, allowances and privileges as are specified in the Second Schedule.
- The emoluments and allowances of the President shall not be diminished during his term of office.

ELECTION PROCESS

Whenever the office becomes vacant, the new President is chosen by an electoral college consisting of the elected members of both houses of Parliament(M.P.), the elected members of the State Legislative Assemblies (Vidhan Sabha) of all States and the elected members of the legislative assemblies (M.L.A.) of two Union Territories i.e., National Capital Territory(NCT) of Delhi and Union Territory of Puducherry.

The nomination of a candidate for election to the office of the President must be subscribed by at least 50 electors as proposers and 50 electors as seconders. Each candidate has to make a security deposit of ₹15,000 (US$240) in the Reserve Bank of India.[109] The security deposit is liable to be forfeited in case the candidate fails to secure one-sixth of the votes polled.

The election is held in accordance to the system of Proportional representation by means of Single transferable vote method. The Voting takes place by secret ballot system. The manner of election of President is provided by Article 55 of the Constitution.[110]

Each elector casts a different number of votes. The general principle is that the total number of votes cast by Members of Parliament equals the total number of votes cast by State Legislators. Also, legislators from larger states cast more votes than those from smaller states. Finally, the number of legislators in a state matters; if a state has few legislators, then each legislator has more votes; if a state has many legislators, then each legislator has fewer votes.

The actual calculation for votes cast by a particular state is calculated by dividing the state's population by 1000, which is divided again by the number of legislators from the State voting in the electoral college. This number is the number of votes per legislator in a given state.Every elected member of the parliament enjoys same number of votes which may be obtained by dividing the total number of votes assigned to the members of legislative assemblies by the total number of elected representatives of the parliament.

Although Indian presidential elections involve actual voting by MPs and MLAs, they tend to vote for the candidate supported by their respective parties.[111]

OATH OR AFFIRMATION

The President is required to make and subscribe in the presence of the Chief Justice of India (or in his absence, the senior-most Judge of the Supreme Court), an oath or affirmation that he/she shall protect, preserve and defend the Constitution as follows:[112]

I, (name), do swear in the name of God (or solemnly affirm) that I will faithfully execute the office of President (or discharge the functions of the President) of the Republic of India, and will to the best of my ability preserve, protect and defend the Constitution and the law, and that I will devote myself to the service and well-being of the people of the Republic of India.

— Article 60, Constitution of India

EMOLUMENTS

President pay		
Date established	**Salary in 1998**	**Salary in 2008**
30 December 2008	₹50000 (US$800)	₹150000 (US$2,400)
Sources:[113]		

The President of India used to receive ₹10,000 (US$200) per month as per the Third Schedule of the Constitution. This amount was increased to ₹50,000 (US$800) in 1998. On 11 September 2008 the Government of India increased the salary of the President to ₹1.5 lakh (US$2,400). However, almost everything that the President does or wants to do is taken care of by the annual ₹22.5 crore (approx. US$5 million) budget that the Government allots for his or her upkeep.[114] Rashtrapati Bhavan, the President's official residence, is the largest Presidential Palace in the world.[119][120] The Rashtrapati Nilayam at Bolarum, Hyderabad and Retreat Building at Chharabra, Shimla are the official Retreat Residences of the President of India.[121] The official state car of the President is a custom-built heavily armoured Mercedes Benz S600 (W221) Pullman Guard.

REMOVAL

The President may be removed before the expiry of the term through impeachment. A President can be removed for violation of the Constitution of India.[122]

The process may start in either of the two houses of the Parliament. The house initiates the process by levelling the charges against the President. The charges are contained in a notice that has to be signed by at least one quarter of the total members of that house. The notice is sent up to the President and 14 days later, it is taken up for consideration.

A resolution to impeach the President has to be passed by a special majority (two-third majority of the total number of members of the originating house). It is then sent to the other house. The other house investigates the charges that have been made. During this process, the President has the right to defend oneself through an authorised counsel. If the second house also approves the charges made by special majority again, the President stands impeached and is deemed to have vacated his/her office from the date when such a resolution stands passed. Other than impeachment, no other penalty can be given to the President for the violation of the Constitution.[89]

No president has faced impeachment proceedings so the above provisions have never been used.[123]

SUCCESSION

In the event of a vacancy created for the President's post due to death, resignation, impeachment, etc., Article 65 of the Indian Constitution says that the Vice President of India will have to discharge the duties. The Vice President reverts to office when a new President is elected and enters office. When the President is unable to act because of absence, illness or any other cause, the Vice President discharges the President's functions until the President resumes the duties.

A Vice President who acts as or discharges the functions of the President has all the powers and immunities of the President and is entitled to the same emoluments as the President.

The Indian Parliament has enacted the law (The President (Discharge Of Functions) Act, 1969)[44] for the discharge of the functions of the President when vacancies occur in the offices of the President and of the Vice President simultaneously, owing to removal, death, resignation of the incumbent or otherwise. In such an eventuality, the Chief Justice, or in his absence, the senior most Judge of the Supreme Court of India available discharges the functions of the President until a newly elected President enters upon his office or a newly elected Vice President begins to act as President under Article 65 of the Constitution, whichever is the earlier.[90]

IMPORTANT PRESIDENTIAL INTERVENTIONS IN THE PAST

The President's role as defender of the Constitution and the powers as Head of State, especially in relation to those exercised by the Prime Minister as leader of the government, have changed over time. In particular, Presidents have made a number of interventions into government and lawmaking, which have established and challenged some conventions concerning Presidential intervention.

PROVING MAJORITY IN THE PARLIAMENT

In 1979, the Prime Minister, Charan Singh, did not enjoy a Parliamentary majority. He responded to this by simply not advising the President to summon Parliament. Since then, Presidents have been more diligent in directing incoming Prime Ministers to convene Parliament and prove their majority within reasonable deadlines (2 to 3 weeks). In the interim period, the Prime Ministers are generally restrained from making policy decisions.

PROOF OF MAJORITY TO FORM A GOVERNMENT

Since the 1990s, Parliamentary elections have generally not resulted in a single party or group of parties having a distinct majority. In such cases, Presidents have used their discretion and directed Prime Ministerial aspirants to establish their credentials before being invited to form the government. Typically, the aspirants have been asked to produce letters from various party leaders, with the signatures of all the MPs who are pledging support to their candidature. This is in addition to the requirement that a Prime Minister prove he has the support of the Lok Sabha (by a vote on the floor of the House) within weeks of being sworn into office.[124][125]

POCKET VETO OF THE POSTAL BILL

Since the Indian Constitution does not provide any time limit within which the President is to declare his assent or refusal, the President could exercise a pocket veto by not taking any action for an indefinite time. Pocket Veto was used in 1986 by the then President Zail Singh in the Postal Bill. The president did not assent the bill by arguing that the scope of the bill was too sweeping which would give the government arbitrary powers to intercept postal communications indiscriminately. [126][127]

RASHTRAPATI BHAVAN COMMUNIQUÉS

In the late 1990s, President K. R. Narayanan introduced the important practice of explaining to the nation (by means of Rashtrapati Bhavan communiqués), the thinking that led to the various decisions he took while exercising his discretionary powers; this has led to openness and transparency in the functioning of the President.[128]

OFFICES OF PROFIT BILL

The constitution gives the President the power to return a bill unsigned but it circumscribes the power to send it back only once for reconsideration. If the Parliament sends back the bill with or without changes, the President is obliged to sign it. In mid-2006, President A. P. J. Abdul Kalam sent back a controversial bill regarding the exclusion of certain offices from the scope of 'offices of profit', the holding of which would disqualify a person from being a member of parliament. The combined opposition, the NDA, hailed the move. The UPA chose to send the bill back to the president without any changes and, after 17 days, Kalam gave his assent on 18 August 2006.

2.2 PRIME MINISTER OF INDIA

The **Prime Minister of India**, as addressed to in the Constitution of India, is the chief of government, chief advisor to the President of India, head of the Council of Ministers and the leader of the majority party in parliament. The prime minister leads the executive branch of the Government of India.

The prime minister is the senior member of cabinet in the executive branch of government in a parliamentary system. The prime minister selects and can dismiss other members of the cabinet; allocates posts to members within the Government; is the presiding member and chairman of the cabinet and is responsible for bringing proposal of legislation. The resignation or death of the prime minister dissolves the cabinet.

The prime minister is appointed by the president to assist the latter in the administration of the affairs of the executive. The incumbent prime minister is **Manmohan Singh**, in office since 22 May 2004.

ORIGINS AND HISTORY

India follows a parliamentary system of government. In parliamentary systems fashioned after the Westminster system, the prime minister is the presiding and actual head of the government and head of the executive branch. In such systems, the head of state or the head of state's official representative (i.e., the monarch, president, or governor-general) usually holds a purely ceremonial position.

The prime minister is expected to become a member of parliament within six months of beginning their tenure, if they are not a member already. They are expected to work with other ministers to ensure the passage of bills through the legislature.

CONSTITUTIONAL FRAMEWORK AND POSITION OF PRIME MINISTER

The Constitution envisages a scheme of affairs in which the President of India is the head of the executive in terms of Article 53 with office of the prime minister as heading the Council of Ministers to assist and advise the president in the discharge of the executive power. To quote, Article 53 and 74 provide as under;

The executive powers of the Union shall be vested in the president and shall be exercised either directly or through subordinate officers, in accordance with the Constitution.

— Article 53(1), Constitution of India

There shall be a Council of Ministers with the prime minister at the head to aid and advise the president who shall, in the exercise of his functions, act in accordance with such advice.

— Article 74(1), Constitution of India

Like most parliamentary democracies, a head of State's duties are mostly ceremonial, the Prime Minister of India is the head of government and has the responsibility for executive power. With India following a parliamentary system of government the prime minister is generally the leader of a party (or coalition of parties) that has a majority in the Lok Sabha, the lower house of the Parliament of India. The prime minister, in common with all other ministers at Central & state level, either has to be a current member of one of the houses of Parliament, or be elected within six months of being appointed.[129]

ROLE AND POWER OF THE PRIME MINISTER

The prime minister leads the functioning and exercise of authority of the Government of India. He is invited by the President of India in the Parliament of India as leader of the majority party to form a government at the federal level (known as Central or Union Government in India) and exercise its powers. In practice the prime minister nominates the members of their Council of Ministers[130][131][132] to the president. They also work upon to decide a core group of Ministers (known as the Cabinet)[130] as in-charge of the important functions and ministries of the Government of India.

The prime minister is responsible for aiding and advising the president in distribution of work of the Government to various ministries and offices and in terms of the Government of India (Allocation of Business) Rules, 1961.[133] The co-ordinating work is generally allocated to the Cabinet Secretariat[134]While generally the work of the Government is divided into various Ministries, the prime minister may retain certain portfolios if they are not allocated to any member of the cabinet.

The prime minister, in consultation with the Cabinet, schedules and attends the sessions of the Houses of Parliament and is required to answer the question from the Members of Parliament to them as the in-charge of the portfolios in the capacity as Prime Minister of India.[135]

Some specific ministries/department are not allocated to anyone in the cabinet but the prime minister himself. The prime minister is usually always in-charge/head of:

- Appointments Committee of the Cabinet;
- Ministry of Personnel, Public Grievances and Pensions;
- Ministry of Planning;
- Department of Atomic Energy; and
- Department of Space.

The prime minister represents the country in various delegations, high level meetings and international organizations that require the attendance of the highest government office[136] and also addresses to the nation on various issues of national or other importance.[137]

APPOINTMENT

ELIGIBILITY

According to Article 84 of the Constitution of India, which sets the principal qualifications for member of Parliament, and Article 75 of the Constitution of India, which sets the qualifications for the minister in the Union Council of Minister, and the argument that the position of prime minister has been described as 'first among equals',[138] A prime minister must:

- be a citizen of India.
- be a member of the Lok Sabha or the Rajya Sabha. If the person chosen as the prime minister is neither a member of the Lok Sabha nor the Rajya Sabha at the time of selection, he must become a member of either of the houses within six months.
- be above 25 years of age if he is a member of Lok Sabha or above 30 years of age if he is a member of the Rajya Sabha.
- not hold any office of profit under the Government of India or the Government of any State or under any local or other authority subject to the control of any of the said Governments.

OATH

The Prime Minister is required to make and subscribe in the presence of President of India before entering office, the oath of office and secrecy, as per the Third Schedule of the Constitution of India.

OATH OF OFFICE:

I, <name>, do swear in the name of God/solemnly affirm that I will bear true faith and allegiance to the Constitution of India as by law established, that I will uphold the sovereignty and integrity of India, that I will faithfully and conscientiously discharge my duties as prime minister for the Union and that I will do right to all manner of people in accordance with the Constitution and the law, without fear or favour, affection or ill-will.

— Constitution of India, Third Schedule, Part I

OATH OF SECRECY:

I, <name>, do swear in the name of God/solemnly affirm that I will not directly or indirectly communicate or reveal to any person or persons any matter which shall be brought under my consideration or shall become known to me as prime minister for the Union except as may be required for the due discharge of my duties as such Minister.

— Constitution of India, Third Schedule, Part II

REMUNERATION

By Article 75 of the constitution of India, remuneration of the prime minister as well as other ministers are to be decided by the Parliament[139] and is renewed from time to time. The original remuneration for prime minister and other ministers were specified in the Part B of the second schedule of the constitution, which was later removed by an amendment.

In 2010, the prime minister's office reported that he did not receive a formal salary, but was only entitled to monthly allowances.[140] That same year The Economist reported that, on a purchasing-power parity basis, the prime minister received an equivalent of $4106 per year. As a percentage of the country's per-capita GDP (Gross Domestic Product), this is the lowest of all countries The Economist surveyed.[141]

Prime Minister monthly pay and allowances		
Salary in Oct 2009	**Salary in Oct 2010**	**Salary in Jul 2012**
₹100000 (US$1,600)	₹135000 (US$2,200)	₹160000 (US$2,600)
Sources: [142]		

LIVING FORMER PRIME MINISTERS

As of February 2014[update], there are only two living former Prime Minister of India (H.D. Deve Gowda and Atal Bihari Vajpayee). The most recent death of a former prime minister was that of I. K. Gujral (1919–2012), on 30 November 2012.

Prime Minister	Term of office	Date of birth
H. D. Deve Gowda	1996–1997	18 May 1933 (age 80)
Atal Bihari Vajpayee	1998–2004	25 December 1924 (age 89)

2.3 COUNCIL OF MINISTERS

Though there is an elected President at the top of the Government structure, the constitution in reality establishes a British cabinet type of Government in India.

Article 74(1) requires the **President** to have a Council of Ministers with the Prime Minister at the head to "aid and advice" him in the exercise of his power. To remove the impression that the advice given by the Council of Ministers may not be binding on the President, the 42nd amendment of the constitution has made the ministerial advice expressly binding on the President.

In terms of Article 74(1) the President is bound to have a Council of Ministers with the Prime Minister at the head. The Prime Minister is appointed by the President and all other ministers are appointed by the President on the advice of the Prime Minister. India has a three-tier ministry consisting of cabinet ministers, ministers of state and the deputy ministers. The term cabinet is absent in the constitution. Usually senior ministers with independent charge of ministries constitute a body that the Prime Minister consults in arriving at policy decisions, constitute the cabinet. The cabinet thus is the policy making part of the ministry. It is an informal body and its members are chosen by the Prime Minister himself.

Article 75 makes the Council of Minister responsible to the House of People. This obliges the President to appoint the leader of the majority party as the Prime Minister and to appoint other ministers on his advice. Thus the Prime Minister is not the President's nominee but the nation's choice. The nation votes a party to power and its leader becomes the Prime Minister. Indian general elections are really elections of the Prime Minister.

The Prime Minister and the members of the council of ministers serve legally "during the pleasure of the President." But the President's pleasure is not personal but political. So long the Prime Minister retains his support in the House of People; the President cannot withdraw pleasure from the Prime Minister and the Council of Ministers.

FUNCTIONS

The executive government in India is really the Prime Minister's government. The cabinet, as in England is the steering wheel of the government. As the nation's chief executive body, the cabinet performs the following principal functions.

- Firstly, it is in charge of administering all the subjects entrusted to the national government by the union list. Principal among these functions are providing for security and defence of the country, maintaining and conducting the nation's foreign affairs, maintaining the system of communication within the country, keeping the national economy in good health, preserving and improving inter-state relations and a host of other things. Ministers are put in charge of administrative departments. The ministers are in reality political heads of administrative departments of governments. An elaborate bureaucracy conducts the day to day administration, under the political control of the ministers. Thus the Cabinet and the Prime Minister administers the country.

- In the sphere of law making the cabinet is equally supreme and the President has only a formal role. The President is no doubt an integral part of the Parliament. The President addresses the joint sessions of the Parliament after every general election and at the beginning of each session of the Parliament. But the President only reads out the address drafted for him by the Cabinet. The President signs the bills passed by the Parliament into law. But the President does exactly what the cabinet asks him to do.

- Again strictly constitutionally, the Parliament is the nation's supreme law making body. But the Prime Minister and the cabinet have a firm control over the Parliamentary majority. Because of this majority support, the Prime Minister and the cabinet can make the Parliament pass whatever law, the Prime Minister wants the Parliament to pass.

Conversely, the Parliament shall never pass a bill which the Prime Minister and the Cabinet oppose. Thus the law making powers of the Parliament is also the powers of the Cabinet.

- The Prime Minister and the Cabinet also have an absolute control over the nation's finances. The annual budget is prepared at the instance of the cabinet. The proposals for taxes and expenditures are really made by the Cabinet, and only formally approved by the Parliament.

- Finally, Indian constitution is partially based on the theory of Parliamentary sovereignty. The sovereignty of the Parliament realistically means the sovereignty of the cabinet. Even the judiciary is not beyond cabinet control. Judges of the Supreme Court and the High Courts are appointed and transferred by the President on Cabinet advice. Similarly the President's rights to grant pardon or reprieve or remission of sentences are also the powers of the Cabinet. Thus the Indian Cabinet, like its British counterpart enjoys powers of dictatorial dimensions.

There is a list of current members of the Council of Ministers of the Government of India. All ministers are based in offices of their respective Union Ministries in New Delhi.

All Cabinet members are mandated by the constitution to be members of either House of the Parliament of India. In a departure from the norm the current Prime Minister, Manmohan Singh, is a member of the upper house, the Rajya Sabha. He remained so for the duration of his entire first term (2004–2009). Most, but not all, previous Prime Ministers have been elected members of the Lok Sabha.[143]

There are three categories of ministers, in descending order of rank:

- Union Cabinet Minister: senior minister in-charge of a ministry. A cabinet minister may also hold additional charges of other Ministries, where no other Cabinet minister is appointed

- Minister of State (Independent Charges): with no overseeing Union cabinet minister for that portfolio

- Minister of State (MoS): junior minister to overseeing cabinet minister usually tasked with a specific responsibility in that ministry. For instance, an MoS in the Finance Ministry may only handle taxation.

UNION MINISTERS

Portfolios	Name	Image	Age	Parliamentary constituency	Party	Educational background
Department of Atomic Energy Department of Space Ministry of Personnel, Public Grievances and Pensions Planning Commission	**Manmohan Singh**		81	Assam (Rajyasabha)	INC	• Panjab University • St John's College • Nuffield College
Ministry of Defence	**A. K. Antony**		72		INC	
Ministry of Agriculture	**Sharad Pawar**		72	Madha	NCP	
Ministry of Finance	**P. Chidambaram**		67	Sivaganga	INC	Harvard University (M.B.A)
Ministry of External Affairs	**Salman Khurshid**		60	Farrukhabad	INC	St Edmund Hall
Ministry of Home Affairs	**Sushilkumar Shinde**		71	Solapur	INC	
Ministry of Communications and Information Technology Ministry of Law and Justice	**Kapil Sibal**		64	Chandni Chowk	INC	
Ministry of Human Resource Development	**Pallam Raju**		50	Kakinada	INC	

Ministry	Name		Age	Constituency	Party	
Ministry of Housing and Urban Poverty Alleviation	**Girija Vyas**		67		INC	
Ministry of Civil Aviation	**Ajit Singh**		73	Baghpat	RLD	
Ministry of Mines	**Dinsha Patel**		75	Kheda	INC	
Ministry of Commerce and Industry	**Anand Sharma**		60	Himachal Pradesh (Rajya Sabha)	INC	
Ministry of Textiles	**Kavuru Samba Siva Rao**		69	Eluru	INC	
Ministry of Petroleum and Natural Gas	**Veerappa Moily**		73	Chikballapur	INC	
Ministry of Culture	**Chandresh Kumari**		68	Jodhpur	INC	
Ministry of Water Resources	**Gulam Nabi Azad**		65	Haridwar	INC	
Ministry of Rural Development	**Jairam Ramesh**		58	Andhra Pradesh (Rajya Sabha)	INC	
Ministry of Urban Development	**Kamal Nath**		66	Chhindwara	INC	
Ministry of Parliamentary Affairs						
Ministry of Overseas Indian Affairs	**Vayalar Ravi**		75	Kerala	INC	
Ministry of Health and Family Welfare	**Ghulam Nabi Azad**		63	Jammu and Kashmir (Rajya Sabha)	INC	
Ministry of Heavy Industries and Public Enterprises	**Praful Patel**		55	Bhandara-Gondiya	NCP	

Ministry	Name		Age	Constituency		Party	
Ministry of Panchayati Raj Ministry of Tribal Affairs	**Kishore Chandra Deo**		65	Araku		INC	
Ministry of Science and Technology Ministry of Earth Sciences	**Jaipal Reddy**		71	Chevella		INC	
Ministry of Road Transport and Highways Ministry of Labour and Employment	**Oscar Fernandes**		72	Karnataka (Rajya Sabha)		INC	
Ministry of Railways Ministry of Social Justice and Empowerment	**Mallikarjun Kharge**		70	Gulbarga		INC	
Ministry of Shipping	**G. K. Vasan**		48	Tamil Nadu (Rajya Sabha)		INC	
Ministry of Steel	**Beni Prasad Verma**		71	Gonda		INC	
Ministry of Coal	**Shriprakash Jaiswal**		68	Kanpur		INC	
Ministry of Minority Affairs	**K. Rahman Khan**		73	Karnataka (Rajya Sabha)		INC	

MINISTERS OF STATE (INDEPENDENT CHARGES)

A 'Minister of State with independent charge' is a junior Minister in the Federal (State) or Central Government of India but is in charge of a ministry, unlike Minister of State who is also a junior Minister but assists a cabinet minister. All the following ministers are from the Indian National Congress.

Sl. No.	Name	Responsible Ministries	Age	Lok Sabha/Rajya Sabha	Party	Educational Qualification
1	Manish Tewari	Information and Broadcasting	47	Lok Sabha (Ludhiana, Punjab)	INC	
2	Chiranjeevi (Konidala Siva Sankara Vara Prasad)	Tourism	58	Rajya Sabha (Andhra Pradesh)	INC	B.Com from Y.N College, Narasapuram, AP

3	Jyotiraditya Madhavrao Scindia	Power	42	Lok Sabha (Guna, Madhya Pradesh)	INC	M.A., M.B.A., Stanford University, U.S.A
4	Bharatsinh Madhavsinh Solanki	Drinking Water and Sanitation	59	Lok Sabha (Anand, Gujarat)	INC	B.E. (Civil)
5	Jitendra Singh	Youth Affairs and Sports	41	Lok Sabha (Alwar, Rajasthan)	INC	B.Com
6	Sachin Pilot	Corporate Affairs	35	Lok Sabha (Ajmer, Rajasthan)	INC	M.B.A. – Wharton Business School, University of Pennsylvania, Philadelphia, USA
7	Krishna Tirath	Women and Child Development	57	Lok Sabha (North West Delhi, Delhi)	INC	M.A., B.Ed. (University of Delhi)
8	K. V. Thomas	Consumer Affairs, Food and Public Distribution	66	Lok Sabha (Ernakulam, Kerala)	INC	M.Sc.(Chemistry)
9	Srikant Kumar Jena	Statistics and Program Implementation and Chemicals and Fertilizers	62	Lok Sabha (Balasore, Odisha)	INC	B.A. Utkal University, Bhubaneswar, Odisha
10	Veerappa Moily	Environment and Forests	58	Rajya Sabha (Tamil Nadu)	INC	B.A., B.L. Ethiraj College and Madras Law College
11	Paban Singh Ghatowar	Development of North Eastern Region, Parliamentary Affairs	62	Lok Sabha (Dibrugarh, Assam)	INC	B.A. Gauhati University, Guwahati
12	K. H. Muniyappa	Micro, Small and Medium Enterprises	64	Lok Sabha (Kolar, Karnataka)	INC	B.A., LL.B.

SOURCE: COUNCIL OF MINISTERS[144]

MINISTERS OF STATE

Sl. No.	Name	Responsible Ministries	Age	Lok Sabha/Rajya Sabha	Party	Educational Qualification
1	E. Ahamed	External Affairs	74	Lok Sabha Malappuram, Kerala	MUL	B.A., B.L.
2	Shashi Tharoor	Human Resource Development	56	Lok Sabha Thiruvananthapuram, Kerala	INC	St. Stephen's College, Delhi (B.A.) Tufts University (M.A.,

						M.A.L.D., Ph.D.)
3	Tariq Anwar	Agriculture	61	Rajya Sabha, Maharastra	NCP	B.Sc.
4	Mullappally Ramachandran	Home Affairs	67	Lok Sabha Vadakara,Kerala	INC	MA, LLB
5	V. Narayanasamy	Personnel, Public Grievances and Pensions and Prime Minister Office	65	Lok Sabha Puducherry	INC	B.A., M.L.
6	Daggubati Purandeswari	Commerce and Industry	53	Lok Sabha, Visakhapatnam Andhra Pradesh	INC	BA
7	Panabaka Lakshmi	Textiles	54	Lok Sabha, Bapatla, Prakasam Dist,Andhra Pradesh	INC	M.A.(Public Administration)
8	Namo Narain Meena	Finance	68	Lok Sabha, Tonk-Sawai Madhopur	INC	M. A. (Geography)
9	Jitin Prasada	Human Resource Development and Defence	38	Lok Sabha Dhaurahra, Uttar Pradesh	INC	M.B.A,
10	Preneet Kaur	External Affairs	68	Lok Sabha Patiala, Punjab	INC	B.A., T.T.C.
11	Tushar Amarsinh Chaudhary	Road Transport and Highways	46	Lok Sabha, Bardoli	INC	M.B.B.S
12	Pratik Prakashbapu Patil	Coal	39	Lok Sabha Sangli	INC	Intermediate, Diploma in Automobile Engineering
13	R. P. N. Singh	Home Affairs	48	Lok Sabha Khushi Nagar	INC	B.A. (Hons.) History
14	Pradeep Jain Aditya	Rural Development	50	Lok Sabha, Jhansi	INC	M.A., M.Com., L.L.B.
15	K. C. Venugopal	Civil Aviation and Power	49	Lok Sabha Alappuzha, Kerala	INC	M.Sc.(Mathematics)
16	Charan Das Mahant	Agriculture and Food Processing Industries	57	Lok Sabha Korba, Chhattisgarh	INC	M.Sc., M.A., LL.B., PhD
17	Milind Murli Deora	Communications and Information Technology	35	Lok Sabha, Mumbai-South	INC	BBA (Bachelor of Science in Business Administration)
18	Rajeev Shukla	Parliamentary Affairs and Planning	53	Rajya Sabha, Maharastra	INC	M.A., LL.B.
19	Kodikunnil	Labor and	50	Lok Sabha	INC	LL.B

	Suresh	Employment		Mavelikara,Kerala		
20	K.J. Surya Prakash Reddy	Railways	61	Lok Sabha Kurnool, Andhra Pradesh	INC	B.A
21	Ranee Narah	Tribal Affairs	46	Lok Sabha Lakhimpur,Assam	INC	B.A
22	Adhir Ranjan Chowdhury	Railways	56	Lok Sabha Berhampore, West Bengal	INC	Under Matriculate
23	Killi Krupa Rani	Communications and Information Technology	46	Lok Sabha Srikakulam, Andhra Pradesh	INC	M.B.B.S
24	Abu Hasem Khan Choudhury	Health and Family Welfare	74	Lok Sabha Malda, West Bengal	INC	Degree in Industrial Psychology (Northampton college,England),University of Guleph, Canada
25	Sarvey Sathyanarayana,	Road Transport and Highways	58	Lok Sabha Malkajgiri, Andhra Pradesh	INC	B.A, LL.B
26	Ninong Ering	Minority Affairs	53	Lok Sabha Arunachal East	INC	B.A
27	Deepa Dasmunsi	Urban Development	52	Lok Sabha Raiganj, West Bengal	INC	M.A.(Dramatics)
28	Lal Chand Kataria	Defence	44	Lok Sabha Jaipur Rural	INC	Intermediate
29	Porika Balram Naik	Social Justice and Empowerment	48	Lok Sabha, Mahabubabad	INC	B.A.

New Ministers of State alongside old ones:[145]

- Manikrao Hodlya Gavit, Social Justice and Empowerment
- Santosh Chowdhary, Health & Family Welfare
- Jesudasu Seelam becomes, Finance
- E.M. Sudarsana Natchiappan, Commerce and Industry

DEMOGRAPHICS OF THE COUNCIL OF MINISTERS

UPA CABINET BY PARTY

SOURCE: VARIOUS NEWS ORGANISATIONS[146][147][148]

The new United Progressive Alliance (UPA) included 77 members, 76 members in the cabinet plus Prime Minister Manmohan Singh. The first 20 cabinet ministers including Manmohan Singh, swore in on 22 May 2009, while the other 59 cabinet members swore in on 27 May 2009.

The non-Congress cabinet ministers, include Sharad Pawar and Praful Patel from Nationalist Congress Party, Farooq Abdullah from National Conference and Chaudhary Ajit Singh from RLD.

Party	# Cabinet Ministers	# Ministers of State (I)	# Ministers of State	Total number of ministers
Indian National Congress	28	12	31	71
Nationalist Congress Party	2	0	1	3
Jammu and Kashmir National Conference	1	0	0	1
Rashtriya Lok Dal	1	0	0	1
Indian Union Muslim League	0	0	1	1
Total	32	12	33	77

2.4 UNION LEGISLATURE OF INDIA

The **Parliament of India**, also popularly known as **Sansad** (Sanskrit: संसद); is the supreme legislative body in India. The Parliament comprises the President of India and the two Houses— Lok Sabha (House of the People) and Rajya Sabha (Council of States). The President has the power to summon and prorogue either House of Parliament or to dissolve Lok Sabha.[149]

India's government is bicameral; Rajya Sabha is the upper house and Lok Sabha is the lower house. The two Houses meet in separate chambers in the Sansad Bhavan (located on the Sansad Marg or "Parliament Street") in New Delhi. Those elected or nominated (by the President) to either house of Parliament are referred to as members of parliament or MPs. The MPs of Lok Sabha are directly elected by the Indian public and the MPs of Rajya Sabha are elected by the members of the State Legislative Assemblies, in accordance with proportional representation. The Parliament is composed of 790 MPs, who serve the largest democratic electorate in the world; 714 million Indians registered to vote in the 2009 general elections.

The Indian Parliament consists of two houses called as Lok Sabha and the Rajya Sabha and the President of India.

PRESIDENT OF INDIA

Similar to most Commonwealth countries, India also includes the Head of State (the President of India in India's case) as a component of Parliament. The President of India is elected, from a group of nominees, by the elected members of the Parliament of India (Lok Sabha and Rajya Sabha) as well as of the state legislatures, and serves for a term of five years. Historically, ruling party (majority in the Lok Sabha) nominees have been elected and run largely uncontested. Incumbents are permitted to stand for re-election, but unlike the president of the United States, who can be elected just twice, incumbents can be elected for any number of terms. A formula is used to allocate votes so there is a balance between the population of each state and the number of votes assembly members from a state can cast, and to give an equal balance between State Assembly members and National Parliament members. If no candidate receives a majority of votes there is a system by which losing candidates are eliminated from the contest and votes for them transferred to other candidates, until one gains a majority. Pranab Mukherjee is the present President of India.[150]

Lok Sabha

Lok Sabha is also known as the "House of the People" or the lower house. All of its members are directly elected by citizens of India on the basis of universal adult franchise, except two who are appointed by the President of India. Every citizen of India who is over 18 years of age, irrespective of gender, caste, religion or race, who is otherwise not disqualified, is eligible to vote for the lok sabha.

The Constitution provides that the maximum strength of the House be 552 members. It has a term of five years. To be eligible for membership in the Lok Sabha, a person must be a citizen of India and must be 25 years of age or older, mentally sound, should not be bankrupt and should not be criminally convicted. At present, the strength of the house is 545 members. The total elective membership is distributed among the States in such a way that the ratio between the number of seats allotted to each State and the population of the State is, so far as practicable, the same for all States.[151]

Up to 530 members represent of the territorial constituencies in States, up to 20 members represent the Union Territories and no more than two members from Anglo-Indian community can be nominated by the President of India if he or she feels that the community is not adequately represented. House seats are apportioned among the states by population .

Several seats are reserved for representatives of Scheduled Castes and Scheduled Tribes, in a practice known as reservation. The Women's Reservation Bill proposes reserving 33% of the seats in Lok Sabha for women.

Rajya Sabha

The Rajya Sabha is also known as "Council of States" or the upper house. Rajya Sabha is a permanent body and is not subject to dissolution. However, one third of the members retire every second year, and are replaced by newly elected members. Each member is elected for a term of six years.[152] Its members are indirectly elected by members of legislative bodies of the States.

The Rajya Sabha can have a maximum of 250 members in all. Elections to it are scheduled and the chamber cannot be dissolved. Each member has a term of 6 years and elections are held for one-third of the seats after every 2 years. 238 members are to be elected from States and Union Territories and 12 are to be nominated by President of India and shall consist of persons having special knowledge or practical experience in respect of such matters as the following, namely literature, science, art and social service. The minimum age for a person to become a member of Rajya Sabha is 30 years.

- Representatives of States are elected by the elected members of the Legislative Assembly of the State in accordance with system of proportional representation by means of single transferable vote.
- Representatives of Union Territories are indirectly elected by members of an electoral college for that territory in accordance with system of proportional representation.

The Council of States is designed to maintain the federal character of the country. The number of members from a state depends on the population of the state (e.g. 31 from Uttar Pradesh and one from Nagaland).

ARCHITECTURE

The parliament is one of the most magnificent buildings in New Delhi. It was designed by Edwin Lutyens and Herbert Baker, who were responsible for planning and construction of New Delhi. The construction of buildings took six years and the opening ceremony was performed on 18 January 1927 by the then Governor-General of India, Lord Irwin. The construction costs for the building were Rs. 8.3 million. The parliament is 570 feet (170 meters) in diameter. It covers an area of nearly six acres. The building has twelve gates among which Gate No. 1 on the Sansad Marg is the main gate.

GENERAL LAYOUT OF THE BUILDING

The centre and the focus of the building is the Central Hall. It consists of chambers of Lok Sabha, Rajya Sabha and the Library Hall and between them lie garden courts. Surrounding these three chambers is the four storyed circular structure providing accommodations for Ministers, Chairmen, Parliamentary committees, Party offices, important offices of Lok Sabha and Rajya Sabha Secretariats and also the offices of the ministry of Parliamentary affairs. The Central Hall is circular in shape and the dome is 98 feet (29.87 meters) in diameter. It is the place of historical importance. The Indian Constitution was framed in the Central Hall. The Central Hall was originally used in the library of erstwhile Central Legislative Assembly and the Council of States.

In 1946, it was converted and refurbished into Constituent Assembly Hall. At present, the Central Hall is used for holding joint sittings of both the houses of parliament and also used for address by the President in the commencement of first session after each general election.

WORKING, PROCEDURES AND COMMITTEES

The Parliament consists of the President of Republic of India and both the Chambers. The House and the Council are equal partners in the legislative process; however, the Constitution grants the House of People some unique powers. Revenue-raising or "Money" bills must originate in the Lok Sabha. The Council of States can only make recommendations suggestions over these bills to the House, within a period of fourteen days – lapse of which the bill is assumed to have been passed by both the Chambers.[149]

SESSION OF PARLIAMENT

The period during which the House meets to conduct its business is called a session. The Constitution empowers the President to summon each House at such intervals that there should not be more than 6-month's gap between the two sessions. Hence the Parliament must meet at least twice a year. In India, the parliament conducts three sessions each year:[149]

- Budget session: In the months of February to May.[149]
- Monsoon session: In the months of July to September.[149]
- Winter session: In the months of November to December[149]

LAWMAKING PROCEDURES

Lawmaking procedures in India are modeled after, and are thus very similar to, those followed by the Parliament of the United Kingdom.

PARLIAMENTARY COMMITTEES

Parliamentary committees play a vital role in the Parliamentary System. They are a vibrant link between the Parliament, the Executive and the general public.

The need for committees arises out of two factors – the first one being the need for vigilance on the part of the Legislature over the actions of the Executive, while the second one is that the modern Legislature these days is over-burdened with heavy volume of work with limited time at its disposal. It thus becomes impossible that every matter should be thoroughly and systematically scrutinized and considered on the floor of the House. If the work is to be done with reasonable care, some Parliamentary responsibility has to be entrusted to an agency in which the whole House has confidence. Entrusting certain functions of the House to the Committees has, therefore, become a normal practice. This has become all the more necessary, as a Committee provides the expertise on a matter which is referred to it.

In a committee, the matter is deliberated at length, views are expressed freely, the matter is considered in depth, in a business-like manner and in a calm atmosphere. In most of the Committees, public is directly or indirectly associated when memoranda containing suggestions and are received, on-the-spot studies are conducted and oral evidence is taken which helps the Committees in arriving at the conclusions.

Parliamentary committees are of two kinds: ad hoc committees and the standing committees. The most powerful committee is the public accounts committee, which is headed by the leader of the opposition.

STANDING COMMITTEES

There are 45 standing committees in the Indian Parliament. Each house of Parliament has standing committees like the Business Advisory Committee, the Committee on Petitions, the Committee of Privileges and the Rules Committee, etc.

Standing committees are permanent and regular committees which are constituted from time to time in pursuance of the provisions of an Act of Parliament or Rules of Procedure and Conduct of Business in Parliament. The work of these committees is of a continuing nature. The Financial Committees, DRSCs and some other committees are standing committees.

AD HOC COMMITTEES

Ad hoc committees are appointed for a specific purpose and they cease to exist when they finish the task assigned to them and submit a report. The principal ad hoc committees are the Select and Joint Committees on Bills. Others like the Railway Convention Committee, the Committees on the Draft Five Year Plans and the Hindi Equivalents Committee were appointed for specific purposes.

Joint Committee on Food Management in Parliament House Complex etc. also come under the category of ad hoc committees.

2001 PARLIAMENT ATTACK

On 13 December 2001, the parliament building was attacked by five Lashkar-e-Taiba and Jaish-e-Mohammed terrorists. In addition to all the attackers, six military personnel and one civilian were killed.[153]

2.5 THE UNION JUDICIARY: THE SUPREME COURT OF INDIA

[Articles 124to147.][154]

INTRODUCTION:

Disputes are endemic in any society. Even in a well-knit family, disputes cannot be ruled out or wished away. It was Bernard Gournay, a French Philosopher, who said several decades ago that the only place which is free from conflicts is the grave yard. But, today, even this proposition is contestable because at grave yards you would, invariably, witness several urchins engaged in gambling. Gamblers, we should suppose, are more inclined to engage in conflicts, The point being emphasized is that disputes/conflicts do arise in various situations and unless resolved quickly would disturb peace in society. Perennial social unrest in a democratic polity would not be a healthy sign. Prudence, therefore, demands that disputes or conflicts should be resolved as expeditiously as possible by an impartial, independent tribunal or Court.

A Constitution is not a static, rigid, lifeless document. It mirrors the ambitions and aspirations of the people who it governs. Its provisions are ever-changing, ever-evolving. It embodies the supreme Law of the Land.

To abide by the constitutional dictates, to promote or achieve the constitutional goals, the legislatures have enacted numerous statutes. These laws may confer rights, impose obligations, The Constitution itself guarantees to its citizens several fundamental rights, like, Freedom of speech and Expression, Freedom of Assembly, Freedom of Association, Freedom of Movement,(Art.19) Equality before the law and Equal protection of the laws (Art.14), Prohibits discrimination on grounds of religion, Race, Caste Sex or Place of Birth (Art.15), guarantees Equality of opportunity in matters of Public Employment (Art.16), promises to protect life and personal liberty (Art.21), Right to Education (Art.21A),Freedom of Religion (Art.25), to mention a few, for illustrative purposes.

Of course, the rights guaranteed under Art.19, like freedom of speech and expression, freedom of assembly, association are not absolute and the State, that is the Central or State Legislatures.... may impose reasonable restrictions upon the same. But who is the final arbiter or authority to determine whether the restrictions imposed are reasonable or unreasonable?

Or, whether the Constitutional Prohibition on discrimination on grounds of race, religion, sex, etc., has been honored by the state or not? Or, whether the law enacted offends the Equality Doctrine which Art.14 propounds?

Further, it is not the Constitution alone that is the repository of the rights of the citizens. Various Statutes enacted by the Legislature do also confer rights. For example, the laws creating rights to pensioner benefits, to gratuity, etc. Who has to ultimately decide the ambit of these rights, the extent of entitlement, whether there has been a violation of these rights?

Also, it would be worthwhile to recall that ours is a written Constitution, which, while creating the various organs of the State, namely, the Executive, the Legislature and the Judiciary, also marks out the jurisdictions within which they have to discharge their constitutionally ordained obligations, functions, duties. That is, the Constitution which grants the powers also limits them. Who has to decide whether the limitations have been crossed or transgressed?

The foregoing would boil down to some significant questions: who has to ensure that the citizens' rights and liberties are secured or protected?

Who has to interpret or expound the statutes and the Constitution? How to ensure the rule of law reigns supreme? If there be no remedy to a citizen when his rights are violated, then, the instruments which confer rights would be worthless. That is the reason why Alexander Hamilton has said: "Laws are a dead letter without Courts to expound and define their true meaning and operation". Thus, an independent impartial judiciary becomes indispensable in a democratic polity. So also, judicial Review of administrative and legislative actions. In fact, Our Supreme Court has ruled that "Judicial Review" and "Independent Judiciary" are among the "Fundamental Features of our Constitution" and are unamendable.

Thus, pronouncements of the Supreme Court acquire great significance when one realizes that "the Government of India is the biggest single litigant in India, and the Govt.(sic) of the States are the biggest single litigants in the states".

Seervai, at p.2836. Seervai, therefore, argues that in ensuring the independence of the judiciary, the Constitutional Provisions bearing upon the appointment of Judges to the Supreme Court and the High Courts should not be interpreted as conferring absolute or unfettered power on the Executive. The learned scholar asserts that "any interpretation of Art.217 ("Appointment – of a Judge of a High Court") which puts judicial independence at the mercy of an Executive, which is the largest single litigant-must be rejected if any other reasonable interpretation can be put on Art.217" Seervai,at p.2836.

With the foregoing introduction, we may now refer to the relevant Constitutional Provisions relating to the establishment of the Supreme Court, the procedure for the appointment of Judges, the qualifications prescribed for such appointments, the manner of removal of Supreme Court Judges and, importantly, the kinds of jurisdiction exercisable by the Highest Court of our land.

Incidentally, it has to be noted that although the Constitution provides for distribution of powers between the centre (union') and the states and there is a dual polity, there are no separate hierarchies of Courts at the state and union levels as exist in some federal systems, for example, the U.S.A.

We have "one unified Judicial system and an integrated judiciary (and) there is one hierarchy of courts". National Commission--- at p.135. The Supreme Court is at the top.

THE SUPREME COURT: ART.124 (1).

Clause (1) of Art.124 declares that there shall be a Supreme Court of India. The Chief Justice of India ("CJI") and twenty-five other Judges constitute the Supreme Court. The Supreme Court and the High Courts enjoy an exalted status under our Constitution. They have been described as the "Protectors" and "Guardians" of the individual's Rights and Liberties and the "Conscience-Keepers of our Constitution". The Supreme Court is the Highest Court and the final Court of Appeal.

CHIEF JUSTICE OF INDIA:

The Constitution offers no indicators for the appointment of the Chief Justice. However, the convention, though breached on a couple of occasions in the past, that the senior-most Judge be appointed as Chief Justice has been followed.

When the CJI presides over a Bench, he is primus inter pares, that is, first amongst equals. CJI Constitutes the Benches of the Supreme Court and assigns matters to be heard. In the appointment of Judges of the Supreme Court and the High Courts, CJI and his senior-most colleagues have an important role to play.

Appointments of officers and servants of the Supreme Court are to be made by the CJI or such other Judge or officer of the Court as he may direct.

APPOINTMENT OF JUDGES: ART.124(2).

The procedure for appointment of Judges to the Supreme Court is spelt out in cl.(2) of Art.124. As per the provisions, it is the President who appoints every judge of the Supreme Court by warrant under his hand and seal. However, the President, before making the appointment is obliged to consult such of the judges of the Supreme Court and of the High Courts as he deems necessary. Further, in the case of appointment of a Judge other than the Chief Justice, the President shall consult the Chief Justice of India ("CJI").

At this Juncture, two important points need be noted. The first one is, although Art.124(2) gives the impression that the appointment of a Judge is made by the President, in reality, it is the union executive that exercises the power. That is, the President has to make the appointment on the advice tendered by the Council of Ministers. The second point is, the Constitution has provided for consultation with a view to fetter the power of the Executive in making judicial appointments so that the Executive would not enjoy absolute power in making the said appointments. For, to concede such a power to the executive would devastate and destroy the prospect of an independent, impartial Judiciary, Seerrai, at p.2854.

There was confusion surrounding the Consultation Process contemplated in the Constitution. The questions being raised were: whether 'Consultation' means "concurrence"? Whether the opinion of CJI should be given primacy? Or, when the CJI and the President differ, whose opinion should prevail? For the time being, at least, the confusion seems to have been removed in the light of the Supreme Court's Advisory opinion in Presidential Reference, AIR 1999 SC 1 Now, CJI'S sole opinion in regard to the appointment of a Judge is of no consequence. "Consultation" means" Consultation of Plurality of Judges". As Prof.M.P.Singh explains: "The process of appointment of Judges is initiated by the CJI through a collegiums consisting of himself and four of the senior-most judges of the Court. Recommendation of the collegiums are binding on the President. However, the President may not appoint a person whom for specific reasons he does not consider suitable for appointment. In such a case, the collegium must reconsider its recommendation. On reconsideration, it may either drop the name of the person not found suitable by the President or reiterate its recommendation.

In the later case, the President is bound to accept the recommendation". Constitution of India Revised by M.P.Singh (Tenth Edition), (2004),at p.413.

TERM OF OFFICE:

A Judge appointed to the Supreme court shall hold office until he attains the age of sixty-five years. Art.124 (2). He may resign before the age of retirement by addressing his letter of resignation to the President. Second proviso to cl.(2) of Art.124.

Impeachment (Removal): Cl.(4) of Art.124 provides that a Judge can be removed from office before he attains the age of sixty five years on grounds of proved misbehavior or incapacity. 'Misbehavior' or 'Incapacity' is not explained under Art.124 (4). Further, what separates 'misbehavior' and 'Incapacity' is 'or', not, 'and'. That is , a Judge can be removed on either of the grounds and there is no need to establish both "misbehavior" and "Incapacity".

'Misbehaviour' may be "misconduct". For example, use of public funds for private purposes. 'Incapacity' may imply either physical or mental incapacity.

Further, a sitting Judge can be removed only when his 'misbehavior' or 'incapacity' is "proved". So, mere allegation, apprehension, or suspicion won't do. 'Misbehavior' or incapacity' has to be investigated, established and proved. Natural Justice demands that the delinquent Judge has to be apprised of the charge and be heard. So, a summary or an informal procedure adopted by the executive for the removal of a Judge is unacceptable because it destroys the independence of the Judiciary.

Therefore, democratic constitutions prescribe an elaborate and, if we can say, a cumbersome procedure for the impeachment of persons holding high Constitutional Offices.

Under our Constitution, a Judge of the Supreme Court can be removed from his office by an order of the President. Such an order can be passed only after an address by each House of Parliament for the removal of the Judge on the ground of proved misbehavior or incapacity is presented to the President. The address must have been supported by a majority of the total membership of the House and by a majority of not less than two-thirds of the members present and voting.

What should be noted is that the address, referred to above, can be presented only after misbehavior or incapacity on the part of the Judge concerned is proved. Now, what is the procedure to be followed to investigate and establish the alleged 'misbehavior' or 'incapacity'? Who has to conduct the investigation?

Cl.(5) of Art.124 says that Parliament may by law regulate the procedure for the presentation of an address and for the investigation and proof of the misbehavior or incapacity of a Judge.

Pursuant to the above provision, Parliament has enacted the Judges (Inquiry) Act, 1968. This Act lays down an elaborate procedure for investigating and establishing 'misbehavior' or 'incapacity' of the Judge by a Committee of Inquiry to be constituted by the Speaker of Lok Sabha or Chairman of Rajya Sabha. The Committee has to frame definite charges and the Judge concerned has to be given a reasonable opportunity to present his defense. Should the committee hold the Judge guilty, then the House can take up the motion for consideration. After the motion is adopted as stipulated in Art.124 (4), the address shall be presented to the President for the removal of the Judge.

Qualifications: The qualifications for appointment of a Judge to the Supreme Court are mentioned in Cl.(3) of Art.124.They are:

1) He must be an Indian citizen.

2) He must have been a Judge of a High Court for at least five years,

3) He must have been an advocate for a High Court of at least Ten Years;

4) In the opinion of the President, he is a distinguished Jurist.

The National commission has observed that "in the last fifty years not a single, distinguished jurist has been appointed". At, p.139. The Commission adds: "From the bar also, less than half a dozen Judges have been appointed" Ibid. The Commission recommends that "suitable meritorious persons from these sources (be) appointed" Ibid.

Apart from the qualifications expressly prescribed by the Constitution, the implied qualifications required are: unimpeachable character and integrity; impartiality, independence; equanimity; incorruptibility.

Dr.Ambedkar had, in the Constituent Assembly, expressed that the Judiciary should be independent of the Executive and competent in itself. Nehru felt :

"They (the Judges) should be first class and seen to be first class".

SUPREME COURT: JURISDICTION AND POWERS:

The Jurisdiction of the Supreme Court under our Constitution is quite wide. It is the final Court of Appeal in respect of civil and criminal matters. What follows would give us an idea about the extensive jurisdiction our Apex Court enjoys as well as the powers conferred upon the Court under our Constitution.

A) POWER TO ENFORCE FUNDAMENTAL RIGHTS (ART.32):

You are, Probably, aware that part III of our Constitution adumbrates our Fundamental Rights. The various Fundamental Rights like 'Right to Equality' 'Right not to be discriminated on the grounds of race, religion, caste, sex or place of birth, 'Equality of opportunity in matters of public employment,' Freedom of Speech and Expression,' 'Freedom of Assembly,' Freedom of Association,' to mention a few, guaranteed to the citizens would remain as pious constitutional declarations if the repositories of the rights are not assured that in case of any violation of those rights they can look up to some authority for their enforcement. It is, at this juncture, Art.32 comes into play and acquires significance. Dr.Ambedkar had remarked that Art.32 "is the soul of the Constitution and the very heart of it" and without this article our constitution would be a nullity." Art. 32 is in the company of other Fundamental Rights in Part. III. But, unlike other rights, "it is remedial and not substantive in nature". (Shukla, Constitution of India, p.277) Art.32(1)declares :"The right to move the Supreme Court by appropriate proceedings for the enforcement of the rights conferred by this part is guaranteed". To be noted is the right to move the Supreme Court for the enforcement of the fundamental Rights is itself a Fundamental Right.

Thus, the Supreme Court is the ultimate protector and guarantor of the fundamental rights and a solemn duty has been cast upon this Court to protect the citizens' fundamental rights "zealously and vigilantly". Clause (2) of Art.32 empowers the Supreme Court to issue writs including the writs of habeas corpus, mandamus, quo warrant, certiorari and prohibition for the enforcement of the fundamental rights. The Court's power is not confined to the issuance of the above writs, It can issue directions or orders which appear to the Court to be appropriate for the enforcement of the fundamental rights. The Court's power is not only preventive, in the sense, preventing violations of fundamental rights, but also remedial , in the sense, the court can award compensation and exemplary costs when the state has violated the fundamental right to life and personal liberty guaranteed under Art.21. Illustrations: Direction that the labour laws be faithfully enforced; that under-trial victims be rehabilitated; that contract labourers be paid minimum wages.

B) Supreme Court's Power to Commit a Person for Contempt (Art.129):

Art.129 declares that the Supreme Court shall be a Court of Record and has all the power of such a court including the power to punish for contempt of itself.

A Court of Record is one where its acts and judicial proceedings are enrolled for a perpetual memorial and testimony and has the power to fine and imprison for contempt of itself. Wharton's Law Lexicon, 14th Edition, p.275.

A Court of Record is a Court whose records are of evidentiary value and cannot be questioned when produced before any court.

Power to punish for contempt is conferred to uphold the majesty and dignity of the court, to prevent scandalisation of the judiciary, to ensure that the stream of justice remains unsullied, to bar interference in the administration of justice. (for more details, see Contempt of Court Act,1971).

The power of the Supreme Court to punish for contempt extends to all Courts and Tribunals subordinate to it.

For the exercise of the power to punish for contempt, no one has to appraise the court. The court can act suo moto.Fair and objective criticism of courts will not amount to contempt.

National Commission has observed:" Judicial decisions have been interpreted to mean that under the law that now prevails even truth cannot be pleaded as a defense to a charge of contempt of court. This is not a satisfactory state of law"---at, p.140. The Commission has recommended that "the law in this area [contempt of court] requires an appropriate change". Ibid.

c) Supreme Court's Original and Exclusive Jurisdiction in Respect of Certain Disputes (Art.131):

The Supreme Court has Original and Exclusive Jurisdiction in any dispute

i) between the Government of India and one or more States; or

ii) between the Government of India and any State on one side and one or more States on the other side; or

iii) between two or more States, if the dispute involves a question of law or fact on which the existence or extent of a legal right depends.

A Court is said to have Original Jurisdiction when it has authority to hear and determine a case in the first instance.

The Court's Jurisdiction is exclusive when no other court has the authority to hear and decide the case.

What is necessary under Art.131 is that the existence or extent of a legal right must be in issue in the dispute between the parties, that is, between the Government of India and one or more States, etc.

The rationale underlying Art.131 is if there be a dispute between two or more states--, it is not proper that the dispute be agitated before the court of one of the disputants that is, disputing parties.

Further, under Art.131, the plaintiff State need not assert a legal or a constitutional right. It is enough if it can challenge the right claimed by the Respondent State.

D) APPELLATE JURISDICTION OF THE SUPREME COURT (ART.132):

a) The Supreme Court shall have the final say on questions involving the interpretation of the Constitution. Different opinions by different High Courts on Constitutional Questions would create confusion among the lawyers and citizens.

Art.132 therefore provides that an Appeal shall lie to the Supreme Court from any Judgment, Decree or Final Order of a High Court, whether in Civil or Criminal or other proceeding, if the High Court certifies that the case involves a substantial question of law as to the interpretation of the Constitution.

E) SUPREME COURT'S APPELLATE JURISDICTION IN CIVIL MATTERS (ART.133):

The Supreme Court is empowered to entertain Appeals from the Judgment, Decree or Final Order of a High Court in Civil Proceedings that is proceedings of civil nature. The Proceedings are civil in nature if a person seeks relief in a Civil Court when his civil rights are infringed by another person or by the State. After the conclusion of the proceedings, the Civil Court may declare that the plaintiff's claim is justified and he is entitled to relief.

To invoke the Supreme Court's appellate Jurisdiction, the following conditions have to be fulfilled:

i) What is being appealed against must be a Judgment, Decree or Final Order of a High Court in a Civil Proceeding.

ii) The High Court must certify that the case involves a substantial question of law of general importance and that it (the High court) is of the opinion that the substantial question of law... needs to be decided by the Apex Court.

It can be said that the Judgment, Decree or Final Order –all seem to convey the same meaning, that is, the Civil Court's pronouncement that finally or conclusively determines the rights of the parties in a controversy or suit.

It should be noted that under Art.133, no appeal can be made against the Judgment, Decree or Final Order of a single Judge of a High Court unless Parliament enacts a law to remove this restriction.

F) APPEALS TO SUPREME COURT IN CRIMINAL MATTERS (ART.134):

The Criminal Appellate Jurisdiction of the Supreme Court can be invoked against the Judgment, Final Order or Sentence of a High Court in a criminal proceeding when the High Court has certified that the case is a fit one for appeal to the Supreme Court.

The grant of certificate by the High Court would be justifiable when difficult questions of law or principles are involved in the case. Ordinarily, the High Court's Certificate would demonstrate that the case involves a substantial question of law or principle.

No doubt, in granting or not granting the certificate under Art.134 (1) (c), the High Court enjoys discretion but the discretion is judicial one which has to be judicially exercised in the light of well-established principles.

The Supreme Court's Criminal Appellate Jurisdiction can be invoked in the following circumstances:

a) When the High Court has reversed the decision of acquittal of the accused by the Sessions Court and sentenced him to death; or

b) When the High Court has withdrawn for trial before itself any case from any court subordinate to it and has convicted the accused person and sentenced him to death.

Parliament may be law enlarges the appellate criminal Jurisdiction of the Supreme Court. In 1970, Parliament enacted a law which enables an accused to appeal to the Supreme Court when the High Court "has not sentenced him to death under Art.134 (2) (6) (1) but has sentenced him to imprisonment for life or for a period of not less than ten years. The Supreme Court (Enlargement of Criminal Appellate Jurisdiction) Act,1970 has substituted the words underlined above for the words "to death".

G) APPEAL TO SUPREME COURT BY SPECIAL LEAVE(ART.136):

Under Art.136, the Supreme Court may, in its discretion, grant special leave to appeal from any judgment, decree, determination sentence or order in any cause or matter passed or made by any court or tribunal in the territory of India.

Under Articles 132 to 135, the Supreme Court's appellate Jurisdiction can be ignited by fulfilling the conditions mentioned there-under. But, under Art,136, Supreme Court's permission or leave is required. Such permission or leave can be granted by the Court in its discretion.

Further, appeal may be allowed against determination, sentence or order (note, need not be a 'final order') of a court (note, need not be a High Court) or tribunal. (Industrial Tribunal, Income Tax Tribunal) Supreme Court may be inclined to grant special leave in situations where a party has suffered gross injustice on account of violation of natural justice or where the tribunal's order or determination is so palpably wrong or absurd as to shock the court's conscience.

Since Art.136 speaks of judgments, decrees, sentence, orders, determinations of Courts or Tribunals, purely admininistrative or executive order or direction cannot be the subject-matter of appeal and the court would be disinclined to accord leave. The Court has to be convinced that there are special circumstances which warrant its intervention. For example, when the Tribunal has been improperly constituted; where the procedure followed is unjust, unfair, and unreasonable; when the Tribunal has assumed a jurisdiction which in law it does not enjoy.

The Supreme Court has no power or Jurisdiction to grant special leave against the Judgment, Decree, Sentence, Determination, Order passed or made by any Court or Trionnal functioning under any law relating to the armed forces.Art.136(2).

H) SUPREME COURT'S POWER TO REVIEW ITS OWN JUDGMENTS, ORDERS. (ART.137):

In Judicial decision-making, the general proposition is that there should be finality attached to Court's Judgments and that there should be an end to law suits. A rigid adherence to this proposition may, in some cases, result in gross and manifest injustice, A court cannot be allowed to be a court of Injustice. If, in a case, the court finds that a particular provision of the Act was not brought to its notice or evidence which would have tilted the scales of Justice was not available at the time of its pronouncement, then, it may be inclined or probably pleased to review its earlier judgment at the instance of the aggrieved. Art.137 expressly empowers the Supreme Court to review its Judgments.

Review is permissible on the following grounds;

i) Discovery of new and important matters of evidence;

ii) Mistake or error of law apparent on the face of the record;19

iii) If there be any other sufficient, justifiable reason.

I)SUPREME COURT'S POWER TO MAKE AN ORDER NECESSARY FOR DOING COMPLETE JUSTICE IN ANY CASE (ART.142);

This is a power which every final court in a democratic polity should possess. When the Constitution of the country does not declare that the Highest Court has this inherent power, then, it should, at least, command the Legislature to provide for this power through law.

Prof M.P.Singh has Observed: "The Supreme Court's power under Art.142 is a residuary power, supplementary and complementary to the powers specifically conferred on he court which it may exercise whenever it is just and equitable to do so and in particular to ensure the observance of due process of law, to do complete justice according to law." Op.cit, p.459. (citing DDAV Skipper Construction Co,(p)Ltd, AIR 1996 SC 2005.

The power conferred on the Supreme Court under Art.142 has been exercised by the court to order payment of compensation to a person who had been illegally detained, to order payment of interim compensation to the victim of rape ,etc. (For case law citations, see Shukla, Constitution of India. (already cited) p.461.

J) ADVISORY JURISDICTION (ART.143);

Normally, the Court's function is to decide the controversy presented to it and render its judgment. Again, Courts do not take suo moto notice of a prevalent controversy and offer their opinions. The Court's Jurisdiction has to be invoked by the aggrieved party through appropriate means, But, Art.143 enables our Supreme Court to render Advisory Opinion in certain contingencies. Such Advisory Opinion of the Supreme Court rendered at the instance of the President of India may enable Parliament to pass appropriate Legislation or to introspect and effect suitable amendments to the existing law.

Art.143 enables the President to refer to the Supreme Court a question of law or fact which in the opinion of the President is of such nature and such public importance that it is expedient to obtain the Court's Opinion on it.

It has to be noted that a question of law which the Supreme Court has already decided in a dispute presented to it cannot be the subject-matter of a reference by the President for Advisory Opinion, Because, the implication would be that the President would be inviting the Apex Court to at act as an Appellate or Reviewing Authority over its earlier decision while seeking its Advisory Opinion under Art.143.

On a Presidential Reference for Advisory Opinion, the Attorney- General would be given notice and all concerned may also be served notices to appear as parties or as interveners.

The Court, after hearing, reports to the President. The Advisory Opinion tendered need not, rather, should not bind the President. Conversely, the Supreme Court for germane reasons may decline to express its opinion, especially, when the reference is vague.

THE HIGH COURTS IN THE STATES (ARTICLES 214 TO 231):

In this segment, we shall examine the composition of the High Courts, the qualifications prescribed for the appointment of Judges, their tenure, procedure prescribed for the removal of Judges and the Powers and Jurisdiction exercisable by the High Courts.

Art.214 declares that there shall be a High Court for each State.

However, Parliament by law may establish a common High Court for two or more States or for two or more States and a union Territory (Art.231). The Constitution also Provides, under Art.230, that Parliament may by law extend the jurisdiction of a High Court or exclude its jurisdiction from any union Territory.

Within its territorial jurisdiction, a High Court may have one or more benches

CONSTITUTION OF HIGH COURTS (ART.216):

Every High Court shall have a Chief Justice and such number of Judges as the President may from time to time determine. Judicial decisions establish that the Chief Justices of the High Courts and the Chief Justice of India ("CJI") may periodically review the strength of the High Courts and in the interest of efficient administration of Justice may recommend to the President that the strength of the High Court be increased.

When the CJI makes such a recommendation, the President is required to act expeditiously. Needless to say, the it is the Executive, in reality, that has to act promptly.

APPOINTMENT AND CONDITIONS OF THE OFFICE OF A JUDGE OF A HIGH COURT (ART.217):

Every Judge of a High Court shall be appointed by the President by warrant under his hand and seal. Before appointing, the President has to consult the Chief Justice of India and the Governor of the State. In the case of appointment of a Judge other than the Chief Justice, the President shall consult the Chief Justice of the High Court.

As regards the 'Consultation Process', see the material provided under 'Union Judiciary'.

Further, it may be noted that as regards the appointment of High Court Judges, the CJI is required to consult two senior-most Judges of the Supreme Court. Hence, the opinion of CJI means the opinion of a collegiums consisting of himself and two senior-most Judges of the Supreme Court.

But, it has to be noted that the process of appointment of a High Court Judge has to be initiated by the Chief Justice of the High Court concerned. His sole opinion is of not much consequence. Because, he must take into account the opinions expressed by two senior-most Judges of his High Court. The Consultation Process should be in writing. That is, all the opinions of consul tees and the one consulting should be in writing. The appointment of a Judge to the High Court must be in conformity with the opinion of the CJI (that is, the Collegium's Opinion, referred to, earlier) In case of disagreement between the President & CJI, the latter's opinion shall prevail.

As regards the appointment of the Chief Justice of the High Court, it appears, that it should be made on the basis of the All India Seniority of High Court Judges. A Judge of the High Court Shall retire on his attaining the age of Sixty-Two years. Art.217 (1).He can, of course, resign by writing to the President of India.

As in the case of a Judge of the Supreme Court, a Judge of a High Court can be impeached on grounds of proved 'misbehaviour' or 'incapacity'. Refer to relevant material under Union Judiciary. Art.217(1(, proviso(b).

QUALIFICATIONS FOR APPOINTMENT ART.217 (2):

a) He/She shall be a citizen of India;
b) Must have held a Judicial Office in our country for atleast ten years;
c) Must have been an advocate of the High Court for atleast ten years.

RESTRICTION ON PRACTICE IN REGARD TO A PERMANENT JUDGE OF A HIGH COURT (ART.220):

A Permanent Judge of a High Court shall not plead or act in any court or before any authority in India except the Supreme Court other High Courts. A reading of the provisions under Art.217 indicates that in so for as the resignation and removal of the High Court Judges are concerned they are mutatis mutandis (with due alteration of details in comparing cases) the same as those for the Judges of the Supreme Court.

POWERS AND FUNCTIONS:

I) APPOINTMENT OF DISTRICT JUDGES. ART.233:

In regard to the appointment, posting and promotion or District Judges, the Governor of State is required to consult the High Court exercising jurisdiction in relation to such State.

II) RECRUITMENT TO JUDICIAL SERVICE. ART.234:

When persons have to be recruited for judicial service (Posts of District Judges excluded), appointments have to be made by the Governor of the State in accordance with the rules made by him after consultation with the State Public Service Commission and the High Court of the State.

III) CONTROL OVER SUBORDINATE COURTS. ART.235:

The control over District Courts and Courts subordinate thereto including the posting and promotion of and grant of leave to persons in Judicial Service holding posts inferior to that of District Judge shall be vested in the High Court. This 'Control' is for ensuring the Independence of the Subordinate Judiciary.

IV) HIGHEST COURT OF APPEAL IN THE STATE:

In the State, the High Court is the Highest Court of Appeal in respect of both civil and criminal matters.

V) TRANSFER OF CERTAIN CASES TO HIGH COURT. ART.228:

On being satisfied that a case pending in a subordinate court involves a substantial question of law as to the interpretation of the Constitution and that the determination of the question is necessary for the disposal of the case, the High Court may withdraw the case and dispose it or may determine the question of law and return the case with its Judgment on the question to the subordinate court which shall then dispose of the case in conformity with such Judgment.

VI) POWER OF SUPERINTENDENCE OVER ALL COURTS BY THE HIGH COURT. ART.227:

Every High Court shall have the power of superintendence over the subordinate courts and tribunals within its Jurisdiction. Interference by the High Court under Art.227 can be suo moto. The High Court can interfere when shown that grave injustice has been done to a party. Or, when the jurisdictional defect of the inferior court or tribunal is established.

Art.227 Jurisdiction is exercisable when lack of Jurisdiction, errors of law, gross violation of Natural Justice or perverse findings is established. or See, P.M.Bakshi, The Constitution of India, (Fifth Edition) (2004), at p.195.

High Court has no power of superintendence over any Court or Tribunal constituted under any law relating to the Armed Forces. The High Court's Power under Art227 is exercisable even in such situations when no appeal or revision lies to the High court.

VII) POWER OF THE HIGH COURTS TO ISSUE CERTAIN WRITS ART.226:

Art.226 is one of the most significant and important Articles in our Constitution. An Article most often invoked by an aggrieved citizen for seeking redress from the High Court. An Article greater in scope than Art.32 because the High Court is empowered under Art.226 to issue to any person or authority in its jurisdiction, directions, orders, or writs, including writs in nature of habeas corpus, mandamus, prohibition, quo warrant and certiorari, ... for the enforcement of the fundamental rights and for any other purpose.

Remedy under Art.226 is discretionary.

Power under Art.226 is to be exercised to examine whether the action under challenge is lawful or unlawful .

The High Court may dismiss the writ petition if there be an alternative, convenient, efficacious remedy.

I suppose the learned Professor who has spoken earlier on :"Fundamental Rights" has already given you an account of the various kinds of writs, their characteristic features, when they would issue, etc. You may please refer to the materials under Art.32.

VIII) POWER TO PUNISH FOR CONTEMPT (ART.215):

Art.215 declares that every High Court shall be a Court of Record and shall have all the powers of such a Court including the power to punish for contempt of itself.

Unit III

SOCIAL BASIS OF INDIAN POLITICS

3.1 CASTE, CLASS AND RELIGION

In India, the caste system is a system of social stratification[155] and which is now also used as a basis for affirmative action.[3][4] Historically, it separated communities into thousands of endogamous hereditary groups called Jātis.[5] Contemporary usage of the term Jātis and caste are synonyms. The Jātis were grouped by the Brahminical texts under four categories, known as varnas: viz Brahmans, Kshatriyas, Vaishyas, Shudras, and Outcastes. Certain groups, now known as "Dalits", were excluded from the varna system altogether, ostracized by all other castes and treated as untouchables.[6][7]

Although strongly identified with Hindus, the caste systems has been carried over to other religions on the Indian subcontinent, including Buddhists, Christians, Muslims,[8][9][10] Sikhs.

Caste is commonly thought of as an ancient fact of Indian life, but various contemporary scholars have argued that the caste system was constructed by the British colonial regime.[3] Between 1860 and 1920, the British segregated Indians by caste, granting administrative jobs and senior appointments only to higher castes. Social unrest during 1920s, led to a change in this policy.[11][12] From 1920s, the British colonial administration began a policy of affirmative action by reserving a certain percentage of government jobs for the lower castes.[13] After India achieved independence, this policy of reservation of jobs and positive discrimination based on caste system was formalized with lists of Scheduled Castes (*Dalit*) and Scheduled Tribes (*Adivassi*).[14]

The caste system has no legality in India[15] and discrimination against lower castes is illegal in India under Article 15 of its constitution.[16] However, sporadic Caste-related discrimination and violence continue to be reported.[17] Since 1950, the country has enacted many laws and social initiatives to protect and improve the socioeconomic conditions of its lower caste population.[18] These caste classifications for college admission quotas, job reservations and other affirmative action initiatives, according to India's Supreme Court, is based on heredity and is not changeable.[19][20] These initiatives by India, over time, have led to many lower caste members being elected to the highest political offices including the election of K.R. Narayanan, a Dalit, as President of the nation from 1997 to 2002.[21]

TERMINOLOGY

In a review published in 1944, D.D. Kosambi noted that "Almost every statement of a general nature made by anyone about Indian castes may be contradicted."[22] The term caste has no universally accepted definition. To some, the term caste traditionally corresponds to endogamous *varnas* of the ancient Indian scripts, and its meaning corresponds in the sense of *estates* of feudal Japan or Europe. To others, endogamous jātis — rather than varnas — are castes, such as the 2378 occupation-classified jātis list created by colonial ethnographers in early 20th century. To others such as Risley, castes in India means endogamous groups that resulted from interactions between what once were different races.[23] Endogamy, the common element in these three definitions, is itself disputed. Ambedkar, who was born in India in a social strata considered untouchable, disagreed that the term castes in India can be defined as endogamous groups of India. According to Ambedkar, India during and before the British colonial rule, was a strictly exogamous society because marriage within blood-relatives and class-relations was culturally forbidden. The term caste, according to Ambedkar, should be defined as a social group that tries to impose endogamy, in an exogamous population.[24]

The use of occupation to define castes is confusing as well. Brahmins have been listed as priests and sometimes rulers or other professions, Kshatriyas include warriors and sometimes rulers or other professions, Vaishyas are listed to include traders and sometimes agriculturists and other professions, while Shudras are listed to include labourers and sometimes agriculturists and other professions. Drekmeier, for example, after his study of Indian castes includes agriculturists as Vaishyas, while Goodrich includes them as Shudras. Drekmeier further notes that official positions of power were not exclusive privilege of the traditionally upper castes; for example, Shudras were sought and included in official administrative appointments in India's history.[25][26]

Castes are poorly defined, confusing concepts. According to William Pinch, the confusion is in part, because the very idea of hierarchical status and relative social identity has been a matter of disagreement in India.[27]

Sociologist Anne Waldrop observes that while outsiders view the term caste as a *static* phenomena of stereotypical tradition-bound India, empirical facts suggest caste has been a radically changing feature of India. The term caste means different thing to different Indians. In the context of politically active modern India, where job and school quotas are reserved for affirmative action based on castes, the term has become a sensitive and controversial subject.[28][29]

G. S. Ghurye wrote in 1932 that, despite much study by many people,

... we do not possess a real general definition of caste. It appears to me that any attempt at definition is bound to fail because of the complexity of the phenomenon. On the other hand, much literature on the subject is marred by lack of precision about the use of the term.[30]

Ghurye did attempt to find a middle-ground between the complexity and the loose usage. He defined six characteristics of the Hindu caste system as a "social philosophy", being its state prior to the relatively modern corruption of this by theories of "rights and duties". He thought that these could be applied across the country, although he acknowledged that there were regional variations on the general theme.[31]

- Strict segmentation of society, with the various groups being rigidly defined and membership of them determined by birth.
- A hierarchical system that defines a ranking place for all of the castes
- Limited choice of occupation, which is enforced within a caste as well as by other castes. A caste might follow more than one traditional occupation but its members would nonetheless be constrained to that range
- The general practice of endogamy, although in some situations hypergamy is acceptable. Endogamy applies to the various sub-groups within a caste itself, preventing marriage between the sub-groups and sometimes imposing an additional geographical constraint, that one can only marry a person from the same gotra and the same place
- Restrictions on dietary and social interactions that defines who could consume what and accept from whom. As with marriage arrangements, these restrictions apply at sub-caste level, not merely at the caste level
- Physical segregation in, for example, villages. This is accompanied by limitations on movement and access, including to religious and educational areas and to basic facilities such as supplies of water. Again, this segregation applies at sub-caste level as well as at the higher level

Not everyone has agreed with the definition proposed by Ghurye, which in any event was intended as an exercise to reduce the gap between lax terminological usage and the realities of an immensely complex system, More recently, Graham Chapman is among those who have reiterated the complexity, and he notes that there are differences between theoretical constructs and the practical reality.[32]

HISTORY

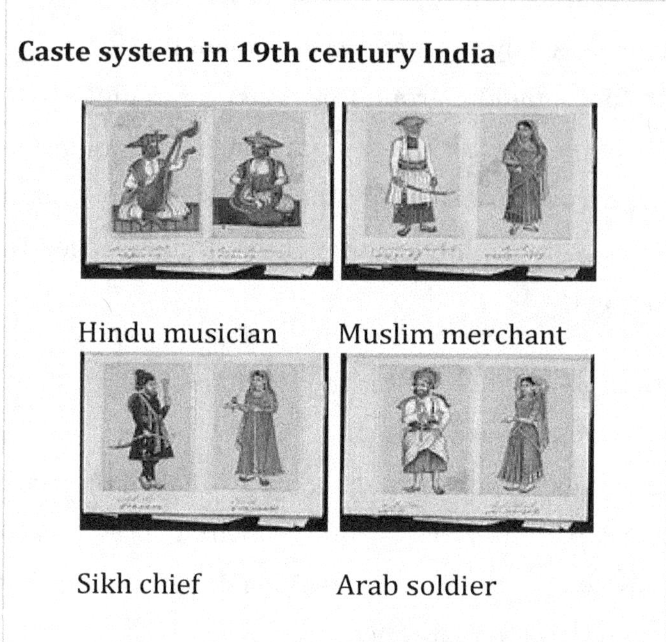

Caste system in 19th century India

Hindu musician   Muslim merchant

Sikh chief   Arab soldier

Pages from *Seventy-two Specimens of Castes in India* according to Christian Missionaries in February 1837. They include Hindu, Muslim, Sikh and Arabs as castes of India.

There are several theories regarding the origins of the Indian caste system. One posits that the Indian and Aryan classes ("*pistras*") show similarity,[33][*full citation needed*] wherein the priests are Brahmins, the warriors are Kshatriya, the merchants are Vaishya, and the artisans are Shudras.[34][35] Another theory is that of Georges Dumézil, who formulated[36][*page needed*] the trifunctional hypothesis of social class. According to the Dumézil theory, ancient societies had three main classes, each with distinct functions: the first judicial and priestly, the second connected with the military and war, and the third class focused on production, agriculture, craft and commerce. Dumézil proposed that Rex-Flamen of the Roman Empire is etymologically similar to Raj-Brahman of ancient India and that they made offerings to deus and deva respectively, each with statutes of conduct, dress and behavior that were similar.

From the Bhakti school, the view is that the four divisions were originally created by Krishna. "According to the three modes of material nature and the work associated with them, the four divisions of human society were created."[37]

Caste can be considered as an ancient fact of Hindu life, but various contemporary scholars have argued that the caste system as it exists today is the result of the British colonial regime, which made caste organisation a central mechanism of administration. According to scholars such as the anthropologist Nicholas Dirks, before colonialism caste affiliation was quite loose and fluid, but the British regime enforced caste affiliation rigorously, and constructed a much more strict hierarchy than existed previously, with some castes being criminalised and others being given preferential treatment.[38] From a sociological point of view Matthew Ward explains that the caste system is inherently embedded in Hindu Religious practices particularly the teachings of samsara, dharma and karma. Samsara views death as a moment of transition and not an end in any person's life. Dharma encourages the belief that our destiny (caste) is fixed and it cannot be changed. Ward says that the Hindu hyper-good has provided a faithful acceptance of ones worldly fate in order to improve one's lot in the next life cycle. "Religion provides such rigorous sanctions for social life and impose such a great fear of falling down that people through their patterned daily activity, find it impossible and abhorrent not to follow religious guidelines"(Ward). Karma is responsible for punishment and reward. This force is influenced by the extent they follow their dharma.[39]

DURING BRITISH RULE

The caste system in India during the British rule extended beyond being hereditary phenomenon. Some people could apply to be re-classified into a caste they preferred. For example, the above order issued in 1937 shows a *Mali* (gardener-agriculturist) being legally awarded the Kshatriya: a warrior caste in ancient India, by British officials. Similarly, many laws such as the Stamp Act required Indians to declare their caste in official documents to be granted lease or licence.[40]

The role of the British on the caste system in India is controversial.[41] Some sources suggest that the caste system became legally rigid during the British Raj, when the British started to enumerate castes during the ten-year census and meticulously codified the system under their rule.[38][42] Zwart, for example, notes in his review article that the caste system used to be thought of as an ancient fact of Hindu life, but some contemporary scholars argue that the system was constructed by the British colonial regime.[3] Other sources suggest that the caste system existed in India prior to the arrival of the British, and enumerating classes and castes do not constitute the act of constructing it. Bouglé, for example, used 17th to 19th century historical reports by Christian missionaries and some Europeans on Indian society to suggest that a rigid caste system existed in India during and before British ruled India, quite similar in many respects to the social stratification found in 17th to 19th century Europe.[43]

Assumptions about the caste system in Indian society, along with its nature, evolved during British rule.[41] For example, some British believed Indians would shun train travel because tradition-bound South Asians were too caught up in caste and religion, and that they would not sit or stand in the same coaches out of concern for close proximity to a member of higher or lower or shunned caste. After the launch of train services, Indians of all castes, classes and gender enthusiastically adopted train travel without any concern for so-called caste stereotypes.[44][45]

Célestin Bouglé, in his essay on the caste system in India, published in 1908, observed the British frequently asserting they had no interest in modifying the caste system in India. The Englishman's motto, claimed Bouglé, was to administer its Indian colony by preserving its customs, caste system, and with a minimum of security or justice or governance. Bouglé acknowledged in his essay the empirical evidence of intermingling between Indians as observed on Indian Railways and the mass adoption of train. Bouglé used the empirical census facts noted by Risley and the direct observation of mutual acceptance of Indians for Indians on its trains to conclude that the historical caste system within 20th century Indian society was fundamentally changing, and that this change was irreversible. British rule, without wanting to, was triggering fundamental social changes in India. The lower castes were becoming officials, the Brahmins were leaving religious occupations and becoming policemen and farmers, and the three pillars of the caste system according to Bouglé—hereditary occupation, social hierarchy and exclusionary repulsion—were crumbling. Bouglé identified the cause for these changes to be economic progress, industrialisation and career mobility inside India between 1880 and 1905. He believed that British rule, without intending to, had accelerated the natural demise of the caste system in India.[43]

Corbridge concludes that British policies of divide and rule of India's numerous princely sovereign states, as well as enumeration of the population into rigid categories during the 10 year census, particularly with the 1901 and 1911 census, contributed towards the hardening of caste identities.[46]

In the round table conference held on August 1932, upon the request of B. R. Ambedkar, the then Prime Minister of Britain, Ramsay Macdonald made a Communal Award which awarded a provision for separate representation for the Muslims, Sikhs, Christians, Anglo-Indians, Europeans and Dalits. These depressed classes were assigned a number of seats to be filled by election from special constituencies in which voters belonging to the depressed classes only could vote. Gandhi went on a hunger strike against this provision claiming that such an arrangement would split the Hindu community into two groups. Fearing a communal reprisal and genocidal acts against untouchables, Ambedkar was coerced into agreeing with Gandhi.[47] This agreement, which saw Gandhi end his fast and Ambedkar drop his demand for a separate electorate, was called the Poona Pact.

CASTE RIGIDITY

An editor has expressed a concern that this section **lends undue weight to certain ideas** relative **to the article as a whole**. Please help to discuss and resolve the dispute before removing this message. *(January 2014)*

In Ancient India

Ancient Hindu texts suggest caste system was not rigid. This flexibility permitted lower caste Valmiki to compose the Ramayana, which was widely adopted and became a major Hindu scripture. Other ancient texts cite numerous examples of individuals moving from one caste to another within their lifetimes.[48]

Fa Xian, a Buddhist pilgrim from China, visited India around 400 AD. "Only the lot of the Chandals he found unenviable; outcastes by reason of their degrading work as disposers of dead, they were universally shunned ... But no other section of the population were notably disadvantaged, no other caste distinctions attracted comment from the Chinese pilgrim, and no oppressive caste 'system' drew forth his surprised censure. Peace and order prevailed."[49] In this period kings of Shudra and Brahmin origin were as common as those of Kshatriya Varna and caste system was not wholly rigid.[50]

DURING BRITISH RULE

Smelser and Lipset in their review of Hutton's study of caste system in colonial India propose the theory that individual mobility across caste lines may have been minimal in British India because it was ritualistic. They theorise that the sub-castes may have changed their social status over the generations by fission, re-location, and adoption of new external ritual symbols. Some of these evolutionary changes in social stratifications, claim Smelser and Lipset, were seen in Europe, Japan, Africa and other regions as well; however, the difference between them may be the relative levels of ritualistic and secular referents. Smelser and Lipset further propose that the colonial system may have affected the caste system social stratification. They note that British colonial power controlled economic enterprises and the political administration of India by selectively cooperating with upper caste princes, priests and landlords. This was colonial India's highest level caste strata, followed by second strata that included favoured officials who controlled trade, supplies to the colonial power and Indian administrative services. The bottom layer of colonial Indian society was tenant farmers, servants, wage labourers, indentured coolies and others. The colonial social strata acted in combination with the traditional caste system. The colonial strata shut off economic opportunity, entrepreneurial activity by natives, or availability of schools, thereby worsening the limitations placed on mobility by the traditional caste system. In America and Europe, they argue individual mobility was better than in India or other colonies around the world, because colonial stratification was missing and the system could evolve to become more secular and tolerant of individual mobility.[51]

CONTEMPORARY INDIA

In the present day India social organization based on caste is considered to be heredity and is not changeable.[19][20] Inter caste marriage is legal in India. Movements started by Gandhi and Ambedkar to decrease the inequality among people practicing caste have had a considerable effect on people's view.[citation needed]

Sociologists such as Srinivas and Damle have debated the question of rigidity in caste. In their independent studies, they claim considerable flexibility and mobility in their caste hierarchies among the Coorgs of South India.[48][52][53]

MODERN STATUS

The massive 2006 Indian anti-reservation protests

The Indian government officially recognises historically discriminated communities of India such as the Untouchables under the designation of Scheduled Castes, and certain economically backward Shudra castes as Other Backward Castes.[6][54] The Scheduled Castes are sometimes referred to as Dalit in contemporary literature. In 2001, the proportion of Dalit population was 16.2 percent of India's total population.[55]

Since 1950, India has enacted and implemented many laws and social initiatives to protect and improve the socio-economic conditions of its Dalit population.[56] Of the highest paying, senior most jobs in government agencies and government controlled enterprises, over 10 percent were held by members of the Dalit community, a tenfold increase in 40 years but yet to fill up the 15 percent reserved quota for them. In 1997, India elected K.R. Narayanan, a Dalit, as the nation's President.[21] Indians who were born in historically discriminated minority castes have been elected to its highest judicial and political offices.[57][58] While the quality of life of Dalit population in India, in terms of metrics such as poverty, literacy rate, access to health care, life expectancy, education attainability, access to drinking water, housing, etc. have seen faster growth amongst the Dalit population between 1986 and 2006, for some metrics, it remains lower than overall non-Dalit population, and for some it is better than poor non-Dalit population.[59][60][61][62]

A 2004 report, compiled by a society of Dalits and people against caste-based discrimination, summarised the developments over previous 60 years, and status of the caste system in modern India, as follows:[63] Article 15 of Indian Constitution, as enacted in 1950, prohibits any discrimination based on caste. Article 17 of Indian Constitution declared any practice of untouchability as illegal.[56] In 1955, India enacted the Untouchability (Offences) Act (renamed in 1976, as the Protection of Civil Rights Act). It extended the reach of law, from intent to mandatory enforcement. The Scheduled Castes and Scheduled Tribes (Prevention of Atrocities) Act, similar to the Hate Crime Laws in the United States, was passed in India in 1989.[64]

- India created National Commission for Scheduled Castes and Scheduled Tribes to investigate, monitor, advise, and evaluate the socio-economic progress of the Scheduled Castes and Scheduled Tribes.[65]
- India implemented a reservation system for its citizens from Scheduled Castes and Scheduled Tribes; this program has been in use in India for over 50 years. This program is similar to Affirmative Action/Equal Opportunities statutes in the United States.
- In India, where the presence of private free market corporations is limited, government jobs have dominated the percentage of jobs in its economy. A 2000 report estimated that most jobs in India were in companies owned by the government or agencies of the government.[66] The reservation system implemented by India over 50 years, has been partly successful, because of all jobs, nationwide, in 1995, 17.2 percent of the jobs were held by those in the lowest castes. In 1995, about 16.1 percent of India's population were the lowest castes.
- The Indian government classifies government jobs in four groups. The Group A jobs are senior most, high paying positions in the government, while Group D are junior most, lowest paying positions. In Group D jobs, the percentage of positions held by lowest caste classified people is 30% greater than their demographic percentage. In all jobs classified as Group C positions, the percentage of jobs held by lowest caste people is about the same as their demographic population distribution. In Group A and B jobs, the percentage of

> positions held by lowest caste classified people is 30% lower than their demographic percentage.

- The presence of lowest caste people in highest paying, senior most position jobs in India has increased by ten-fold, from 1.18 percent of all jobs in 1959 to 10.12 percent of all jobs in 1995.[67]

- In 2007, India elected K. G. Balakrishnan, a Dalit, to the office of Chief Justice.[68]

- In 2007, Uttar Pradesh, the most populous state of India, elected Mayawati as the Chief Minister, the highest elected office of the state. BBC claims, "Mayawati Kumari is an icon for millions of India's Dalits, or untouchables as they used to be known."[57]

- In 2009, the Indian parliament unanimously elected a Dalit,[58] Meira Kumar, as the first female speaker.

In addition to taking affirmative action for people of schedule castes and scheduled tribes, India has expanded its effort to include people from poor, backward castes in its economic and social mainstream. In 1990, the Government of India introduced reservation of 27% for Backward Classes on the basis of the Mandal Commission's recommendations. This became the law with the issuance of Gazette notice 36012/31/90-Estt. (SCT) dated 13 August 1990. Since then, India has reserved 27 percent of job opportunities in government-owned enterprises and agencies for Socially and Educationally Backward Classes (SEBCs). The 27 percent reservation is in addition to 22.5 percent set aside for India's lowest castes for last 50 years.[69]

In a 2008 study, Desai et al. focussed on education attainments of children and young adults aged 6–29, from lowest caste and tribal populations of India. They completed a national survey of over 100,000 households for each of the four survey years between 1983 and 2000.[62] They found a significant increase in lower caste children in their odds of completing primary school. The number of dalit children who completed either middle-, high- or college-level education increased three times faster than the national average, and the total number were statistically same for both lower and upper castes. The number of dalit girls in India who attended school doubled in the same period, but still few percent less than national average. Other poor caste groups as well as ethnic groups such as Muslims in India have also made improvements over the 16 year period, but their improvement lagged behind that of dalits and adivasis. The net percentage school attainment for Dalits and Muslims were statistically the same in 1999.

A 2007 nationwide survey of India by the World Bank found that over 80 percent of children of historically discriminated castes were attending schools. The fastest increase in school attendance by Dalit community children occurred during the recent periods of India's economic growth.[59] The quality and quantity of schools are now major issues in India.[70]

A study by Darshan Singh presents data on health and other indicators of socio-economic change in India's historically discriminated castes. He claims:[61]

- In 2001, the literacy rates in India's lowest castes was 55 percent, compared to a national average of 63 percent.
- The childhood vaccination levels in India's lowest castes was 40 percent in 2001, compared to a national average of 44 percent.
- Access to drinking water within household or near the household in India's lowest castes was 80 percent in 2001, compared to a national average of 83 percent.
- The poverty level in India's lowest castes dropped from 49 percent to 39 percent between 1995 and 2005, compared to a national average change from 35 to 27 percent.

The table below presents this data for various caste groups in modern India. Both 1998 and 2005 data is included to ascertain the general trend. The Mohanty and Ram report suggests that poverty, not caste, is the bigger differentiator in life expectancy in modern India.[60]

Life expectancy statistics for Indian caste groups

Castes group	Life expectancy at birth (in years)	
	1998–1999	**2005–2006**
Lowest castes	61.5	64.6
Other backward castes	63.5	65.7
Poor, tribal populations	57.5	56.9
Poor, upper castes	61.9	62.7
National average	63.8	65.5

Leonard and Weller have surveyed marriage and genealogical records to empirically study patterns of exogamous inter-caste and endogamous intra-caste marriages in a regional population of India, between 1900 to 1975. They report a striking presence of exogamous marriages across caste lines over time, particularly since the 1970s. They propose education, economic development, mobility and more interaction between youth as possible reasons for these exogamous marriages.[71]

A 2003 article in The Telegraph claimed that inter-caste marriage and dating are common in urban India. Indian societal and family relationships are changing because of female literacy and education, women at work, urbanisation, need for two-income families, and global influences through the television. Female role models in politics, academia, journalism, business, and India's feminist movement have accelerated the change.[72]

SCHEDULED CASTES (SC)

Scheduled castes generally consist of Dalit. By 2007, the population was 16% of the total population of India (around 165 million).[73]

SCHEDULED TRIBES (ST)

Scheduled tribes generally consist of tribal groups. The present population is 7% of the total population of India i.e. around 70 million.[citation needed]

OTHER BACKWARDS CASTES (OBC)

The Mandal Commission covered more than 3000 castes under Other Backwards Castes (OBC) category, regardless of their affluence or economic status and stated that OBCs form around 53% of the Indian population. However, the National Sample Survey puts the figure at 32%.[74][75] There is substantial debate over the exact number of OBCs in India; it is generally estimated to be sizable, but many believe that it is lower than the figures quoted by either the Mandal Commission or the National Sample Survey.[76]

The caste-based reservations in India have led to widespread protests, such as the 2006 Indian anti-reservation protests, with many complaining of reverse discrimination against the forward castes (the castes that do not qualify for the reservation).[citation needed]

In May 2011, the government approved a caste census with the intention of verifying the claims and counterclaims by various sections of the society about their actual numbers.[77] The census would also help the government to re-examine and possibly undo some of the policies which were formed in haste such as the Mandal commission in order to bring more objectivity to the policies with respect to contemporary realities.[78] Critics of the reservation system believe that there is actually no social stigma at all associated with belonging to a backward caste and that because of the huge constitutional incentives in the form of educational and job reservations, a large number of people will falsely identify with a backward caste to receive the benefits. This would not only result in a marked inflation of the backward castes' numbers, but also lead to enormous administrative and judicial resources being devoted to social unrest and litigation when such dubious caste declarations are challenged.[79]

AMONG RELIGIONS

Although strongly identified with Hinduism, the caste systems has been carried over to other religions on the Indian subcontinent, including small groups of Buddhists, Christians, Muslims, Sikhs.[8][9][10]

CHRISTIANS

In some parts of India, Christians are stratified by sect, location, and the castes of their predecessors.[80] In many ways this presence of social strata system has been witnessed elsewhere, such as the society structured by Christian Spaniards who, according to Cahill, established a caste system in their colonial possessions: the West Indies, East Indies, New Spain and the Viceroyalty of Peru, within the last 500 years.[81][82][83]

The earliest reference to caste among Indian Christians comes from Kerala. Duncan Forrester observes that "... Nowhere else in India is there a large and ancient Christian community which has in time immemorial been accorded a high status in the caste hierarchy. ... Syrian Christian community operates very much as a caste and is properly regarded as a caste or at least a very caste-like group."[84] Amidst the Hindu society, the Saint Thomas Christians of Kerala had inserted themselves within the Indian caste society by the observance of caste-rules and were regarded by the Hindus as a caste occupying a high place within their caste hierarchy.[85][86] Their traditional belief that their ancestors were high-caste Hindus such as Namboodiris and Nairs, who were evangelised by St. Thomas, has also supported their upper-caste status.[87] With the arrival European missionaries and their evangelistic mission among the so-called lower castes in Kerala, two new groups of Christians, called Latin Rite Christians and New Protestant Christians, were formed but they continued to be considered as lower castes by higher ranked communities, including the Saint Thomas Christians.[88]

MUSLIMS

Contrary to the Qur'anic worldview, Muslims in India have a caste system. Ashrafs are presumed to have a superior status,[89][90] while the Ajlafs have a lower status. The *Arzal* caste among Muslims was regarded as the equivalent of untouchables, by anti-caste activists like Ambedkar, and by the colonial British ethnographer Herbert Risley who claimed more than 60 percent of Muslims in British India were of a caste equivalent in status as the Hindu Shudras and Untouchables,[91][92][93] While other sources state an estimate between 75 and 80 percent.[94][95] In the Bengal region of India, some Muslims stratify their society according to 'Quoms.'[96] Some scholars have asserted that the Muslim "castes" are not as acute in their discrimination as those of the Hindus,[97] while other scholars argue that the social evils in South Asian Muslim society were worse than those seen in Hindu society.[91][93]

SIKH

Although the Sikh Gurus criticised the hierarchy of the caste system, one does exist in Sikh community. In the Shiromani Gurdwara Prabandhak Committee, 20 of the 140 seats are reserved for low-caste Sikhs.[98][99]

BUDDHISTS

When Ywan Chwang traveled to South India after the period of the Chalukyan Empire, he noticed that the caste system had existed among the Buddhists and Jains.[100]

In parts of India, such as Ladakh, with significant historical presence of Buddhists, a caste system existed in a manner similar to caste structure in Tibet.[101] The upper castes belongs to *sger gzhis*, and they are called *sgar pa*. The priestly caste belonged to monastery, and are called *chos-gzhis*. *Miser* are the serf caste. Serfs, the majority of the people, farmed and paid taxes. An individual's social status and lifelong occupation was destined by birth, closed, and depending on the family one was born into, the individual inherited a tenure document known as *khral-rten*. Buddhist castes had sub-castes, such as *nang gzan*,[102] *khral pa* and *dud chung*. Buddhist also had castes that were shunned by their community and ostracised, such as hereditary fishermen, butchers and undertakers. The untouchables in Buddhist regions, as in Tibet, are known as *Ragyappa*, who lived in isolated ghettos, and their occupation was to remove corpses (human or animal) and dispose of sewage.[103][104]

JAINS

Jains also had castes in places such as Bihar. For example, in the village of Bundela, there were several exclusionary *jaats* amongst the Jains. Martin claims these castes avoided eating with each other.[105] Walter Hamilton in his trip to the Tulava region of South India noticed that the Jains there do not accept Shudras into their sect.[106]

CASTE AND SOCIAL STATUS

Doctrinally, caste was defined as a system of segregation of people, each with a traditional hereditary occupation. The Jātis were grouped by the Brahminical texts under the four well-known caste categories (the varnas): viz Brahmins, Kshatriyas, Vaishyas, and Shudras. Certain people were excluded altogether, ostracised by all other castes and treated as untouchables.[7]

This ideological scheme was theoretically composed of 3000 sub-castes, which in turn was claimed to be composed of 90,000 local endogamous sub-groups.This theory of caste was applied to what was then British India in the early 20th century, when the population comprised about 200 million people, across five major religions, and over 500,000 agrarian villages, each with a population between 100 to 1000 people of various age groups, variously divided into numerous rigid castes (British India included what is now India, Pakistan, Bangladesh and Burma).[3][38][42][107][108]

VIEWS OF AMBEDKAR

Ambedkar, was born in a caste that was classified as untouchable, became a leader of human rights in India, a prolific writer, and a key person in drafting modern India's constitution in the 1940s. Ambedkar wrote extensively on discrimination, trauma and tragic effects of the caste system in India.[109]

From the 1850s, photography was used in Indian subcontinent by the British for anthropological purposes, helping classify the different castes, tribes and native trades. Included in this collection were Hindu, Muslim and Buddhist (Sinhalese) people classified by castes.[110] Above is an 1860s photograph of Rajpoots, classified as the highest secular Hindu caste. Amongst the Rajpoot clans, Chohans, descendents of warrior princes, were classified to have the highest position.

Ambedkar described the Untouchables as belonging to the same religion and culture, yet shunned and ostracised by the community they lived in. The Untouchables, observed Ambedkar, recognised the sacred as well as the secular laws of India, but they derived no benefit from this. They lived on the outskirts of a village. Segregated from the rest, bound down to a code of behaviour, they lived a life appropriate to a servile state. According to this code, an Untouchable could not do anything that raised him or her above his or her appointed station in life. The caste system stamped an individual as untouchable from birth. Thereafter, observed Ambedkar, his social status was fixed, and his economic condition was permanently set. The tragic part was that the Mahomedans, Parsis and Christians shunned and avoided the Untouchables, as well as the Hindus. Ambedkar acknowledged that the caste system wasn't universally absolute in his time; it was true, he wrote, that some Untouchables had risen in Indian society above their usually low status, but the majority had limited mobility, or none, during Britain's colonial rule. According to Ambedkar, the caste system was irrational. Ambedkar listed these evils of the caste system: it isolated people, infused a sense of inferiority into lower-caste individuals, and divided humanity. The caste system was not merely a social problem, he argued: it traumatised India's people, its economy, and the discourse between its people, preventing India from developing and sharing knowledge, and wrecking its ability to create and enjoy the fruits of freedom. The philosophy supporting the social stratification system in India had discouraged critical thinking and cooperative effort, encouraging instead treatises that were full of absurd conceits, quaint fancies, and chaotic speculations. The lack of social mobility, notes Ambedkar, had prevented India from developing technology which can aid man in his effort to make a bare living, and a life better than that of the brute. Ambedkar stated that the resultant absence of scientific and technical progress, combined with all the transcendentalism and submission to one's fate, perpetrated famines, desolated the land, and degraded the consciousness from respecting the civic rights of every fellow human being.[109][111][112]

According to Ambedkar, castes divided people, only to disintegrate and cause myriad divisions which isolated people and caused confusion. Even the upper caste, the Brahmin, divided itself and disintegrated. The curse of caste, according to Ambedkar, split the Brahmin priest class into well over 1400 sub-castes. This is supported by census data collected by colonial ethnographers in British India (now South Asia).[111]

VIEWS OF GANDHI

Gandhi, disagreed with some of Ambedkar's observations, rationale and interpretations about the caste system in India. Caste he claimed has saved Hinduism from disintegration. But like every other institution it has suffered from excrescences. He consider the four divisions of Varnas to be fundamental, natural and essential. The innumerable subcastes or Jātis he considered to be a hindrance. He advocated to fuse all the Jātis into a more global division of Varnas. He also advocated for the idea of heredity in caste to be rejected.[113]

He claimed that Varnashrama of the shastras is today nonexistent in practice. The present caste system is theory antithesis of varnashrama. Caste in its current form, claimed Gandhi, had nothing to do with religion. The discrimination and trauma of castes, argued Gandhi, was the result of custom, the origin of which is unknown. Gandhi said that the customs' origin was a moot point, because one could spiritually sense that these customs were wrong, and that any caste system is harmful to the spiritual well-being of man and economic well-being of a nation. The reality of colonial India was, Gandhi noted, that there was no significant disparity between the economic condition and earnings of members of different castes, whether it was a Brahmin or an artisan or a farmer of low caste. India was poor, and Indians of all castes were poor. Thus, he argued that the cause of trauma was not in the caste system, but elsewhere. Judged by the standards being applied to India, Gandhi claimed, every human society would fail. He acknowledged that the caste system in India spiritually blinded some Indians, then added that this did not mean that every Indian or even most Indians blindly followed the caste system, or everything from ancient Indian scriptures of doubtful authenticity and value. India, like any other society, cannot be judged by a caricature of its worst specimens. Gandhi stated that one must consider the best it produced as well, along with the vast majority in impoverished Indian villages struggling to make ends meet, with woes of which there was little knowledge.[1][111]

Gandhi also advocated that no one should have a superior status merely by virtue of the caste he was born into. Gandhi said he believes that caste system, even as distinguished from varnashrama, to be an "odious and viciousdogma." It has its limitations and defects, but there is nothing sinful about it, as there is about Untouchability;

A 1922 stereograph of Hindu children of high caste, Bombay. This was part of Underwood & Underwood stereoscope journey of colonial world. This and related collections became controversial for staging extreme effects and constructing identities of various colonised nations. Christopher Pinney remarks such imaging was a part of surveillance and imposed identities upon Indians that were resented.[114][115][116]

CASTE-RELATED VIOLENCE

Independent India has witnessed caste-related violence. According to a UN report, approximately 110,000 cases of violent acts committed against Dalits were reported in 2005.[73][117] The report claimed 6.7 cases of violent acts per 10000 Dalit people. For context, the UN reported between 40 and 55 cases of violent acts per 10000 people in developed countries in 2005.;[118][119] and the total number of cases pending in various courts of India, on Dalit related and non-Dalit related matters were 31.28 million as of 2010.[120] One example of such violence is the Kherlanji Massacre of 2006.

CASTE POLITICS

B. R. Ambedkar and Jawaharlal Nehru had radically different approaches to caste, especially concerning constitutional politics and the status of untouchables.[121] Since the 1980s, caste has become a major issue in the politics of India.[121]

The Mandal Commission was established in 1979 to "identify the socially or educationally backward" and to consider the question of seat reservations and quotas for people to redress caste discrimination.[122] In 1980, the commission's report affirmed the affirmative action practice under Indian law, whereby additional members of lower castes—the other backward classes— were given exclusive access to another 27 percent of government jobs and slots in public universities, in addition to the 23 percent already reserved for the Dalits and Tribals. When V. P. Singh's administration tried to implement the recommendations of the Mandal Commission in 1989, massive protests were held in the country. Many alleged that the politicians were trying to cash in on caste-based reservations for purely pragmatic electoral purposes.

Many political parties in India have indulged in caste-based votebank politics. Parties such as Bahujan Samaj Party (BSP), the Samajwadi Party and the Janata Dal claim that they are representing the backward castes, and rely on OBC support, often in alliance with Dalit and Muslim support, to win elections.[123] Remarkably, in what is called a landmark election in the history of India's most populated state of Uttar Pradesh,[*by whom?*] the Bahujan Samaj Party was able to garner a majority in the state assembly elections with the support of the high caste Brahmin community.

CRITICISM

There has been criticism of the caste system from both within and outside of India.[124] Criticism of the Caste system in Indian society came both from the Indian fold and without.

HISTORICAL VIEWS

The caste system has been criticised by many Indian social reformers over India's history.

For example, Jyotirao Phule vehemently criticised any explanations that the caste system was natural and ordained by the *Creator* in Hindu texts. If *Brahma* wanted castes, argued Phule, he would have ordained the same for other creatures. There are no castes in species of animals or birds, so why should there be one among human animals. In his criticism Phule added, "Brahmins cannot claim superior status because of caste, because they hardly bothered with these when wining and dining with Europeans." Professions did not make castes, and castes did not decide one's profession. If someone does a job that is dirty, it does not make them inferior; in the same way that no mother is inferior because she cleans the excreta of her baby. Ritual occupation or tasks, argued Phule, do not make any human being superior or inferior.[125]

Dadabhai Naoroji (1825-1917) regarded that the Caste system had been strengthened by the British, and they had been using it in order to exploit the Indian people, Dadabhai Naoroji wrote that:-

It may be said that Hindus of high caste may not respect those of lower castes in the service. Is it for the British to maintain and encourage such distinction and feeling? Or is it the mission of Britain.[126]

Vivekananda similarly criticised caste as one of the many human institutions that bars the power of free thought and action of an individual. Caste or no caste, creed or no creed, any man, or class, or caste, or nation, or institution that bars the power of free thought and bars action of an individual is devilish, and must go down. Liberty of thought and action, asserted Vivekananda, is the only condition of life, of growth and of well-being.[127]

CONTEMPORARY CRITICISM

People winnowing in a Dalit village near Madurai, Tamil Nadu, India

AS DISCRIMINATION

The maltreatment of Dalits in India has been described by some authors as "India's hidden apartheid".[128][129] Critics of the accusations point to substantial improvements in the position of Dalits in post-independence India, consequent to the strict implementation of the rights and privileges enshrined in the Constitution of India, as implemented by the Protection of Civil rights Act, 1955.[130] They also argue that the practise had disappeared in urban public life.[131]

Sociologists Kevin Reilly, Stephen Kaufman and Angela Bodino, while critical of caste system, conclude that modern India does not practice apartheid since there is no state-sanctioned discrimination.[132] They write that casteism in India is presently "not apartheid. In fact, untouchables, as well as tribal people and members of the lowest castes in India benefit from broad affirmative action programmes and are enjoying greater political power."[133]

Allegations that caste amounts to race has been rejected by prominent[134] scholars.[135][136][137] Ambedkar, for example, wrote that "The Brahmin of Punjab is racially of the same stock as the Chamar of Punjab. The Caste system does not demarcate racial division. The Caste system is a social division of people of the same race." Prominent sociologists, anthropologists and historians have rejected the racial origins and racial emphasis of caste and consider the idea to be one that has purely political and economical undertones. Beteille writes that "the Scheduled Castes of India taken together are no more a race than are the Brahmins taken together. Every social group cannot be regarded as a race simply because we want to protect it against prejudice and discrimination", and that the 2001 Durban conference on racism hosted by the U.N. is "turning its back on established scientific opinion".[137]

Other scholars propose that caste and race based discrimination may be related.[2] Cahill, for example, suggests that the social structure engineered by colonial Spaniards, with *limpieza de sangre*, in South America, one based on race, ethnicity and economic condition was a caste system.[138] The Spanish colonial rule posited, according to Cahill, that the character and quality of people varied according to their colour, race and origin of ethnic types. Caste system and racism have empirically been the two faces of the same coin in recent human history, in a colonial migrant society outside of India. Martínez calls the discriminatory social structure in New Spain as a caste system that was race based colonial order, inspired in part by degrees of racial impurity.[139][140][141] Haviland suggests that race and caste systems are related and each a type of social stratification. Both create social classes determined by birth and fixed for life. Both are opposite of the principle that all humans are born equal, both tend to be endogamous, and offsprings are automatically members of parent's social strata. As examples, Haviland describes castelike situations in Central and South America where wealthy, upper class European-descent population rarely intermarried with people of non-European descent; the social strata in current practice by the royal families and nobility in modern Europe; racial segregation and castelike separation of people by their ethnicity in townships of modern South Africa.[129]

CASTE AND ECONOMICS

A 1995 study suggests that the caste system in India must be viewed as a system of exploitation of poor low-ranking groups by more prosperous high-ranking groups.[142] Such qualitative theories have been questioned though by other studies. Haque reports that over 90 percent of both scheduled castes (low-ranking groups) and all other castes (high-ranking groups) either do not own land or own very small land area only capable of producing less than $1000 per year of food and income per household. Over 99 percent of India's farms are less than 10 hectares, and 99.9 percent of the farms are less than 20 hectares, regardless of the farmer or landowner's caste. Indian government has, in addition, vigorously pursued agricultural land ceiling laws which prohibit anyone from owning land greater than mandated limits. India has used this law to forcibly acquire land from some, then redistribute tens of millions of acres to the landless and poor of the low-caste. However, but for some short term exceptions in some states, these laws have not met the expectations.[143][144] In a 2011 study, Aiyar too notes that such qualitative theories of economic exploitation and consequent land redistribution within India between 1950 and 1990 had no effect on the quality of life and poverty reduction. Instead, economic reforms since the 1990s and resultant opportunities for non-agricultural jobs have reduced poverty and increased per capita income for all segments of Indian society.[145] For specific evidence, Aiyar mentions the following

Critics believe that the economic liberalisation has benefited just a small elite and left behind the poor, especially the lowest Hindu caste of dalits. But a recent authoritative survey revealed striking improvements in living standards of dalits in the last two decades. Television ownership was up from zero to 45 percent; cellphone ownership up from zero to 36 percent; two-wheeler ownership (of motorcycles, scooters, mopeds) up from zero to 12.3 percent; children eating yesterday's leftovers down from 95.9 percent to 16.2 percent... Dalits running their own businesses up from 6 percent to 37 percent; and proportion working as agricultural labourers down from 46.1 percent to 20.5 percent.

Cassan has studied the differential effect within two segments of India's Dalit community. He finds India's overall economic growth has produced the fastest and more significant socio-economic changes. Cassan further concludes that legal and social program initiatives are no longer India's primary constraint in further advancement of India's historically discriminated castes; further advancement are likely to come from improvements in the supply of quality schools in rural and urban India, along with India's economic growth.[28]

3.2 MODERNITY IN INDIAN POLITICS

Caste in Indian society refers to a social group where membership is largely decided by birth. By the early 1990s there began a shift in caste politics. The continuation of a one party system, which was the Congress party, composed mostly of upper-caste leadership, came to an end. This was partly due to economic liberalization in India which reduced the control the state had on the economy and thus the lower casts, and partly due to an upsurge in caste based parties that made the politics of lower caste empowerment a central part of their political agenda. It should be pointed out that these new political parties emerged not on a national level but on a village and regional level, and were most dominant in North India. It is easier for the youth to maintain their status by rallying rather than remain loyal to a specific party. This also weakened the influence of caste and clientelism on Indian politics.

As explained by experts in the field such as Dr Susan Bayly, caste is not the essence of Indian culture and civilization. It is rather a contingent and variable response to the enormous changes that occurred in the subcontinent's political landscape both before and after the colonial conquest1. The New Shorter Oxford English Dictionary defines Caste as "a Hindu hereditary class of socially equal persons, united in religion and usually following similar occupations, distinguished from other castes in the hierarchy by its relative degree of purity or pollution."[2]

The term Caste is commonly used to refer to two distinct concepts of corporate affiliation: the 'Jāti' (birth group) and the Varna (order, class or kind). The term Jāti is used for the units of thousands or sometimes millions of people with whom one may identify oneself for such purposes as marriage. There are thousands of titles associated with specific Jātis in different parts of the country: Rajput, Chamar and Jat – these terms have come to be widely recognised. But these terms are unfamiliar to people outside a limited geographical area. In contrast to this profusion of Jātis or birthgroups, the concept of Varma involves a scheme with only four divisions. Thus what would now be called Hindu society is conceived of as beingdivisible into four very large units which transcend specific regional associations. These are: Brāhmana, Kstriya, Vaisya and Sudra. They are commonly understood as a ranked order of precedence.

Then there is another caste called the 'fifth' one (called Pañcama), the so-called 'untouchable' (the hill and forest population who are called tribals, inclusive). This group occupies a place below, outside this Varna scheme. The Brāhmanas are commonly identified with those who fulfil the calling of priests and spiritual preceptors. The Ksatriyas (etymologically, the 'protectors') are usually rulers and warriors. The Vai.yasare those who have commercial livelihood, and are associated with other producers and wealth-creators as well. The Sudras are toilers and artisans. People belonging to the 'fifth' group perform 'unclean' services such as cremation, killing animals for food, etc.[3] But in real life, these principles have often been widely contested and modified. The implication would be that all who are born into the so called 'clean' castes,rank as high and pure, regardless of wealth, achievement or other individual circumstances. Dr M.N. Srinivas has brought in the 'theory of Sanskritization', an historical process of a group moving upward socially through the embrace of the high or 'Sanskritic' practices, as opposed to local or popular forms of social and religious practices. Thus in his view, castesociety is mobile and fluid, rather than static and inflexible [4].

Caste and Politics

Caste has always been central to modern Indian politics. Even the power structure of mediaeval India was based on caste. Caste also operated as the central principle in the distribution of power and material resources in the colonialperiod. Colonialism in India created a democratic and modernist space; nevertheless this space was also predominantly captured by upper-caste groups. The nationalist struggle against the imperial power was aimed at establishing the caste-class hegemony. Non- Brahmin and low-caste movements were active during the colonial era, broadly pursuing two aims: achieving upward caste-class mobility and annihilation of caste.

The caste system played a significant role in determining the content and direction of the processes of political socialisation, political mobilisation and institutionalisation within the framework of modern democracy.. The dynamics of caste and class were at the root of the complexity of Indian politics in its functioning.

Behind the seemingly religious and communal movements in post-independent India, it was the dynamics of caste-class hegemony that was the real operational factor. Both the anti-caste and the upwardly mobile caste movements are guiding the proreservation movement, which aims at upward class mobility of the hitherto excluded castes. The pro-imperialist bourgeois policies of the ruling class and the struggles against these policies are also influenced and shaped by the tensions and contradictions in caste-class dynamics.

In the years following independence, the traditional upper castes continued to rule in most parts of India. For example, until 1977, upper castes continued to hold prominent elected positions in Uttar Pradesh, the most populous state in the Indian union [5,6]. Untill 1962, as many as 63% of ruling Congress members of the Legislative Assembly came from elite castes [7]. Soon, however, traditional peasant castes such as Ahirs, Kurmis, Koeri, LodhRajputs, and Jats began to dominate the political scape of northern India. In the southern state of Tamilnadu, the Vanniyars and Thevars have become assertive, and in Karnataka, control was wrested in the mid- 1950s from the traditional rural elite within the Congress party by the Vokkaligas and Linagayats [8, 9]. In the North Indian Hindi speaking belt, upper caste members of parliament fell below 50% for the first time in 1977. The challenge to the established Congress was mounted in Uttar Pradesh rather effectively in the late 1960s by a coalition of peasant castes led by Charan Singh. In Bihar, also, there was a significant decline of upper caste members of the legislative assembly after 1977 [10].

DALIT IN POLITICS

The binary relationship between caste and politics is trotted out for re-examination whenever there's a major election. That caste affiliation is a fundamental determinant of political calculation and voting patterns is a commonplace of academic and street discourse.Even when the relationship is complex, and not easily reducible to a limited set of factors, it acts as a matrix which encloses the electoral field. This is usually denied or deplored by the urban upper class which occupies the apex of the social structure and whose concerns and ideology are reflected in the mainstream media. But for the overwhelming majority of the Indian bourgeoisie, attached in some way or the other to the countryside, caste considerations usually govern political affiliation either directly or indirectly.[11]

The Republican party was founded by the legendary BabasahebAmbedkar in 1957. He later led his people to renounce Hinduism and embrace Buddhism instead [12]. It is true that most of the votaries of the Republican party of India (RPI) belong to the Mahar caste because other formerly untouchable castes of the region, such as the Mangs, Matangs, and Chambars, have stayed away from it. In fact, they often veer toward supporting the BharaiyaJanata party [13], which is, ironically, a right-wing Hindu organization. This is because many members of these other castes believe that the RPI is a vehicle of upward mobility for the Mahars alone. They have also desisted from becoming Buddhists. Nevertheless, BabasahebAmbedkar's shadow looms large today in the politics of the former untouchables. They resent the term "Harijan" (children of God) that Gandhi used for them as they consider it toopatronizing. They would rather be known as "Dalits," or the oppressed.

Ambedkar was the first to use this term to denote the Scheduled Castes for its obvious combative edge [14]. Ambedkar, today, has been deified among the Buddhist Mahars of Maharashtra and has a similar iconic status to Buddha in many Mahar families [15].Ambedkar's death anniversary in 1981 provided the occasion for Kanshi Ram to inaugurate the Dalit ShoshitSamajSangharshSamit (or DS-4). In its attempt to attract as wide a range as possible, the DS-4 also called out to Muslims to help fight the privileges of the traditional elite castes. According to Vora, no Dalit leader after Ambedkar paid any consistent attention to economic issues [16]. Dalits are, however, very active when it comes to voting in elections. As Yadav notes, the turnout of Scheduled Caste (or Dalit) voters was as high as 62.2% in the 1998 elections [17].

In all, caste has become an important determinant in Indian society and politics, the new lesson of organised politics and consciousness of caste affiliations learnt by the hitherto despised caste groups have transformed the contours of Indian politics encountered. The impact of these mobilizations along caste-identities has resulted not only in the empowerment of newly rising groups but has amplified the power of stimulating politics and possibly leading to a growing crisis of governability.

MODERN INDIA

At the beginning of the twentieth century, caste rank was not a good indicator of material deprivation. It is highly unlikely that the heterogeneity within a caste and between castes sharing the same administrative rank would have diminished over time, while observed economic inequalities have been very high. Clearly, the caste-based public policy lacks empirical foundation. However, the Indian state is actually conveying the benefits to the privileged by treating the rich and the poor belonging to the caste categories as equals. Thus the ruling coalition co-opts the elite of the lower castes, strengthens itself and weakens the depressed groups. At the same time the policy and its regular extensions, by persistently focusing on caste, keep the poor divided along caste lines. Thus caste quotas are extremely useful as a tool of governance. It is hypocritical to argue that this policy does anything to eliminate acute, long standing deprivation [18].

Relationships between castes have become more relaxed today. There is more food sharing between castes and a lot more eating done at local restaurants where caste distinctions are less likely to be made. One of the biggest changes that took place in India was occupational pursuits among men [19] (and women later on). Earlier, most men did not veer away from their caste-linked occupations, such as blacksmithing and pottery making. Many have now taken up newer occupations that do not relate to their caste, such as government jobs, teaching, retail and services, and machine repair. Wealth and power in the village is now less associated with caste than before, and landownership has become more diversified [19]. Also, the idea that purity and pollution is caused by the lower castes has diminished a good amount. It has, however, only somewhat diminished in the public, whereas behind closed doors and on ceremonial occasions, purification rituals related to caste status are still observed.

Although discrimination on the basis of caste has been outlawed in India, caste has become a means for competing for access to resources and power in modern India, such as educational opportunities, new occupations, and improvement in life chances [19]. This trend is associated to India's favored policies and the execution.

We have to come to certain conclusions and offer viable solutions to the problems created by a wrong understanding and application of the standard of Caste in India. What has been there for centuries cannot be undone in a day or two. Therefore there is change all over the place – in the thinking of people about caste, community, religious and philosophical values. Nothing is objectionable so long as there is no compulsion, hatred, animosity. The world is created by God in a wonderful and mysterious way. Diversity is the Art of Nature; but Unity is the Heart of God. This is what the Rgveda (I.164.46) declared ages ago: *'ekaˆ sad viprābahudhāvadanti'* (What exists is One but wise men call it by different names). Let people do what they think is right and good for them; but let them not battle in the name of religion, philosophy, race, caste, class, community or political affiliations.

Unit IV

Political Parties: National and Regional

4.1 Meaning and Role of Politics

Human beings have always organised themselves in groups and larger formations. Political parties have emerged as one of these human organisations. In modern age the ideal form of government is run through one or the other method of representative institutions. All representative governments and representative institutions require the existence of political parties.

A political party is an organised body of people who share certain common principles and goals regarding the political system of a country. The main purpose of political parties is to acquire and retain political power. Political parties which run the government are called the ruling party. In a coalition government, there may be more than one ruling party. Those who sit in the opposition and criticise and analyse the performance of the ruling party/parties generally or on specific issues are called opposition parties. A political party as such should have the following essential features:

i) it must be an organised body of people with a formal membership;

ii) it must have clearly spelt out policies and programmes;

iii) its members should agree with its ideology, policies and programmes;

iv) it must aim at getting power through the democratic process;

v) it must have a clear and acceptable leadership; and

vi) it must focus on broad issues and major areas of government policies. [321]

Types of Party System

India has a multi-party system. Indian politics is dominated by several national and regional parties. There are countries where there is one-party system or two-party system. Erstwhile Soviet Union and Yugoslavia had single party systems. Similarly, China has one-party system. Earlier in Germany there existed only one-party – the Nazi Party; so was the case in Italy where the only party was known as the Fascist Party. In a two party or bi-party system there are two main political parties. The United Kingdom (UK), the United States of America (USA), Australia and New Zealand have bi-party systems. There may exist other parties but their role is generally insignificant. For example in UK, there are two main parties, the Conservative Party and the Labour Party. In the USA the two main parties are the Republican Party and the Democratic Party. Japan, France, Germany and Switzerland have multi-party systems.

EVOLUTION OF PARTY SYSTEM IN INDIA

The evolution of Indian party system can be traced to the formation of the Congress, as a political platform in 1885. Other parties and groups originated later. The Indian National Congress was formed as a response to the colonial rule and to achieve independence from the British rule. After independence and with the adoption of a democratic Constitution, a new party system emerged in the wake of the first general elections based on universal adult franchise in 1952. In preceding lesson you have learnt about the universal adult franchise in detail.

During the post-independence period, the party system passed through various phases. The first phase is known as the phase of one-party dominance because with the exception of Kerala during 1956–59, the ruling party both at the Centre and in the states was the Congress. The second phase (1967–1975) saw the emergence of a multi-party system in India. In the Assembly elections in 1967, Congress was defeated in eight States. For the first time non-Congress parties formed governments in these states. These parties formed coalition governments. Then came the split in Congress into Congress (O) and Congress (N). However, the Congress again became a dominant force at the Centre after winning 1971 mid-term poll. Then came the emergency period (1975–77) which is known as the authoritarian period of Indian democracy.

With the lifting of emergency, the dominance of Congress ended. In the general elections of 1977 Congress was defeated by the Janata Party. Janata Party came into existence as a result of the merger of many opposition parties. But again in 1980 general elections Congress came back to power and remained in power till 1989.

Janata Party emerged out of the merger of Congress (O) led by Morarji Desai, Bharatiya Lok Dal led by Ch. Charan Singh, Congress for Democracy (CFD) led by Jagjivan Ram and H.N. Bahuguna, the socialists led by George Fernandes and Jana Sangh led by L.K. Advani.

In 1989 elections, the National Front joined government with the support of BJP and the Left Front. But this formation could not last its tenure and elections for the tenth Lok Sabha were held in May-June, 1991. Congress again formed government at the Centre. In 1996 general elections BJP emerged as the single largest party and was asked to form government at the Centre. Since it could not prove its majority within the given time it had to resign. The United Front which was a combination of thirteen parties, formed the government at the Centre with the external support of the Congress and the CPI(M). But this government also could not last its full term. Although the coalition government formed under the leadership of BJP after 1998 elections was defeated in Lok Sabha, the 1999 elections again provided them the opportunity to form government which lasted its full term under a multi-party coalition, known as National Democratic Alliance (NDA).

In the 14th general elections held in 2004, Congress emerged as the single largest party. It formed alliance with like minded parties and formed government at the Centre. The phase of

Indian party system which began in 1989 and is still continuing has been aptly called a phase of coalition politics. No single party has been able to form government on its own at the Centre.

NATIONAL PARTIES AND REGIONAL PARTIES

India has two types of political parties – national parties and regional parties. National parties are those which generally have influence all over the country. It is not necessary that a national party will have equal strength in all the states; it varies from State to State.

A party is recognised as a national party by the Election Commission on the basis of a formula. The political party which has secured not less than four percent of the total valid votes in the previous general elections at least in four states, is given the status of a national party.

The number of national parties has been changing. In the year 2006, Indian National Congress, Bharatiya Janata Party, Communist Party of India (Marxist) [CPI(M)], Communist Party of India (CPI), Bahujan Samaj Party, and the Nationalist Congress Party were national parties.

However, there are other parties in India, which do not enjoy national influence. Their activities and influence are restricted to particular states or regions. Sometimes these parties are formed to voice demands of a specific region. These parties are neither weak nor short-lived. Sometimes they prove to be very powerful in their respective regions.

These are known as regional parties. Major regional parties are AIADMK and DMK in Tamil Nadu, Telugu Desam in Andhra Pradesh, Akali Dal in Punjab, National Conference in Jammu and Kashmir, Jharkhand Mukti Morcha in Jharkhand, Asom Gana Parishad in Assam and Nationalist Congress Party and Shiv Sena in Maharashtra. About the regional parties you will read in the following lesson.

4.2   MAJOR NATIONAL PARTIES IN INDIA

1. INDIAN NATIONAL CONGRESS

As you have already read, Indian National Congress was formed in the year 1885 in Bombay. W.C. Bonnarjee was the first President of the Indian National Congress. To begin with, Congress was an organisation of middle class intellectuals who were primarily concerned with political reforms in the British colonial rule. In the twenties under the leadership of Mahatma Gandhi, the Congress became a mass based organisation. The party started enjoying the support of the common people and played a very significant role in the freedom struggle.

After independence Jawahar Lal Nehru became the Prime Minsiter and led the Congress till his death in 1964. As already mentioned in an earlier paragraph, this was known as the 'Nehru era'. The Congress party won first five general elections in 1952, 1957, 1962, 1967 and 1971. In 1975 national emergency was declared which went on till 1977. In the elections of 1977, the Congress was defeated. However, in 1980 general elections, the Congress Party led by Indira Gandhi came back to power. Indira Gandhi was assassinated in 1984 and during 1985 general elections, Rajiv Gandhi was the leader of the party. Congress won the 1985 general elections with a larger majority. In 1989 though Congress could not get absolute majority, it was the single largest party. In the tenth general elections in 1991,Congress again emerged as the single largest party and formed the government at the Centre. In the 1996, general elections Congress could not form government at the Centre.

In the 12th general elections in 1998, Congress could get only 140 Lok Sabha seats. In the 1999 general elections Congress's strength was further reduced to 112. But in the 14th general elections Congress entered into alliance with other secular parties and secured the number of seats that provided it an opportunity to form a coalition government.

2. THE BHARATIYA JANATA PARTY (BJP)

The Bharatiya Janata Party (BJP) was formed in 1980. Since then it has extended its influence in the Hindi belt, Gujarat and Maharashtra. Since 1989, it has been trying to extend its base in South India also.

Since its formation in 1980, the BJP has been increasing its number of seats in the Lok Sabha gradually. In 1984, general elections it secured only two seats. In 1989 the number of seats increased to 88. In 1991 general elections BJP's strength in the Lok Sabha increased to 122 which rose to 161 in the 1996 elections. In 1998 it won 180 seats and in 1999 its number in Lok Sabha increased to 182. In the 1999 general elections, BJP contested as an alliance partner in the National Democratic Alliance (NDA). In the recent 2004 general elections BJP as an alliance of NDA could not get the required majority. It is playing the role of the opposition party. The BJP has emerged as a significant national party but its support base as yet is limited to certain areas, rather than spread all over India.

3. THE COMMUNIST PARTIES

The two communist parties are the Communist Party of India (CPI) and the Communist Party of India (Marxist) [CPI(M)]. Next to the Congress, the Communist Party is the oldest in India. The communist movement began in the early twenties and the Communist Party was founded in 1925. The communists participated in the national movement, though often they had serious differences with the Congress. The communists assert that the people should be economically equal and the society should not be divided into classes of rich and poor. The workers and peasants and other toiling people who do most of the productive work for the society, should be given due recognition and power.

The communists were the main opposition in the Lok Sabha throughout the Nehru Era. In the first Lok Sabha they had 26 members, in the second and the third Lok Sabha, they had 27 and 29 members respectively. In 1957, the CPI won absolute majority in the Kerala Assembly and formed the first Communist government in India. In the early sixties specially after the Chinese aggression of 1962 there were serious differences among the members of the Communist Party. As a result, the party split into two. Those who broke away from CPI, formed CPI(M) in 1964. The CPI(M)'s main support base has been concentrated in West Bengal, Kerala and Tripura, though it has registered its presence in Andhra Pradesh, Assam, Bihar, Maharashtra, Orissa and Punjab. The CPI has its pockets of influence in states like Andhra Pradesh, Assam, Bihar, Manipur, Orissa, Pondicherry, Punjab, etc.

Moreover CPI has been a part of the left front coalition in Kerala and West Bengal. In the Lok Sabha elections of 2004, both the CPI and the CPI (M) were alliance partners of the Congress. They are supporting the United Progressive Alliance (UPA) government at the Centre from outside.

4. Bahujan Samaj Party (BSP)

The BSP acquired the status of a national party in 1996. The BSP champions the cause of those sections which belong to low castes, deprived groups and minorities. In fact, these sections of Indian society (the Bahujan Samaj) form the majority of the Indian population.

The BSP believes that this 'samaj' should be freed from the exploitation of the upper castes and by forming their own government. BSP's influence lies in states like Madhya Pradesh, Uttar Pradesh and Punjab. In 1995 and 1997 BSP was a partner in the coalition governments in Uttar Pradesh.

4.3   Role and Programme; Electoral system and Voting Behavior

Elected political agents are expected to fulfill the various demands of their constituents; however, their actions may be more in line with fostering their own welfare at the expense of the citizens. The public choice framework is used to model this behavior of the government and political agents. Politicians are modeled as vote maximizing agents who attempt to influence voters by using various tactics. While influencing voters by large campaign expenditures, handing out jobs to supports are examined,2 the use of economic policies to examine voter behavior is the focus of most extant literature.

Interestingly, while the theoretical models emphasize the use of economic policies as tactical instruments to influence voter behavior, empirically this is not examined directly. Models of opportunistic behavior by the government,3 examine the presence of election cycles in tax collections, government expenditures and deficits i.e., whether the government tries to reduce (increase) taxes (expenditures) in the election year. Models of strategic behavior4 on the other hand attempt to discern the pattern of political redistribution i.e., who are the ultimate beneficiaries of these actions, the longtime supporters or swing voters. Though these do provide insight into the workings of the government, they do not attempt to examine whether these policies did in fact influence voter behavior. To do this one would need to examine whether opportunistic or strategic actions by politicians in the election period influenced voters to vote for them in the forthcoming elections. This can be accomplished by examining the effect of election or pre-election year expenditure (taxes), economic outcomes such as income growth, unemployment and inflation on voter turnout, vote share and the probability of winning of the incumbent.

In keeping with the Indian theme instituted in this exercise; an attempt to establish a relationship between pre-election government behavior and various outcomes of elections in India is undertaken. India, a fertile ground for these kinds of excursions has been a serious matter of inquiry for many years. While electoral cycles, strategic redistributions and patronage through favorable regulations have been found to exist here; researchers concur that there is a need to examine whether voters condition their vote on economic policies and outcomes.

Though voting behavior of the Indian electoral has been studied extensively; they have generally been based on surveys or case studies of individual voters.6 Most studies that use aggregate election data do not employ rigorous econometric methodology but rather use measures of correlation to eke out a relationship between voter turnout, vote share of parties and various socio-economic variables. Kondo (2003) uses regression analysis to examine relationship between these variables and concludes that literacy, urbanization, agricultural development and political competition positively influences voter turnout, however, the importance of socio-economic variables reduce over time.

Studies that use individual survey data conclude that while gender, caste, religion,education and income are important in explaining political awareness and exposure to propaganda; they matter less in case of party preference. Recent surveys show that rising prices and unemployment are major issues that affect the electorate. Meyer (1989) concludes that Indian voters vote retrospectively, and are sensitive to short term shifts in agricultural output and the economy. This holds true even when we account for formation of new parties (Meyer and Malcolm 1993).

We intend to use previous research on electoral cycles and political economy of intergovernmental transfers as a stepping stone to examine the effects of pre-election behavior of political agents on voter behavior. While there is widespread acknowledgement of the presence of electoral cycles in taxes and expenditures prior to national and state elections; these studies tend to use less comprehensive and older data.

Also, though research indicating the presence of political manipulation of grants also exists, there has been no systematic study on the presence of cycles with respect to the most important element of fiscal policy in the hands of the central government–the intergovernmental transfer system. This dissertation therefore attempts to provide a comprehensive analysis of political cycles in the different elements of fiscal policies available to the various governments and an exploration of economic voting effects in India.

The incorporation of political variables in the study of a few purely economic relationships brings abstract models closer to reality. In the vast field of political economy, the study of how elections and politics interact with the economy is accorded tremendous importance. The main strands of this literature focus on the phenomenon of tactical redistribution (Cox and McCubbins 1986, Dixit and Londregan 1998), political business cycles (Nordhaus 1975, Rogoff and Sibert 1988, Rogoff 1990, Alesina 1987), and the economic voting behavior of the electorate in response to actions carried out by politicians (Ferejohn 1986). While theories of tactical distribution examine which type of voter, core supporters or swing voters, benefit from the incumbent" s largesse,10 political business cycles examine the presence of election cycles in economic outcomes such as inflation and unemployment,11 tax collections, government transfers, expenditures and deficits. Economic voting on the other hand analyzes the voter response to economic policies of the incumbent, and outcomes of economic policies of incumbents such as inflation, unemployment and income growth.

Empirical studies that attempt to find relationships between economic and policy outcomes and electoral fortunes of the incumbent are based on the reward-punishment or responsibility hypothesis. In its simplest version, voters condition their responses on economic policies and outcomes such as income, inflation, inequality and are assumed to reward incumbents who perform well and punish those who perform unsatisfactorily.

Recent research has enriched this model by incorporating measures for clarity of responsibility, economic geography and yard stick effects. In India, a fertile ground for such excursions, these phenomena have been a serious matter of inquiry for many years. Political economy studies in India have focused on models of opportunistic and strategic behavior by the government. The former examine the presence of election cycles in tax collections, government expenditures and deficits i.e., whether the government tries to reduce (increase) taxes (expenditures) in the election year;12 while models of strategic behavior attempt to discern the pattern of political redistribution i.e., who are the ultimate beneficiaries of these actions, the longtime supporters or swing voters.13 Interestingly, while the theoretical models emphasize the use of economic policies as tactical instruments to influence voter behavior; there is a lack of studies on voting behavior in India which would validate these propositions. While electoral cycles, strategic redistributions and patronage through favorable regulations have been found to exist here; researchers concur that there is a need to examine whether voters condition their vote on economic policies.

In this section, an attempt to establish a relationship between pre-election government behavior and various outcomes of elections in India is undertaken. There are many reasons why India is an excellent country to base our exercise. Extant research in economic voting behavior has focused on explaining this phenomenon in western countries with established democracies and a developed economy. Though other countries have in been included in cross-country voting studies, the inherent instability of vote functions across nations behooves a greater need of country specific studies; so such an exercise involving India, a dynamic young democracy and developing economy would be a valuable addition to the literature. Economic voting behavior has found to be weak in countries with a low clarity of vertical responsibility,15 i.e., when voters are unable to assign responsibility of the economic policies or performance to the different levels of government; economic factors play a less important role in decisions of voting. However, in India there is a clear delineation of the functional responsibility of each level of government in the constitution and so examining economic voting effects of elections to different levels of government is easier to justify.16 The argument for decentralization centers on the fact that bringing the government closer to its citizens improves its functioning by enhancing the relationship between citizen needs and government services. Proponents of greater decentralization have argued that it promotes economic development and growth. Countries have been encouraged to decentralize in an effort to promote a closer matching of needs and development. But inherent in this argument is that incumbents of these levels of governments would be held accountable for their actions, free and fair elections therefore are a necessary condition for decentralization to reap its potential benefits. Therefore a result indicating the presence of economic voting in India can be interpreted as voters holding governments accountable. Finally, having established previously the nature of political economy in India, examination of economic voting behavior is the next logical step which would enhance the current state of literature in this area in India.

This study also extends the literature on political cycles in India by examining Inter-governmental transfers, incorporating a larger number of states and including more recent elections. To accomplish the task of examining economic voting behavior in India, this exercise proposes to analyze the following questions.

Studies involving U.S. states have analyzed the effect of macro economic outcomes such an income growth, unemployment and inflation on Presidential, Gubernatorial and state assembly elections. Such an exercise would be an interesting undertaking within the Indian context. Hence the first question is:

Proposition 1: Are Central and State incumbents rewarded electorally for increases in income growth and central incumbents penalized for increases in inflation prior to elections?

Chaudhuri and Dasgupta (2006) have unearthed electoral cycles in social and developmental spending, commodity taxes and current account expenditure, while Khemani (2006) has found cycles in excise tax collections and public investment spending in various Indian states. Ghosh (2006) finds that the property crime rate significantly drops prior to an election, so if this was due to changes in expenditure on police we can expect voters to positively react to increases in expenditure on public safety.

Proposition 2a: How do voters react in elections for state legislative assemblies to increases (decreases) in government spending (taxes) by state level incumbents?

Proposition 2b: Are political cycles persistent in state fiscal policies prior to state legislative elections? Khemani (2003), Dutta et al. (2007), Rao and Singh (2000), Rodden and Wilkinson (2004) examine the political economy of intergovernmental transfers. They argue that a central incumbent interested in maximizing votes across the Indian states would attempt to manipulate central grants to favor either their core supporters or swing voters. Findings from these indicate that manipulable grants are provided to co-partisans at the sub-national level and to states co-partisan with central coalition partners. Given this, we can analyze the effect of such grants on vote shares of incumbents in elections to the Lower House of the parliament. A caveat however is in order; since most of these grants are not directly „visible" to the individual voter, it may be hard to establish such a relationship.

Proposition 3a: In elections to the Lower House of the parliament, are central incumbents rewarded by voters for increases in central grants to states? Given the previous research, economic voting effects may be greater in co-partisan states.

Proposition 3b: Are political cycles persistent in grants and loans provided by the center prior to national elections? How does alignment of the states matter?

Interestingly, the Indian set up also allows us to analyze a perhaps unintended political consequence of federalism. While empirical works on voting behavior of other countries focus on the effects of national and state government policies on elections to congruent levels of government; the fiscal dependence of Indian states on the national governments affords us an opportunity to examine whether the incumbent at the center manipulates policies to aid his supporters to win state elections.

Proposition 4a: How do voters react in state assembly elections to grants and transfers provided by the center?

Proposition 4b: Are political cycles persistent in grants and loans provided by the center prior to state assembly elections?

Since grants and loans from the center in India are used to finance a majority of the state's expenditures; state fiscal policy can be affected by both central and state incumbents. Therefore we also attempt to establish a relationship between vote shares of central and state incumbents and state fiscal policy instruments in national elections.

Proposition 5a: Do voters reward or penalize state (central) incumbents for changes in government expenditure and taxation at the time of national elections?

While these propositions are reasonably simple, complexities can be easily incorporated. In case of the first proposition, one can include variables to measure a state's growth relative to national growth so it would mean that voters only respond to growth in state incomes that diverges from trends in national growth. Similarly, economic policy variables for other states can be included in the tests for the second proposition to account for yardstick competition. Research indicates that the reward and punishment effects in the U.S. are tinged by partisan flavor; Republican incumbents are more severely punished for tax increases than their Democratic counterparts while the magnitude of punishment is larger for Democratic incumbents who cut spending that when Republicans do the same. However, these effects may not be found in the Indian scenario given the fact that Indian political parties are generally populist in nature and seem to have no such distinct differences in ideology.20 Interestingly, it has been argued that when there is low clarity of horizontal responsibility, i.e., in the case of divided or coalition governments, economic voting effects are muted. India has enjoyed a wide variety of government types, from single party government to coalitions, so variables to indicate divided governments can be incorporated to test the importance of clarity of horizontal responsibility in India.

Voting Behavior

Voting behavior is a form of political behavior. Understanding voters' behavior can explain how and why decisions were made either by public decision-makers, which has been a central concern for political scientists, or by the electorate. To interpret voting behavior both political science and psychology expertise where necessary and therefore the field of political psychology emerged. Political psychology researchers study ways in which **affective influence** may help voters make more informed voting choices, with some proposing that affect may explain how the electorate makes informed political choices in spite of low overall levels of political attentiveness and sophistication.

To make inferences and predictions about behavior concerning a voting decision, certain factors such as gender, race, culture or religion must be considered. Moreover, key public influences include the role of emotions, political socialization, tolerance of diversity of political views and the media. The effect of these influences on voting behavior is best understood through theories on the formation of attitudes, beliefs, schema, knowledge structures and the practice of information processing. For example, surveys from different countries indicate that people are generally happier in individualistic cultures where they have rights such as the right to vote. The degree to which voting decision is affected by internal processing systems of political information and external influences, alters the quality of making truly democratic decisions.

VOTING BEHAVIOR TYPES

The existing literature does not provide an explicit classification of voting behavior types. However, research following the Cypriot referendum of 2004, identified **four distinct voting behaviors** depending on the election type. Citizens use different decision criteria if they are called to exercise their right to vote in **i) presidential, ii) legislative, iii) local elections** or in a **iv) referendum.**[3] In national elections it is usually the norm that people vote based on their political beliefs. Local and regional elections differ, as people tend to elect those who seem more capable to contribute to their area. A referendum follows another logic as people are specifically asked to vote for or against a clearly defined policy.

Interestingly, an older study in postwar Japan identified that urban citizens were more likely to be supportive of socialist parties, while rural citizens were favorable of conservative parties. Regardless of the political preference, this is an interesting differentiation that can be attributed to affective influence.

AFFECTIVE INFLUENCE

A growing literature on the significance of affect in politics finds that affective states play a role in public voting behavior that can be both beneficial and biasing. Affect here refers to the experience of emotion or feeling, which is often described in contrast to cognition. This work largely follows from findings in psychology regarding the ways in which affective states are involved in human judgment and decision-making.

Research in political science has traditionally ignored non-rational considerations in its theories of mass political behavior, but the incorporation of social psychology has become increasingly common. In exploring the benefits of affect on voting, researchers have argued that affective states such as anxiety and enthusiasm encourage the evaluation of new political information and thus benefit political behavior by leading to more considered choices. Others, however, have discovered ways in which affect such as emotion and mood can significantly bias the voting choices of the electorate. For example, evidence has shown that a variety of events that are irrelevant to the evaluation of candidates but can stir emotions, such as the outcome of football matches and weather, can have a significant impact on voting decisions.

Several variables have been proposed that may moderate the relationship between emotion and voting. Researchers have shown that one such variable may be political sophistication, with higher sophistication voters more likely to experience emotions in response to political stimuli and thus more prone to emotional biases in voting choice. Affective intensity has also been shown to moderate the relationship between affect and voting, with one study finding a doubling of estimated impact for higher-intensity affective shocks.

4.4   MECHANISMS OF AFFECTIVE INFLUENCE ON VOTING

The differential impact of several specific emotions have been studied on voting behavior:

Surprise – Recent research suggests that the emotion of surprise may magnify the impact of emotions on voting. In assessing the impact of home-team sports victories on voting, Healy et al. showed that surprising victories provided close to twice the benefit to the incumbent party compared to victories overall.

Anger – Affective theory would predict that anger increases the use of generalized knowledge and reliance upon stereotypes and other heuristics. An experiment on students at the University of Massachusetts Amherst showed that people who had been primed with an anger condition relied less upon issue-concordance when choosing between candidates than those who had been primed with fear. In a separate laboratory study, subjects primed with the anger emotion were significantly less likely to seek information about a candidate and spent less time reviewing a candidate's policy positions on the web.

Anxiety – Affective intelligence theory identifies anxiety as an emotion that increases political attentiveness while decreasing reliance on party identification when deciding between candidates, thus improving decision-making capabilities. Voters who report anxiety regarding an election are more likely to vote for candidates whose policies they prefer, and party members who report feeling anxious regarding a candidate are twice as likely to defect and vote for the opposition candidate.[6] Others have denied that anxiety's indirect influence on voting behavior has been proven to the exclusion of alternative explanations, such as the possibility that less preferred candidates produce feelings of anxiety, as opposed to the reverse.

Fear – Studies in psychology has shown that people experiencing fear rely on more detailed processing when making choices. One study found that subjects primed with fear spent more time seeking information on the web before a hypothetical voting exercise than those primed with anger.

Pride - Results from the American National Elections Survey found that pride, along with hope and fear, explained a significant amount of the variance in peoples' 2008 voting choices. The size of the effect of expressions of pride on voting for McCain was roughly one third of the size of the effect of party identification, typically the strongest predictor. Appeals to pride were also found to be effective in motivating voter turnout among high-propensity voters, though the effect was not as strong as appeals to shame.

EFFECTS OF VOTING ON EMOTION

The act of voting itself can produce emotional responses that may bias the choices voters make and potentially impact subsequent emotional states.

A recent study on voters in Israel found that voters' cortisol levels, the so-called "stress hormone," were significantly higher immediately before entering a polling place than personal baseline levels measured on a similar, non-election day. This may be significant for voting choices since cortisol is known to have an impact on memory consolidation, memory retrieval, and reward- and risk-seeking behavior. Acute stress may disrupt decision making and impact cognition. Additionally, research done on voters in Ann Arbor and Durham after the US 2008 elections showed partial evidence that voting for the losing candidate may lead to increased cortisol levels relative to levels among voters who chose the winning candidate.

PRACTICAL IMPLICATIONS

POLITICAL CAMPAIGNS

The use of emotional appeals in political campaigns to increase support for a candidate or decrease support for a challenger is a widely recognized practice and a common element of any campaign strategy. Campaigns often seek to instill positive emotions such as enthusiasm and hopefulness about their candidate among party bases to improve turnout and political activism while seeking to raise fear and anxiety about the challenger. Enthusiasm tends to reinforce preferences, whereas fear and anxiety tends to interrupt behavioral patterns and leads individuals to look for new sources of information.

POLITICAL SURVEYS

Research findings illustrate that it is possible to influence a persons' attitudes toward a political candidate using carefully crafted survey questions, which in turn may influence his or her voting behavior. A laboratory study in the UK focused on participants' attitude toward former Prime Minister Tony Blair during the 2001 pre-election period via a telephone survey. After gauging participants' interest in politics, the survey asked the participants to list either i) two positive characteristics of the Prime Minister, ii) five positive characteristics of the Prime Minister, iii) two negative characteristics of the Prime Minister, or iv) five negative characteristics of the Prime Minister. Participants were then asked to rate their attitude toward Blair on a scale from 1 to 7 where higher values reflected higher favorability.

Listing five positive or negative characteristics for the Prime Minister was challenging; especially for those with little or no interest in politics. The ones asked to list five positive characteristics were primed negatively towards the politicians because it was too hard to name five good traits. On the contrary, following the same logic, those who were to list five negative, came to like the politician better than before. This conclusion was reflected in the final survey stage when participants evaluated their attitude toward the Prime Minister.

LOSS AVERSION

The loss aversion theory by Amos Tversky and Daniel Kahneman is often associated with voting behavior as people are more likely to use their vote to avoid the impact of an unfavorable policy rather than supporting a favorable policy. From a psychological perspective, value references are crucial to determine individual preferences. For instance, tax breaks are a value which voters don't want to lose thus they are more likely to vote for the candidate that promises such benefit, instead of voting for a candidate closer to their political beliefs.

4.5 PROCEDURE OF AMENDMENTS

Amendment of the Constitution of India is the process of making changes to the nation's fundamental law or supreme law. The procedure of amendment in the constitution is laid down in Part XX (Article 368) of the Constitution of India. This procedure ensures the sanctity of the Constitution of India and keeps a check on arbitrary power of the Parliament of India.

However, there is another limitation imposed on the amending power of the constitution of India.

There has been a conflict between the Supreme Court and Parliament, where Parliament wants to exercise discretionary use of power to amend the constitution while the Supreme Court wants to restrict that power. This has led to the laying down of various doctrines or rules in regards to checking the validity/legality of an amendment, the most famous among them is the Basic structure doctrine as laid down by the Supreme Court in the case of *Kesavananda Bharati v. State of Kerala*.

CONSTITUENT ASSEMBLY DEBATES

The framers of the Constitution were neither in favour of the traditional theory of federalism, which entrusts the task of constitutional amendment to a body other than the Legislature, nor did they favour a rigid special procedure for such amendments. They also never wanted to have a British-style system where Parliament is supreme. The framers, instead, adopted a combination of the "theory of fundamental law", which underlies the written Constitution of the United States with the "theory of parliamentary sovereignty" as existing in the United Kingdom. The Constitution of India vests constituent power upon the Parliament subject to the special procedure laid down therein.

During the discussion in the Constituent Assembly on this aspect, some members were in favour of adopting an easier mode of amending procedure for the initial five to ten years. Explaining why it was necessary to introduce an element of flexibility in the Constitution, Jawaharlal Nehru observed in the Constituent Assembly on 8 November 1948, "While we want this Constitution to be as solid and as permanent a structure as we can make it, nevertheless there is no permanence in Constitutions. There should be a certain flexibility. If you make anything rigid and permanent, you stop a nation's growth, the growth of a living, vital, organic people. Therefore, it has to be flexible ... while we, who are assembled in this House, undoubtedly represent the people of India, nevertheless I thinks it can be said, and truthfully, that when a new House, by whatever name it goes, is elected in terms of this Constitution, and every adult in India has the right to vote - man and woman - the House that emerges then will certainly be fully representative of every section of the Indian people. It is right that House elected so - under this Constitution of course it will have the right to do anything - should have an easy opportunity to make such changes as it wants to. But in any event, we should not make a Constitution, such as some other great countries have, which are so rigid that they do not and cannot be adapted easily to changing conditions. Today especially, when the world is in turmoil and we are passing through a very swift period of transition, what we may do today may not be wholly applicable tomorrow. Therefore, while we make a Constitution which is sound and as basic as we can, it should also be flexible ..."

Dr. P.S. Deshmukh believed that the amendment of the Constitution should be made easier as there were contradictory provisions in some places which would be more and more apparent when the provisions were interpreted, and that the whole administration would suffer, if the amendment to the Constitution was not made easy. Brajeshwar Prasad also favoured a flexible Constitution so as to make it survive the test of time. He was of the opinion that rigidity tends to check progressive legislation or gradual innovation. On the other hand, H.V. Kamath favoured ensuring procedural safeguards to avoid the possibility of hasty amendment to the Constitution.

"It is said that the provisions contained in the Draft make amendment difficult. It is proposed that the Constitution should be amendable by a simple majority at least for some years. The argument is subtle and ingenious. It is said that this Constituent Assembly is not elected on adult suffrage while the future Parliament will be elected on adult suffrage and yet the former has been given the right to pass the Constitution by a simple majority while the latter has been denied the same right. It is paraded as one of the absurdities of the Draft Constitution. I must repudiate the charge because it is without foundation. To know how simple are the provisions of the Draft Constitution in respect of amending the Constitution one has only to study the provisions for amendment contained in the American and Australian Constitutions. Compared to them those contained in the Draft Constitution will be found to be the simplest. The Draft Constitution has eliminated the elaborate and difficult procedures such as a decision by a convention or a referendum ... It is only for amendments of specific matters—and they are only few—that the ratification of the State Legislatures is required. All other Articles of the Constitution are left to be amended by Parliament. The only limitation is that it shall be done by a majority of not less than two-thirds of the members of each House present and voting and a majority of the total membership of each House. It is difficult to conceive a simpler method of amending the Constitution.

What is said to be the absurdity of the amending provisions is founded upon a misconception of the position of the Constituent Assembly and of the future Parliament elected under the Constitution. The Constituent Assembly in making a Constitution has no partisan motive. Beyond securing a good and workable Constitution it has no axe to grind. In considering the Articles of the Constitution it has no eye on getting through a particular measure. The future Parliament if it met as Constituent Assembly, its members will be acting as partisans seeking to carry amendments to the Constitution to facilitate the passing of party measures which they have failed to get through Parliament by reason of some Article of the Constitution which has acted as an obstacle in their way. Parliament will have an axe to grind while the Constituent Assembly has none. That is the difference between the Constituent Assembly and the future Parliament. That explains why the Constituent Assembly though elected on limited franchise can be trusted to pass the Constitution by simple majority and why the Parliament though elected on adult suffrage cannot be trusted with the same power to amend it."

— B.R. Ambedkar, speaking in the Constituent Assembly on 4 November 1948

PROCEDURE

The Constitution of India provides for a distinctive amending process when compared to the Constitutions of other nations. It can be described as partly flexible and partly rigid. The

Constitution provides for a variety in the amending process. This feature has been commended by Australian academic Sir Kenneth Wheare who felt that uniformity in the amending process imposed "quite unnecessary restrictions" upon the amendment of parts of a Constitution. An amendment of the Constitution can be initiated only by the introduction of a Bill in either House of Parliament. The Bill must then be passed in each House by a majority of the total membership of that House and by a majority of not less than two-thirds of the members of that House present and voting. There is no provision for a joint sitting in case of disagreement between the two Houses. The Bill, passed by the required majority, is then presented to the President who shall give his assent to the Bill. If the amendment seeks to make any change in any of the provisions mentioned in the proviso to article 368, it must be ratified by the Legislatures of not less than one-half of the States. Although, there is no prescribed time limit for ratification, it must be completed before the amending Bill is presented to the President for his assent.

Every constitutional amendment is formulated as a statute. The first amendment is called the "Constitution (First Amendment) Act", the second, the "Constitution (Second Amendment) Act", and so forth. Each usually has the long title "An Act further to amend the Constitution of India".

TYPES OF AMENDMENTS

The Constitution provides for three categories of amendments. The first category of amendments are those contemplated in articles 4 and 169, para 7(2) of Schedule V and para 21(2) of Schedule VI. These amendments can be effected by Parliament by a simple majority such as that required for the passing of any ordinary law. The amendments under this category are specifically excluded from the purview of article 368 which is the specific provision in the Constitution dealing with the power and the procedure for the amendment of the Constitution. Article 4 provides that laws made by Parliament under article 2 (relating to admission or establishment of new States) and article 3 (relating to formation of new States and alteration of areas, boundaries or names of existing States) effecting amendments in the First Schedule or the Fourth Schedule and supplemental, incidental and consequential matters, shall not be deemed to be amendments of the Constitution for the purposes of article 368. For example, the *States Reorganisation Act, 1956*, which brought about reorganisation of the States in India, was passed by Parliament as an ordinary piece of legislation. In *Mangal Singh v. Union of India* (A.I.R. 1967 S.C. 944), the Supreme Court held that power to reduce the total number of members of Legislative Assembly below the minimum prescribed under article 170 (1) is implicit in the authority to make laws under article 4. Article 169 empowers Parliament to provide by law for the abolition or creation of the Legislative Councils in States and specifies that though such law shall contain such provisions for the amendment of the Constitution as may be necessary, it shall not be deemed to be an amendment of the Constitution for the purposes of article 368. *The Legislative Councils Act, 1957,* which provided for the creation of a Legislative Council in Andhra Pradesh and for increasing the strength of the Legislative Councils in certain other States, is an example of a law passed by Parliament in exercise of its powers under article 169. The Fifth Schedule contains provisions as to the administration and control of the Schedule Areas and Scheduled Tribes. Para 7 of the Schedule vests Parliament with plenary powers to enact laws amending the Schedule and lays down that no such law shall be deemed to be an amendment of the Constitution for the purposes of article 368. Under Para 21 of the Sixth Schedule, Parliament has full power to enact laws amending the Sixth Schedule which contains provisions for the administration of Tribal Areas in the States of Assam, Meghalaya, Tripura and Mizoram. No such law, will be deemed to be an amendment of the Constitution for the purposes of article 368.

The second category includes amendments that can be effected by Parliament by a prescribed 'special majority'; and the third category of amendments includes those that require, in addition to such "special majority", ratification by at least one half of the State Legislatures. The last two categories are governed by article 368.

Ambedkar speaking in the Constituent Assembly on 17 September 1949, pointed out that there were "innumerable articles in the Constitution" which left matters subject to laws made by Parliament. Under article 11, Parliament may make any provision relating to citizenship notwithstanding anything in article 5 to 10. Thus, by passing ordinary laws, Parliament may, in effect, provide, modify or annul the operation of certain provisions of the Constitution without actually amending them within the meaning of article 368. Since such laws do not in fact make any change whatsoever in the letter of the Constitution, they cannot be regarded as amendments of the Constitution nor categorised as such. Other examples include Part XXI of the Constitution— "Temporary, Transitional and Special Provisions" whereby "Notwithstanding anything in this Constitution" power is given to Parliament to make laws with respect to certain matters included in the State List (article 369); article 370 (1) (d) which empowers the President to modify, by order, provisions of the Constitution in their application to the State of Jammu and Kashmir; provisos to articles 83 (2) and 172 (1) empower Parliament to extend the lives of the House of the People and the Legislative Assembly of every State beyond a period of five years during the operation of a Proclamation of Emergency; and articles 83(1) and 172 (2) provide that the Council of States/Legislative Council of a State shall not be subject to dissolution but as nearly as possible one-third of the members thereof shall retire as soon as may be on the expiration of every second year in accordance with the provisions made in that behalf by Parliament by law.

AMENDMENTS UNDER ARTICLE 368

Article 368 of the Constitution of India grants constituent power to make formal amendments and empowers Parliament to amend the Constitution by way of addition, variation or repeal of any provision according to the procedure laid down therein, which is different from the procedure for ordinary legislation. Article 368 has been amended by the 24th and 42nd Amendments in 1971 and 1976 respectively. The following is the full text of Article 368 of the Constitution, which governs constitutional amendments. Clause 3 was inserted by the 24th Amendment in 1971, which also added a new clause (4) in article 13 which reads, "Nothing in this article shall apply to any amendment of this Constitution made under article 368." The provisions in *italics* were inserted by the 42nd Amendment, but were later declared unconstitutional by the Supreme Court in *Minerva Mills v. Union of India* in 1980.

---

368. POWER OF PARLIAMENT TO AMEND THE CONSTITUTION AND PROCEDURE THEREFORE:

(1) Notwithstanding anything in this Constitution, Parliament may in exercise of its constituent power amend by way of addition, variation or repeal any provision of this Constitution in accordance with the procedure laid down in this article.

(2) An amendment of this Constitution may be initiated only by the introduction of a Bill for the purpose in either House of Parliament, and when the Bill is passed in each House by a majority of the total membership of that House and by a majority of not less than two-thirds of the members of that House present and voting, it shall be presented to the President who shall give his assent to the Bill and thereupon the Constitution shall stand amended in accordance with the terms of the Bill:

Provided that if such amendment seeks to make any change in –

(a) article 54, article 55, article 73, article 162 or article 241, or

(b) Chapter IV of Part V, Chapter V of Part VI, or Chapter I of Part XI, or

(c) any of the Lists in the Seventh Schedule, or

(d) the representation of States in Parliament, or

(e) the provisions of this article,

the amendment shall also require to be ratified by the Legislatures of not less than one-half of the States by resolutions to that effect passed by those Legislatures before the Bill making provision for such amendment is presented to the President for assent.

(3) Nothing in article 13 shall apply to any amendment made under this article.

(4) No amendment of this Constitution (including the provisions of Part III) made or purporting to have been made under this article whether before or after the commencement of section 55 of the Constitution (Fortysecond Amendment) Act, 1976 shall be called in question in any court on any ground.

(5) For the removal of doubts, it is hereby declared that there shall be no limitation whatever on the constituent power of Parliament to amend by way of addition, variation or repeal the provisions of this Constitution under this article.

As per the procedure laid out by article 368 for amendment of the Constitution, an amendment can be initiated only by the introduction of a Bill in either House of Parliament. The Bill must then be passed in each House by a majority of the total membership of that House and by a majority of not less than two-thirds of the members of that House present and voting. There is no provision for a joint sitting in case of disagreement between the two Houses. Total membership in this context has been defined to mean the total number of members comprising the House irrespective of any vacancies or absentees on any account vide Explanation to Rule 159 of the Rules of Procedure and Conduct of Business in Lok Sabha. "Abstentions" in any voting are not taken into consideration in declaring the result of any question. A member who votes "abstention" either through the electronic vote recorder or on a voting slip or in any manner, does so only to indicate his presence in the House and his intention to abstain from voting; he does not record his vote within the meaning of the words "present and voting". The expression, "present and voting" refers to those who vote for "ayes" and for "noes".

The Bill, passed by the required majority, is then presented to the President who shall give his assent to the Bill. If the amendment seeks to make any change in any of the provisions mentioned in the proviso to article 368, it must be ratified by the Legislatures of not less than one-half of the States. These provisions relate to certain matters concerning the federal structure or of common interest to both the Union and the States viz., the election of the President (articles 54 and 55); the extent of the executive power of the Union and the States (articles 73 and 162); the High Courts for Union territories (article 241); The Union Judiciary and the High Courts in the States (Chapter IV of Part V and Chapter V of Part VI); the distribution of legislative powers between the Union and the States (Chapter I of Part XI and Seventh Schedule); the representation of States in Parliament; and the provision for amendment of the Constitution laid down in article 368. Ratification is done by a resolution passed by the State Legislatures. There is no specific time limit for the ratification of an amending Bill by the State Legislatures. However, the resolutions ratifying the proposed amendment must be passed before the amending Bill is presented to the President for his assent.

RULES OF PROCEDURE IN PARLIAMENT

Article 368 does not specify the legislative procedure to be followed at various stages of enacting an amendment. There are gaps in the procedure as to how and after what notice a Bill is to be introduced, how it is to be passed by each House and how the President's assent is to be obtained. This point was decided by the Supreme Court in *Shankari Prasad Singh Deo v. Union of India* (AIR 1951 SC 458). Delivering the judgment, Patanjali Sastri J. observed, "Having provided for the constitution of a Parliament and prescribed a certain procedure for the conduct of its ordinary legislative business to be supplemented by rules made by each House (article 118), the makers of the Constitution must be taken to have intended Parliament to follow that procedure, so far as it may be applicable consistently with the express provisions of article 368, when they entrusted to it power of amending the Constitution." Hence, barring the requirements of special majority, ratification by the State Legislatures in certain cases, and the mandatory assent by the President, a Bill for amending the Constitution is dealt with the Parliament following the same legislative process as applicable to an ordinary piece of legislation. The Rules of the House in the Rajya Sabha do not contain special provisions with regard to Bills for the amendment of the Constitution and the Rules relating to ordinary Bills apply, subject to the requirements of article 368.

The Rules of Procedure and Conduct of Business make certain specific provisions regarding amendment bills in the Lok Sabha. They relate to the voting procedure in the House at various stages of such Bills, in the light of the requirements of article 368; and the procedure before introduction in the case of such Bills, if sponsored by Private Members. Although the "special majority", required by article 368 is prima facie applicable only to the voting at the final stage, the Lok Sabha Rules prescribe adherence to this constitutional requirement at all the effective stages of the Bill, i.e., for adoption of the motion that the Bill be taken into consideration; that the Bill as reported by the Select/Joint Committee be taken into consideration, in case a Bill has been referred to a Committee; for adoption of each clause or schedule or clause or schedule as amended, of a Bill; or that the Bill or the Bill as amended, as the case may be, be passed.

This provision was arrived at after consultation with the Attorney-General and detailed discussions in the Rules Committee. It has been described as "evidently *ex abundanti cautela*", a Latin phrase, which in law, describes someone taking precautions against a very remote contingency. By strictly adhering to article 368, the provision is intended to ensure the validity of the procedure adopted, but also guard against the possibility of violation of the spirit and scheme of that article 29 by the consideration of a Bill seeking to amend the Constitution including its consideration clause by clause being concluded in the House with only the bare quorum present. Voting at all the above stages is by division. However, the Speaker may, with the concurrence of the House, put any group of clauses or schedules together to the vote of the House, provided that the Speaker will permit any of the clauses or schedules be put separately, if any member requests that. The Short Title, Enacting Formula and the Long Title are adopted by a simple majority. The adoption of amendments to clauses or schedules of the Bill, requires a majority of members present and voting in the same manner as in the case of any other Bill.[7]

PRIVATE MEMBERS' BILLS

A Bill for amendment of the Constitution by a Private Member is governed by the rules applicable to Private Members' Bills in general. The period of one month's notice applies to such a Bill also. In addition, in Lok Sabha, such a Bill has to be examined and recommended by the Committee on Private Members' Bills before it is included in the List of Business. The Committee has laid down the following principles as guiding criteria in making their recommendations in regard to these Bills:

"(i) The Constitution should be considered as a sacred document — a document which should not be lightly interfered with and it should be amended only when it is found absolutely necessary to do so. Such amendments may generally be brought forward when it is found that the interpretation of the various articles and provisions of the Constitution has not been in accordance with the intention behind such provisions and cases of lacunae or glaring inconsistencies have come to light. Such amendments should, however, normally be brought by the Government after considering the matter in all its aspects and consulting experts, and taking such other advice as they may deem fit.

(ii) Some time should elapse before a proper assessment of the working of the Constitution and its general effect is made so that any amendments that may be necessary are suggested as a result of sufficient experience.

(iii) Generally speaking, notice of Bills from Private Members should be examined in the background of the proposal or measures which the Government may be considering at the time so that consolidated proposals are brought forward before the House by the Government after collecting sufficient material and taking expert advice.

(iv) Whenever a Private Member's Bill raises issues of far-reaching importance and public interest, the Bill might be allowed to be introduced so that public opinion is ascertained and gauged to enable the House to consider the matter further. In determining whether a matter is of sufficient public importance, it should be examined whether the particular provisions in the

Constitution are adequate to satisfy the current ideas and public demand at the time. In other words, the Constitution should be adapted to the current needs and demands of the progressive society and any rigidity which may impede progress should be avoided."

ROLE OF STATE LEGISLATURES

The role of the States in constitutional amendment is limited. State Legislatures cannot initiate any Bill or proposal for amendment of the Constitution. They are associated in the process of the amendment only through the ratification procedure laid down in article 368, in case the amendment seeks to make any change in the any of the provisions mentioned in the proviso to article 368. The only other provision for constitutional changes by State legislatures is to initiate the process for creating or abolishing Legislative Councils in their respective Legislatures, and to give their views on a proposed Parliamentary Bill seeking to affect the area, boundaries or name of any State or States which has been referred to them under the proviso to article 3. However, this referral does not restrict Parliament's power to make any further amendments of the Bill.[1]

Article 169 (1) reads, "Notwithstanding anything in article 168, Parliament may by law provide for the abolition of the Legislative Council of a State having such a Council or for the creation of such a Council in a State having no such Council, if the Legislative Assembly of the State passes a resolution to that effect by a majority of the total membership of the Assembly and by a majority of not less than two-thirds of the members of the Assembly present and voting." The proviso of article 3 provides that no Bill for the purpose shall be introduced in either House of Parliament except on the recommendation of the President and unless, where the proposal contained in the Bill affects the area, boundaries or name of any of the States, the Bill has been referred by the President to the Legislature of the State for expressing its views thereon within such period as may be specified in the reference or within such further period as the President may allow and the period so specified or allowed has expired.

ROLE OF UNION TERRITORIES

Union territories have no say in constitutional amendments, including the ratification process which is only open to States. Delhi and Puducherry are two union territories that are entitled, by special constitutional amendments, to have an elected Legislative Assembly and a Cabinet of ministers, thereby enjoying partial statehood powers. However, neither of these territories can participate in the ratification process because they are not States, as defined by the Constitution.

LIMITATIONS

The Constitution can be amended only by Parliament; and only in the manner provided. In *Abdul Rahiman Jamaluddin v. Vithal Arjun (*AIR 1958 Bombay, 94, (1957)), the Bombay High Court held that any attempt to amend the Constitution by a Legislature other than Parliament, and in a manner different from that provided for, will be void and inoperative. Although Parliament must preserve the basic framework of the Constitution, there is no other limitation placed upon the amending power, meaning that there is no provision of the Constitution that cannot be amended.

The Supreme Court first struck down a constitutional amendment in 1967, ruling in the case of *I.C. Golak Nath* and *Ors. vs. State of Punjab and Anr.* An amendment was struck down on the basis that it violated Article 13: "The State shall not make any law which takes away or abridges the rights conferred by [the charter of Fundamental Rights]". The term "law" in this article was interpreted as including a constitutional amendment. Parliament responded by enacting the twenty-fourth Amendment of the Constitution of India which declared that "nothing in Article 13 shall apply to any amendment of this Constitution".

The current limitation on amendments comes from *Kesavananda Bharati v. The State of Kerala,*where the Supreme Court ruled that amendments of the constitution must respect the "basic structure" of the constitution, and certain fundamental features of the constitution cannot be altered by amendment. Parliament attempted to remove this limitation by enacting the Forty-second Amendment, which declared, among other provisions, that "there shall be no limitation whatever on the constituent power of Parliament to amend ...this Constitution". However, this change was itself later declared invalid by the Supreme Court in *Minerva Mills v. Union of India.*

The issue of whether an entire constitutional amendment is void for want of ratification or only an amended provision required to be ratified under proviso to clause (2) of article 368 was debated before the Supreme Court in *Kihota Hollohon v. Zachilhu* (AIR 1993 SC 412), in which the constitutional validity of the Tenth Schedule of the Constitution inserted by the 52nd Amendment in 1985 was challenged. The decisions of the Speakers/Chairmen on disqualification, which had been challenged in different High Courts through different petitions, were heard by a five-member Constitution Bench of the Supreme Court. The case, now popularly known as Anti-Defection case, was decided in 1992. The Constitution Bench in its majority judgement upheld the validity of the Tenth Schedule, but declared Paragraph 7 of the Schedule invalid because it was not ratified by the required number of the Legislatures of the States as it brought about in terms and effect, a change in articles 136, 226 and 227 of the Constitution. While doing so, the majority treated Paragraph 7 as a severable part from the rest of the Schedule. However, in the dissenting opinion, the minority of the Judges held that the entire Amendment is invalid for want of ratification.

PARTS FREQUENTLY AMENDED

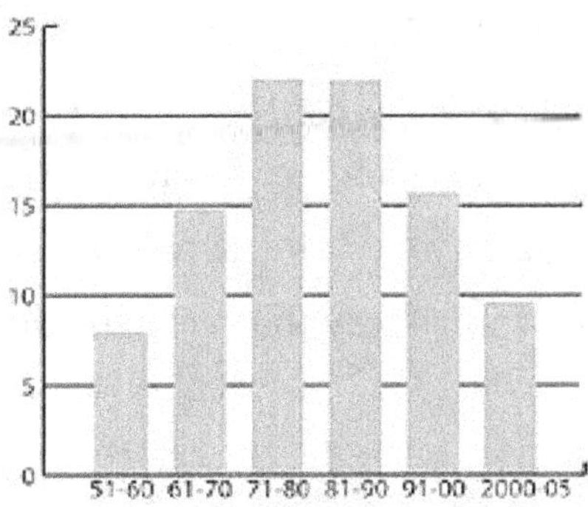

Number of constitutional amendments in India per decade.[9]

Despite the super majority requirement in the Constitution, it is one of the most frequently amended governing documents in the world; amendments have averaged about two a year. This is partly because the Constitution is so specific in spelling out government powers that amendments are often required to deal with matters that could be addressed by ordinary statutes in other democracies. As a result, it is the longest constitution of any sovereign nation in the world. It currently consists of over 117,000 words (450 articles plus 115 amendments). Another reason is that the Parliament of India is elected by means of single seat districts, under the plurality voting system, used in the United Kingdom and the United States. This means that, it is possible for a party to win two thirds of the seats in Parliament without securing two thirds of the vote. For example, in the first two Lok Sabha elections held under the Constitution, the Indian National Congress party won less than one half of the national vote but roughly two thirds of seats in the chamber.

FUNDAMENTAL RIGHTS

The most important and frequent reason for amendments to the Constitution is the curtailment of the Fundamental Rights charter. This is achieved by inserting laws contrary to the fundamental rights provisions into Schedule 9 of the Constitution. Schedule 9 protects such laws from judicial review. The typical areas of restriction include laws relating to property rights, and affirmative action in favour of minority groups such as the "scheduled castes", "scheduled tribes", and other "backward classes" and also lower classes people.

In a landmark ruling in January 2007, a nine judge constitutional bench of the Supreme Court of India confirmed that all laws (including those in Schedule 9) would be open to judicial review if they violate the basic structure of the constitution. Chief Justice Yogesh Kumar Sabharwal noted, "If laws put in the Ninth Schedule abridge or abrogate fundamental rights resulting in violation of the basic structure of the constitution, such laws need to be invalidated".

TERRITORIAL CHANGES

Constitutional amendments have been made to facilitate changes in the territorial extent of the Republic of India due to the incorporation of the former French colony of Pondicherry, the former Portuguese colony of Goa, and a minor exchange of territory with Pakistan. Amendments are also necessary with regard to littoral rights over the exclusive economic zone of 200 mi and the formation of new states and union territories by the reorganization of existing states.

TRANSITIONAL PROVISIONS

The constitution includes transitional provisions intended to remain in force only for a limited period. These need to be renewed periodically. For example, for continuing reservation in parliamentary seats for scheduled castes and scheduled tribes an constitutional amendment is enacted once in every ten years.

DEMOCRATIC REFORM

Amendments have been made with the intent of reform the system of government and incorporating new "checks and balances" in the Constitution. These have included the following:

- Creation of the National Commission for Scheduled Castes.
- Creation of the National Commission for Scheduled Tribes.
- Creation of mechanisms for *Panchayati Raj* (local self governance).
- Disqualification of members from changing party allegiance.
- Restrictions on the size of the cabinet.
- Restrictions on imposition of an internal emergency.

Unit V

STATE POLITICS

5.1 STATE POLITICS WITH REFERENCE TO DELHI

GOVERNORS

The **governors** and **lieutenant-governors** of the states and union territories of India have similar powers and functions at the state level as that of the President of India at Union level. Governors exist in the states while lieutenant-governors exist in union territories and in the National Capital Territory of Delhi. The governor acts as the nominal head whereas the real power lies in the hand of the chief ministers of the states and the chief minister's Council of Ministers.

In India, a lieutenant governor is in charge of a Union Territory. However the rank is present only in the union territories of Andaman and Nicobar Islands, Delhi and Pondicherry (the other territories have an administrator appointed, who is an IAS officer). Lieutenant-governors hold the same rank as a governor of a state in the list of precedence.

The governors and lieutenant-governors are appointed by the president for a term of 5 years.

QUALIFICATIONS

Article 157 and Article 158 of the Constitution of India specify eligibility requirements for the post of governor. They are as follows:

A governor must:

- be a citizen of India;
- be at least thirty-five (35)years old;
- not be a member of the either house of the parliament or house of the state legislature.
- not hold any other office of profit.

POWERS AND FUNCTIONS

The governor enjoys many different types of powers:

- **Executive powers** related to administration, appointments and removals,
- **Legislative powers** related to lawmaking and the state legislature, that is Vidhan Sabha or Vidhan Parishad,
- **Discretionary Powers** to be carried out according to the discretion of the governor.

EXECUTIVE POWERS

The Constitution vests in the governor all the executive powers of the state government. The governor appoints the chief minister, who enjoys the support of the majority in the Vidhan Sabha. The governor also appoints the other members of the Council of Ministers and distributes portfolios to them on the advice of the chief minister.

The Council of Ministers remains in power during the 'pleasure' of the governor, but in the real sense it means the pleasure of the Vidhan Sabha. As long as the majority in the Vidhan Sabha supports the government, the Council of Ministers cannot be dismissed.

The governor appoints the chief minister of a state. He/she also appoints the Advocate General and the chairman and members of the State Public Service Commission. The president consults the governor in the appointment of judges of the High Courts and the governor appoints the judges of the District Courts. All administrations are carried on his name.

LEGISLATIVE POWERS

The governor summons the sessions of both houses of the state legislature and prorogues them. The governor can even dissolve the Vidhan Sabha. These powers are formal and the governor while using these powers must act according to the advice of the Council of Ministers headed by the chief minister.

The governor inaugurates the state legislature by addressing it after the assembly elections and also at the beginning of the first session every year. The governor's address on these occasions generally outlines new policies of the state government. A bill that the state legislature has passed can become a law only after the governor gives assent. The governor can return a bill to the state legislature, if it is not a money bill, for reconsideration. However, if the state legislature sends it back to the governor for the second time, the governor must assent to it. The governor has the power to reserve certain bills for the president.

When the state legislature is not in session and the governor considers it necessary to have a law, then the governor can promulgate ordinances. These ordinances are submitted to the state legislature at its next session. They remain valid for no more than six weeks from the date the state legislature is reconvened unless approved by it earlier.

FINANCIAL POWERS

Money bills can be introduced in the State Legislative Assembly only on the prior recommendation of the governor. He also causes to be laid before the State Legislature the annual financial statement which is the State Budget. Further no demand for grant shall be made except on his recommendation. He can also make advances out of the Contingency Fund of the State to meet any unforeseen expenditure. Moreover, he constitutes the State Finance Commission. In vidhan sabha he nominates 1 person. The annual budget of the country presented in the parliament in the name of the president.

DISCRETIONARY POWERS

The governor can use these powers: a) If no party gets an absolute majority, the governor can use his discretion in the selection of the chief minister; b) During an emergency he can override the advice of the council of ministers. At such times, he acts as an agent of the president and becomes the real ruler of the state; c) He uses his direction in submitting a report to the president regarding the affairs of the state; and d) He can withhold his assent to a bill and send it to the president for his approval. e) He can pardon the punishment awarded to any criminal under the state rules.

EMOLUMENTS

Governor's pay

Date established Salary (per month)

1 January 2006 ₹1.1 lakh (US$1,800)

Various Emoluments, Allowances and Privileges available to a governor are determined by the Governors (Emoluments, Allowances and Privileges) Act, 1982.

In addition to the monthly salary, the governor is entitled to rent free official residence, free household facilities and conveyance. The governor and his family are provided with free medical attendance, accommodation and treatment for life.

REMOVAL

The term of governor's office is normally 5 years but it can be terminated earlier by:

1. Dismissal by the president on the advice of the prime minister of the country, at whose pleasure the governor holds office.

2. Resignation by the governor.

There is no provision of impeachment, as it happens for the president.

CHIEF MINISTER

The **Chief Minister of Delhi** is the chief of government, head of the Council of Ministers and the leader of the majority party in the Delhi assembly. The Chief Minister leads the executive branch of the Government of Delhi. The former Chief Minister of Delhi was Arvind Kejriwal of the Aam Aadmi Party.

The leader of the party with the largest representation of seats in the unicameral Legislative Assembly of Delhi usually takes on the role. Delhi and Pondicherry are the only union territories of India, which have been given partial statehood according to the Seventh Schedule of the Constitution in which Delhi is defined as National Capital Territory of India or NCT-Delhi. Due to this special right of partial statehood, unlike other union territories which are governed by special administrators appointed by the President of India, governments of Delhi and Pondicherry both are headed by their respective chief ministers and Lieutenant Governors, appointed by the president acting as the head of state. A former chief minister, Sheila Dikshit, was India's longest serving woman chief minister. Arvind Kejriwal remained the Chief Minister of Delhi for 49 days and he has resigned from the post on 14-02-2014.

ELECTION

Every five years the Delhi State Election Commission, under the supervision of the Election Commission of India, conducts assembly elections in the National Capital Territory of Delhi by universal adult suffrage, in which Delhi's electorate choose the members of the Vidhan Sabha (or Legislative/State Assembly). An aspirant member is either the nominee of any political party or runs as an independent candidate.

APPOINTMENT OF CABINET AND CHIEF MINISTER

To form a government, any party must have won a majority of assembly seats (at present, at least 36). The Lieutenant Governor then invites the party concerned to form a government within a specified time limit, during which time the majority party has to nominate appointees for the post of chief minister and other members of the cabinet. The selected member of the assembly is appointed as Chief Minister by the Lieutenant Governor, who also administers the oath of office.

ELIGIBILITY

Article 84 of the Constitution sets the principal qualifications one must meet to be eligible to the office of the Chief Minister. A Chief Minister must be:

- a citizen of India,

- a member of the Legislative Assembly of Delhi,
- aged 25 or older.

A person shall not be eligible for election as Chief Minister if he holds any office of profit under the Government of India, the Government of any State, or under any local or other authority subject to the control of any of the said Governments.

ROLE AND POWER OF THE CHIEF MINISTER

On 2 January 1992 after passing the Government of National Capital Territory of Delhi act in parliament, the central government approved more autonomy for Delhi's government, which made it able to make its own law and regulations. Certain categories of bills, however, still require the prior approval of the central government for introduction in the legislative assembly. Some bills passed by the legislative assembly of Delhi are required to be reserved for consideration and assent of the President.

The chief minister is the most senior minister of cabinet in the executive branch of government in a legislative assembly. The chief minister selects and can dismiss other members of the cabinet, allocates posts to members within the Government, is the presiding member and chairman of the cabinet and is responsible for bringing proposals for legislation.

LIST OF CHIEF MINISTERS OF DELHI

Sheila Dikshit was Chief Minister of New Delhi for three consecutive terms and held the post for longest duration.

This is a complete list of the chief ministers of Delhi who assumed office from 1952 until present.

Key:	INC Indian National Congress	BJP Bharatiya Janata Party	AAP Aam Aadmi Party

S No.	Name	Took Office	Left Office	Political Party
1	Chaudhary Brahm Prakash	1952	1955	Indian National Congress
2	G N Singh	1955	1956	Indian National Congress

†	President's Rule	1956	1993	State ceased to exist, became a centrally administered union territory (President's Rule)[citation needed]
3	Madan Lal Khurana	1993	1996	Bharatiya Janata Party
4	Sahib Singh Verma	1996	1998	Bharatiya Janata Party
5	Sushma Swaraj	1998	1998	Bharatiya Janata Party
6	Sheila Dikshit	2 December 1998	28 December 2013	Indian National Congress
7	Arvind Kejriwal	28 December 2013	14 February 2014	AAP Aam Aadmi Party
†	President's Rule			(President's Rule)

5.2 VIDHAN SABHA (DELHI LEGISLATIVE ASSEMBLY)

The **Legislative Assembly of Delhi**, also known as Vidhan Sabha, is a unicameral law making body of the National Capital Territory of Delhi, one of the 7 union territories in India. It is situated at Delhi, the state capital of Delhi, with 70 Members of the Legislative Assembly (MLA).

The seat of assembly is the Old Secretariat building, which is also the seat of the Delhi Government.

HISTORY

Delhi State Assembly was first constituted on 7 March 1952 under the Government of Part C States Act, 1951, it was inaugurated by then Home Minister K. N. Katju. The Assembly has 48 members, and a council of Minister in an advisory role to the Chief Commissioner of Delhi, though it also powers to make laws. The first Council of Ministers leads by Chaudhary Brahm Prakash, who became the first Chief Minister of Delhi.

However, States Reorganization Commission set up in 1953, led to the Constitution amendment through States Reorganization Act, 1956, which came into effect on 1 November 1956. This meant that Delhi was no longer a Part-C State and was made a Union Territory under the direct administration of the President of India. Also the Delhi Legislative Assembly and the Council of Ministers were abolished simultaneously. Subsequently, the Delhi Municipal Corporation Act, 1957 was enacted which led to the formation the Municipal Corporation.

Then in September 1966, with "The Delhi Administration Act, 1966", the assembly was replaced by the Delhi Metropolitan Council with 56 elected and 5 nominated members with the Lt. Governor of Delhi as its head. The Council however had no legislative powers, only an advisory role in the governance of Delhi. This set up functioned till 1990.

This Council was finally replaced by the Delhi Legislative Assembly through the Constitution (Sixty-ninth Amendment) Act, 1991, followed by the Government of National Capital Territory of Delhi Act, 1991 the Sixty-ninth Amendment to the Constitution of India, which declared the Union Territory of Delhi to be formally known as National Capital Territory of Delhi also supplements the constitutional provisions relating to the Legislative Assembly and the Council of Ministers and related matters. The Legislative Assembly is selected for period of five years, and presently it is fifth assembly, which was selected through the Delhi state assembly elections, 2013.

ASSEMBLY BUILDING

Originally built 1912, designed by E. Montague Thomas to hold the Imperial Legislative Council and subsequently the Central Legislative Assembly (after 1919), till the newly constructed Parliament House of India in New Delhi (Sansad Bhawan)was inaugurated on 18 January 1927.

The building also housed in the Secretariat of the Government of India, and was built after the capital of India shifted to Delhi from Calcutta, the temporary secretariat building was constructed in a few months' time in 1912, it functioned as the Secretariat for another decade, before the offices shifted to the present Secretariat Building on Raisina Hill.

LIST OF ASSEMBLIES

Election Year	Assembly	Government formed by	Chief Minister
1993	First Assembly	Bharatiya Janata Party	Madan Lal Khurana Sahib Singh Verma Sushma Swaraj
1998	Second Assembly	Indian National Congress	Sheila Dikshit
2003	Third Assembly	Indian National Congress	Sheila Dikshit
2008	Fourth Assembly	Indian National Congress	Sheila Dikshit
2013	Fifth Assembly	Aam Aadmi Party President's rule	Arvind Kejriwal President's rule

POWERS OF LEGISLATIVE ASSEMBLY

Under the current(February 2014) constitutional framework, the National Capital Territory of Delhi (NCTD) is not a full fledged State as is evident from Schedule I of the Constitution, where it is listed as a Union Territory (UT). Despite that, the NCTD occupies a unique position among the UTs in the Constitution. Article 246(4) gives the power to Parliament to make laws on all subjects for

UTs, including those listed in the State List of Schedule VII. This widely stated power for Parliament operates without any further qualifications for all UTs except Pondicherry and the NCTD. As far as the NCTD is concerned, Article 239-AA requires a legislative assembly to be formed and gives it the power to legislate on all subjects contained in the State List of Schedule VII except some fields that have no real relevance in this instance. Article 239-AA(3)(b) makes it amply clear that despite giving this power to the Delhi State Assembly, it does not derogate from the power of Parliament to make a law on any subject. In case of conflict between the laws of Parliament and those of the Delhi Legislative Assembly, the law passed by the Delhi Legislative Assembly would prevail if the President gave assent to such a law.

5.3 Delhi High Court

The **High Court of Delhi** (Hindi: दिल्ली उच्च न्यायालय, IAST: *dillī ucca nyāyālaya*) was established on 31 October 1966. The High Court of Delhi was established with four judges. They were Chief Justice K. S. Hegde, Justice I. D. Dua, Justice H. R. Khanna and Justice S. K. Kapur.

History

On 21 March 1919, the High Court of Judicature at Lahore was established with jurisdiction over the provinces of Punjab and Delhi. This jurisdiction lasted till 1947 when India was partitioned.

The High Courts (Punjab) Order, 1947 established a new High Court for the province of East Punjab with effect from 15 August 1947. The India (Adaptation of Existing Indian Laws) Order, 1947 provided that any reference in an existing Indian law to the High Court of Judicature at Lahore be replaced by a reference to the High Court of East Punjab.

The High Court of East Punjab started functioning from Shimla in a building called "Peterhoff". This building burnt down in January, 1981.

When the Secretariat of the Punjab Government shifted to Chandigarh in 1954-55, The High Court also shifted to Chandigarh. The High Court of Punjab, as it later came to be called, exercised jurisdiction over Delhi through a Circuit Bench which dealt with the cases pertaining to the Union Territory of Delhi and the Delhi Administration.

In view of the importance of Delhi, its population and other considerations, the Indian Parliament, by enacting the Delhi High Court Act, 1966, established the High Court of Delhi effective from 31 October 1966.

By virtue of Section 3(1) of the Delhi High Court Act, the Central Government was empowered to appoint a date by a notification in the official gazette, establishing a High Court for the Union Territory of Delhi. The appointed date was 31st October, 1966.

The High Court of Delhi initially exercised jurisdiction not only over the Union Territory of Delhi, but also Himachal Pradesh. The High Court of Delhi had a Himachal Pradesh Bench at Shimla in a building called Ravenswood. The High Court of Delhi continued to exercise jurisdiction over Himachal Pradesh until the State of Himachal Pradesh Act, 1970 came into force on 25 January 1971.

BACKLOG

As per the report released on 2006-08, Delhi High court has a long list of pending cases.The backlog is such that it would take 466 years to resolve them.In a bid to restore public trust and confidence, Delhi court spent 5 minutes per case and disposed of 94,000 cases in 2008-10.

CHIEF JUSTICES

- Justice K. S. Hegde (31 October 1966 – 17 July 1967)
- Justice M K M Ismail (25th May 1967 - 13th November 1967)[3]
- Justice I. D. Dua (17 July 1967 – 1 August 1969)
- Justice H. R. Khanna (1 August 1969 – 22 September 1971)
- Justice Hardayal Hardy (22 September 1971 – 15 May 1972)
- Justice Narain Andley (15 May 1972 – 4 June 1974)
- Justice T. V. R. Tatachari (4 June 1974 – 16 October 1978)
- Justice V. S. Deshpande (16 October 1978 – 27 March 1980)
- Justice Prakash Narain (8 January 1981 – 6 August 1985)
- Justice Rajinder Sachar (6 August 1985 – 22 December 1985)
- Justice D. K. Kapur (22 December 1985 – 20 August 1986)
- Justice T.P.S. Chawla (20 August 1986 – 16 August 1987)
- Justice R. N. Aggarwal (16 August 1987 – 21 August 1987)
- Justice Yogeshwar Dayal (21 August 1987 – 18 March 1988)
- Justice Rabindranath Pyne (18 March 1988 – 28 September 1990)
- Justice Milap Chand Jain (28 November 1990 – 21 July 1991)
- Justice G. C. Mittal (5 August 1991 – 4 March 1994)
- Justice M. Jagannadha Rao (12 April 1994 – 21 March 1997)
- Justice Mahinder Narain (21 March 1997 – 30 December 1999)
- Justice Sam Nariman Variava (31 December 1999 – 15 March 2000)
- Justice Arijit Pasayat (10 May 2000 – 19 October 2001)
- Justice S. B. Sinha (26 November 2001 – 1 October 2002)
- Justice B. C. Patel (5 March 2003 – 7 August 2005)

- Justice Markandey Katju (12 October 2005 – 10 April 2006)
- Justice Mukundakam Sharma (4 December 2006 – 9 April 2008)
- Justice Ajit Prakash Shah (11 May 2008 – 12 February 2010)
- Justice Dipak Misra (24 May 2010 – 10 October 2011)
- Justice D Murugesan (26 September 2012 – 10 June 2013)
- Justice Badar Durrez Ahmed (Acting) (10 June 2013 - 1 September 2013)
- Justice N. V. Ramana (2 September 2013 - 16 February 2014)
- Justice Badar Durrez Ahmed (Acting) (17 February 2014)

SUBORDINATE COURTS OF DELHI HIGH COURT

Today, the National Capital Territory of Delhi has six District Courts that function under the Delhi High Court:

- Tis Hazari Courts Complex, established 1958
- Patiala House Courts Complex, established 1977
- Karkardooma Courts Complex, established 1993
- Rohini Courts Complex, established 2005
- Dwarka Courts Complex, established 2008
- Saket Courts Complex, established 2010

The above are six physical locations of the district courts, whereas actually there are nine district courts headed by individual District Judges. The Tis Hazari complex hosts three district courts, the Karkarddoma complex hosts two district courts and the remaining complexes host one district court each.

5.4 SOCIAL AND ECONOMIC BASES OF POLITICS IN DELHI ACCORDING TO CASTE AND CLASS

The government officially recognises historically discriminated communities of India such as the Untouchables under the designation of Scheduled Castes, and certain economically backward Shudra castes as Other Backward Castes. The Scheduled Castes are sometimes referred to as Dalit in contemporary literature. In 2001, the proportion of Dalit population was 16.2 percent of total population.

Since 1950, India has enacted and implemented many laws and social initiatives to protect and improve the socio-economic conditions of its Dalit population. Of the highest paying, senior most jobs in government agencies and government controlled enterprises, over 10 percent were held by members of the Dalit community, a tenfold increase in 40 years but yet to fill up the 15 percent reserved quota for them. In 1997, India elected K.R. Narayanan, a Dalit, as the nation's President.

Indians who were born in historically discriminated minority castes have been elected to its highest judicial and political offices. While the quality of life of Dalit population in India, in terms of metrics such as poverty, literacy rate, access to health care, life expectancy, education attainability, access to drinking water, housing, etc. have seen faster growth amongst the Dalit population between 1986 and 2006, for some metrics, it remains lower than overall non-Dalit population, and for some it is better than poor non-Dalit population.

A 2004 report, compiled by a society of Dalits and people against caste-based discrimination, summarised the developments over previous 60 years, and status of the caste system in modern India, as follows: Article 15 of Indian Constitution, as enacted in 1950, prohibits any discrimination based on caste. Article 17 of Indian Constitution declared any practice of untouchability as illegal. In 1955, India enacted the Untouchability (Offences) Act (renamed in 1976, as the Protection of Civil Rights Act). It extended the reach of law, from intent to mandatory enforcement. The Scheduled Castes and Scheduled Tribes (Prevention of Atrocities) Act, similar to the Hate Crime Laws in the United States, was passed in India in 1989.

- India created National Commission for Scheduled Castes and Scheduled Tribes to investigate, monitor, advise, and evaluate the socio-economic progress of the Scheduled Castes and Scheduled Tribes.
- India implemented a reservation system for its citizens from Scheduled Castes and Scheduled Tribes; this program has been in use in India for over 50 years. This program is similar to Affirmative Action/Equal Opportunities statutes in the United States.
- In India, where the presence of private free market corporations is limited, government jobs have dominated the percentage of jobs in its economy. A 2000 report estimated that most jobs in India were in companies owned by the government or agencies of the government. The reservation system implemented by India over 50 years, has been partly successful, because of all jobs, nationwide, in 1995, 17.2 percent of the jobs were held by those in the lowest castes. In 1995, about 16.1 percent of India's population were the lowest castes.
- The Indian government classifies government jobs in four groups. The Group A jobs are senior most, high paying positions in the government, while Group D are junior most, lowest paying positions. In Group D jobs, the percentage of positions held by lowest caste classified people is 30% greater than their demographic percentage. In all jobs classified as Group C positions, the percentage of jobs held by lowest caste people is about the same as their demographic population distribution. In Group A and B jobs, the percentage of

positions held by lowest caste classified people is 30% lower than their demographic percentage.

- The presence of lowest caste people in highest paying, senior most position jobs in India has increased by ten-fold, from 1.18 percent of all jobs in 1959 to 10.12 percent of all jobs in 1995.

- In 2007, India elected K. G. Balakrishnan, a Dalit, to the office of Chief Justice.

- In 2007, Uttar Pradesh, the most populous state of India, elected Mayawati as the Chief Minister, the highest elected office of the state. BBC claims, "Mayawati Kumari is an icon for millions of India's Dalits, or untouchables as they used to be known."

- In 2009, the Indian parliament unanimously elected a Dalit, Meira Kumar, as the first female speaker.

In addition to taking affirmative action for people of schedule castes and scheduled tribes, India has expanded its effort to include people from poor, backward castes in its economic and social mainstream. In 1990, the Government of India introduced reservation of 27% for Backward Classes on the basis of the Mandal Commission's recommendations. This became the law with the issuance of Gazette notice 36012/31/90-Estt. (SCT) dated 13 August 1990. Since then, India has reserved 27 percent of job opportunities in government-owned enterprises and agencies for Socially and Educationally Backward Classes (SEBCs). The 27 percent reservation is in addition to 22.5 percent set aside for India's lowest castes for last 50 years.

In a 2008 study, Desai et al. focussed on education attainments of children and young adults aged 6–29, from lowest caste and tribal populations of India. They completed a national survey of over 100,000 households for each of the four survey years between 1983 and 2000. They found a significant increase in lower caste children in their odds of completing primary school. The number of dalit children who completed either middle-, high- or college-level education increased three times faster than the national average, and the total number were statistically same for both lower and upper castes. The number of dalit girls in India who attended school doubled in the same period, but still few percent less than national average. Other poor caste groups as well as ethnic groups such as Muslims in India have also made improvements over the 16 year period, but their improvement lagged behind that of dalits and adivasis. The net percentage school attainment for Dalits and Muslims were statistically the same in 1999.

A 2007 nationwide survey of India by the World Bank found that over 80 percent of children of historically discriminated castes were attending schools. The fastest increase in school attendance by Dalit community children occurred during the recent periods of India's economic growth. The quality and quantity of schools are now major issues in India.

A study by Darshan Singh presents data on health and other indicators of socio-economic change in India's historically discriminated castes. He claims:

- In 2001, the literacy rates in India's lowest castes were 55 percent, compared to a national average of 63 percent.
- The childhood vaccination levels in India's lowest castes was 40 percent in 2001, compared to a national average of 44 percent.
- Access to drinking water within household or near the household in India's lowest castes was 80 percent in 2001, compared to a national average of 83 percent.
- The poverty level in India's lowest castes dropped from 49 percent to 39 percent between 1995 and 2005, compared to a national average change from 35 to 27 percent.

The table below presents this data for various caste groups in modern India. Both 1998 and 2005 data is included to ascertain the general trend. The Mohanty and Ram report suggests that poverty, not caste, is the bigger differentiator in life expectancy in modern India

5.5 Elections in Delhi

Elections in Delhi, a territory and capital of India are conducted in accordance with the Constitution of India. The Assembly of Delhi creates laws regarding the conduct of local body elections unilaterally while any changes by the state legislature to the conduct of state level elections need to be approved by the Parliament of India. In addition, the state legislature may be dismissed by the Parliament according to Article 356 of the Indian Constitution and President's rule may be imposed.

Lok Sabha elections

Year	Lok Sabha Election	Winning Party/Coalition
1951	First Lok Sabha	Indian National Congress
1957	Second Lok Sabha	Indian National Congress
1962	Third Lok Sabha	Indian National Congress
1967	Fourth Lok Sabha	Bharatiya Jana Sangh
1971	Fifth Lok Sabha	Indian National Congress
1977	Sixth Lok Sabha	Janata alliance (BLD)
1980	Seventh Lok Sabha	Indian National Congress (Indira)

1984	Eighth Lok Sabha	Indian National Congress
1989	Ninth Lok Sabha	Bharatiya Janata Party
1991	Tenth Lok Sabha	Bharatiya Janata Party
1996	Eleventh Lok Sabha	Bharatiya Janata Party
1998	Twelfth Lok Sabha	Bharatiya Janata Party (BJP+)
1999	Thirteenth Lok Sabha	Bharatiya Janata Party (NDA)
2004	Fourteenth Lok Sabha	United Progressive Alliance (INC)
2009	Fifteenth Lok Sabha	United Progressive Alliance (INC)

References

REFERENCES

1. Smith, William Roy, Nationalism and reform in India, New Haven Yale University Press 1938

2. Shah, K. T., Federal Structure (under the Government of India act, 1935), Bombay, Vora, 1937

3. Keith, A. Berriedale, A Constitutional history of India, 1600-1935, 2nd rev. ed. Metheun, 1937

4. Ross, Alan, The Emissary: G. D. Birla, Gandhi and Independence, London, Collins Harvill 1986.

5. Anatole FRANCE, The Red Lily, 1894.

6. Moore, R. J., The Crisis of Indian Unity, Oxford University Press, 1974

7. http://storyofpakistan.com/government-of-india-act-1935 retrieved on dt.24 FEB 2014

8. http://storyofpakistan.com/fourteen-points-of-m-a-jinnah retrieved on dt.24 FEB 2014

9. Cell, John W., Hailey : A Study in British Imperialism, 1872-1969, Cambridge University Press, 1992

10. Gwyer, Sir Maurice and Appadorai, A. (editors), Speeches and Documents on the Indian Constitution, 1921-1947 (2 volumes), OUP 1957**

11. Glendevon, John Hope, The Viceroy at Bay: Lord Linlithgow in India, 1936-1943, Collins 1971

12. GANGULEE, The making of federal India, p. 165.

13. Prof. Dr. Helmut Weber: Who Guards the Constitution?, English version of a paper delivered on 22 October 1999 at the Centre for British Studies, Humboldt University Berlin, Colloquium of the Graduiertenkolleg "Das neue Europa

14. Barnett, H. (2005). Constitutional and Administrative Law (5 ed.). London: Cavendish. p. 9. "Conversely, "A written constitution is one contained within a single document or a [finite] series of documents, with or without amendments", id."

15. Chrimes, S B (1967). English Constitutional History. London: Oxford University Press. p. 42

16. This principle was famously enunciated by the legal scholar Albert Venn Dicey, and can be found, for example, in Justice Megarry's judgment in the 1982 case of Manuel v Attorney General.

17. Turpin, Colin; Tomkins, Adam (2007). British government and the constitution: text and materials. Cambridge: Cambridge University Press. p. 41. ISBN 978-0-521-69029-4. Cite uses deprecated parameters (help)

18. Beatson, Jack (1998). Constitutional reform in the United Kingdom: practice and principles. London: Hart Publishing. p. 45. ISBN 978-1-901362-84-8.

19. Bogdanor, Vernon (1997). The Monarchy and the Constitution. Oxford University Press. p. 131. ISBN 0-19-829334-8.

20. Jeffrey Goldsworthy's study The Sovereignty of Parliament, OUP 1999.

21. http://www.publications.parliament.uk/pa/ld200506/ldjudgmt/jd051013/jack-1.html

22. retrieved on dt. 24FEB2014

23. Craig, Paul; Grainne De Burca , P. P. Craig (2007). EU Law: Text, Cases and Materials (4th ed.). Oxford: Oxford University Press. pp. 344–378. ISBN 978-0-19-927389-8.

24. Steiner, Josephine; Woods, Lorna; Twigg-Flesner, Christian; Jo Steiner, Lorna Woods and Christian Twigg-Flesner (2006). EU Law (9th ed.). Oxford: Oxford University Press. p. 72. ISBN 978-0-19-927959-3.

25. Tomkins, Adam (2003). Public Law. Oxford University Press. p. 120. ISBN 978-0-19-926077-5. "As far as English public law is concerned, even after Factortame Parliament may relatively easily legislate in violation of Community law and moreover may do so in such a way that the domestic courts have no option but to uphold and enforce the legislation."

26. Craig, Paul; Grainne De Burca , P. P. Craig (2007). EU Law: Text, Cases and Materials (4th ed.). Oxford: Oxford University Press. p. 371. ISBN 978-0-19-927389-8. "It is however unclear as yet what the UK courts would do if Parliament sought expressly to derogate from a provision of EU law, while still remaining in the EU." Cite uses deprecated parameters (help)

27. Quoted in Steiner, Josephine; Woods, Lorna; Twigg-Flesner, Christian (2006). EU Law (9th ed.). Oxford: Oxford University Press. p. 79. ISBN 978-0-19-927959-3.

28. European Union Act 2011

29. Smits, Jan (Jan 2002). The Making of European Private Law: Towards a Ius Commune Europaeum as a Mixed Legal System. Intersentia Publishers. p. 113. ISBN 978-90-5095-191-3. "Formerly, of course, Scots law like other Civilian systems did not recognise the strict doctrine of stare decisis, and even today it is probable that the only single decision that the Court of Session could not disregard is a precedent established by the House of Lords in a Scottish appeal."

30. Bradley and Ewing, p.24

31. Maier, Pauline. "Ratification: the people debate the constitution, 1787-1788". 2010. ISBN 978-0-684-86854-7, p. 35.

32. Paul Rodgers (2011). United States Constitutional Law: An Introduction. McFarland. p. 109.

33.   "Amendments to the Constitution of the United States of America". The Constitution of the United States of America: Analysis and Interpretation. U.S. Government Printing Office. 1992. p. 25 n.2.

34.   "The Declining Influence of the United States Constitution". JournalistsResource.org, retrieved April 4, 2012

35.   Law, David S.; Versteeg, Mila (2012). "The Declining Influence of the United States Constitution". New York University Law Review 87 (3).

36.   Armstrong, Virginia Irving (1971). I Have Spoken: American History Through the Voices of the Indians. Pocket Books. p. 14. ISBN 671-78555-9. See also, House Concurrent Resolution 331, October 21, 1988. United States Senate. Retrieved November 23, 2008.. In October 1988, the U.S. Congress passed Concurrent Resolution 331 to recognize the influence of the Iroquois Constitution upon the U.S. Constitution and Bill of Rights.

37.   Greymont, Barbara. The Iroquois in the American Revolution 1972. ISBN 0-8156-0083-6, p.vii.

38.   Morgan, Edmund S., Benjamin Franklin 2002. ISBN 0-300-10162-7 (pbk) p.80-81 Viewed December 29, 2011.

39.   Mee, Charles L., Jr. The Genius of the People. New York: Harper & Row, 1987. p. 237

40.   Greymont, Barbara. Op.cit. p.66 These intrigues were mounted by (a) the French and British empires, (b) the colonies, then states of New York, Pennsylvania and Virginia, and (c) the United States as the Continental Congress, the Articles Congress and subsequently.

41.   NARA. "National Archives Article on the Bill of Rights". Retrieved December 16, 2007.

42.   "Constitution of Ireland Bunreacht Na hÉireann". The All-Party Oireachtas Committee on the Constitution. Archived from the original on 21 July 2011. Retrieved 24 August 2008.

43.   Dáil Éireann – Volume 64 – 12 December, 1936. Executive Authority (External Relations) Bill, 1936 – Committee Stage.

44.   Emmett Larkin, of the University of Chicago in Church, State, and Nation in Modern Ireland, 1975; The Historical Dimensions of Irish Catholicism, 1976; Irish Times 25 November 2006 by Stephen Collins based on Republic of Ireland state papers released under 30-year rule.

45.   "Referendum Results 1937–2009". Department of the Environment, Community and Local Government. Retrieved 8 March 2010.

46.   ULSTER'S INCLUSION BARRED BY BRITAIN; London Protests Claim That Belfast Eventually Must Be Ruled by Dublin; LITTLE CHANGE IS SEEN; Premier of Northern Ireland Attacks Constitution as an 'Affront to His Majesty' – New York Times, 30 December 1937]

47. Circular dated 1 April 1949 from the Canadian Secretary of State for External Affairs to Heads of Post Abroad (Circular Document No.B38, 836. DEA/7545-B-40)

48. The Manchester Guardian, 30 December 1937 Britain accepts new name for the Free State. Full text of British Government's communiqué cited in Clifford, Angela, The Constitutional History of Eire/Ireland, Athol Books, Belfast, 1985, p153.

49. In May 1938 the British government enacted the Eire (Confirmation of Agreements) Act 1938.

50. The Canberra Times – Thursday 13 January 1938

51. Tidridge, Nathan (2010), Canada's Constitutional Monarchy: An Introduction to Our Form of Government, Toronto: Dundurn Press, p. 54, ISBN 9781459700840

52. New Brunswick Broadcasting Co. v. Nova Scotia [1993] 1 S.C.R. 319

53. Dupras, Daniel (3 April 2000). "INTERNATIONAL TREATIES: CANADIAN PRACTICE". Depository Services Program. Public Works and Government Services Canada. Retrieved 17 December 2010.

54. Senate of Canada (20 March 2013). "LCJC Meeting No. 74". Queen's Printer for Canada. Retrieved 24 March 2013.

55. Supreme Court of Canada (28 September 1981), Re: Resolution to amend the Constitution, [1981] 1 SCR 753, Queen's Printer for Canada, p. 785

56. [1998] 2 S.C.R. 217

57. "ARCHIVED - Key Terms - Provinces and Territories - Canadian Confederation - Library and Archives Canada". Collectionscanada.gc.ca. Retrieved 17 April 2013.

58. Parliamentary Government in Canada: Basic Organization and Practices |http://www.mapleleafweb.com/features/parliamentary-government-canada-basic-organization-and-practices

59. Encyclopaedia of Contemporary Russian, Routledge, 2007, ISBN 0415320941 (page 250)

60. "State and Society Under Stalin: Constitutions and Elections in the 1930s," article by J. Arch Getty in Slavic Review, Vol. 50, No. 1 (Spring, 1991). p. 19, 22.

61. Leonard Schapiro, The Communist Party of the Soviet Union, 2nd ed., Random House, New York, 1971, pp. 410-411.

62. Fitzpatrick, Sheila. 1999. Everyday Stalinism: Ordinary Life in Extraordinary Times: Soviet Russia in the 1930s. New York: Oxford University Press, 179.

63. "Walter Duranty Explains Changes In Soviet Constitution," Miami News, Feb. 6 1944

64. League of Nations Timeline - Chronology 1944

65. Constitutional Development in the USSR: A Guide to the Soviet Constitutions, by Aryeh L. Unger, Universe Pub, 1981, ISBN 0876637322 (page 197)

66. The Ukrainian Resurgence by Bohdan Nahaylo, University of Toronto Press, 1999, ISBN 0802079776 (page 402)

67. Encyclopaedia of Contemporary Russian, Routledge, 2007, ISBN 0415320941 (page 250)

68. S.V.Kallistratova. Comments about Project of Constitution of 1977. (in Russian, Некоторые замечания по поводу «Проекта Конституции СССР» 1977 г.), in the book "Заступница", editor:Е.Э.Печуро; publisher: "Звения", Moscow, 2003. http://www.memo.ru/library/books/sw/chapt43.html

69. "France backs constitution reform". BBC News. 21 July 2008. Retrieved 4 September 2009.

70. Decision nr. 71-44 DC, granting constitutional authority to the preambles of 1789 and 1946

71. "The Constitution: The certification process". Constitutional Court of South Africa. Retrieved 13 October 2009.

72. Barnes, Catherine; de Klerk, Eldred (2002). "South Africa's multi-party constitutional negotiation process". Owning the process: Public participation in peacemaking. Conciliation Resources. Retrieved 19 October 2011.

73. Goldstone, Richard (1997). "The South African Bill of Rights". Texas International Law Journal 32: 451–470.

74. Certification of the Constitution of the Republic of South Africa, 1996 [1996] ZACC 26, 1996 (4) SA 744, 1996 (10) BCLR 1253 (6 September 1996), Constitutional Court (South Africa)

75. Certification of the Amended Text of the Constitution of the Republic of South Africa [1996] ZACC 24, 1997 (2) SA 97, 1997 (1) BCLR 1 (4 December 1996), Constitutional Court (South Africa)

76. Mark A. Levin, Essential Commodities and Racial Justice: Using Constitutional Protection of Japan's Indigenous Ainu People to Inform Understandings of the United States and Japan (2001). New York University of International Law and Politics, Vol. 33 (2001), pp. 484, 488. Available at SSRN: http://ssrn.com/abstract=1635451.

77. Mark A. Levin, Civil Justice and the Constitution: Limits on Instrumental Judicial Administration in Japan. Pacific Rim Law & Policy Journal, Volume 20, No. 2, March 2011. Available at SSRN: http://ssrn.com/abstract=1653992; Eiji Sasada, Saibankan Seido (The Court System) (Yuhikaku 1997) at 86.

78. Ramseyer, J. Mark; Rasmusen, Eric (January 2001). "Why is the Japanese Conviction Rate So High?". Journal of Legal Studies 30 (1): 53–88. doi:10.1086/468111

79. Constitution of India (PDF). Ministry of Law and Justice, Government of India. 1 December 2007. p. 26. Retrieved 27 May 2013.

80. Larson, Gerald James (1995). India's Agony Over Religion. SUNY Press. p. 2. ISBN 978-0-7914-2411-7.

81. Singh, Manisha (22 July 2012). "Pranab Mukherjee: The 13th President of India". Zee News. Retrieved 27 May 2013.

82. Pradhan, Bibhudatta (19 July 2007). "Patil Poised to Become India's First Female President". Bloomberg.com. Retrieved 20 July 2007.

83. "India and Pakistan Become Nations; Clashes Continue" - New York Times Retrieved on 20 July 2013.

84. Sharma, Brij Kishore (2007). Introduction to the Constitution of India. PHI Learning. ISBN 978-81-203-3246-1.

85. Jai, Janak Raj (2003). Presidents of India, 1950–2003. Regency Publications. ISBN 978-81-87498-65-0.

86. Pratiyogita Darpan (March 2007). Pratiyogita Darpan (9). Pratiyogita Darpan. p. 60. Retrieved 10 May 2012

87. Roy Chowdhury, Biswaroop (2006). Memory Unlimited. Diamond Pocket Books. ISBN 978-81-8419-017-5.

88. Gupta, V. P. (26 August 2002). "The President's role". The Times of India. Retrieved 4 January 2012.

89. Bakshi, P.M. (June 1956). "Comparative Law: Separation of Powers in India". ABA Journal (American Bar Association) 42: 554. ISSN 0747-0088.

90. Kumar, Rajesh (2011). Universal's Guide to the Constitution of India. Universal Law Publishing. ISBN 978-93-5035-011-9.

91. Bakshi, P. M. (2010). The Constitution Of India. Universal Law Publishing Company. ISBN 978-81-7534-840-0.

92. Deogaonkar, S.G. (1997). Parliamentary System in India. Concept Publishing. p. 25. ISBN 978-81-7022-651-2.

93. The Constitution of India: For all Academic and Competitive Examinations. Bright Publications. p. 48. ISBN 978-81-7199-054-2.

94. Woods, Patricia J. (2008). Judicial Power and National Politics: Courts and Gender in the Religious-Secular Conflict in Israel. SUNY Press. p. 185. ISBN 978-0-7914-7400-6.

95. Laxmikanth, M (2010). Indian Polity for Civil Services Examinations. Tata McGraw-Hill Education. ISBN 978-0-07-015316-5.

96. Thorpe, Vandana (2008). The Pearson Guide To Bank Probationary Officer Recruitment Examinations. Pearson Education India. p. 12. ISBN 978-81-317-1568-0.

97.   Barrington, Lowell W.; Bosia, Michael J.; Bruhn, Kathleen (2009). Comparative Politics: Structures and Choices. Cengage Learning. p. 267. ISBN 978-0-618-49319-7.

98.   Omar, Imtiaz (2002). Emergency Powers and the Courts in India and Pakistan. Martinus Nijhoff Publishers. p. 129. ISBN 978-90-411-1775-5.

99.   Arora, N.D. (2010). Political Science for Civil Services Main Examination. Tata McGraw-Hill Education. ISBN 978-0-07-009094-1

100.   History & Civics. Rachna Sagar. p. 14. ISBN 978-81-8137-037-2.

101.   New ICSE History and Civics. Frank Brothers. p. 3. ISBN 978-81-8409-587-6.

102.   Hardgrave, Robert L.; Kochanek, Stanley A. (2008). India: Government and Politics in a Developing Nation. Cengage Learning. ISBN 978-0-495-00749-4.

103.   Srivastava, Meera (1980). Constitutional Crisis in the States in India. Concept Publishing Company. p. 17. GGKEY:0BS5QYU7XF2. Retrieved 31 May 2012.

104.   "President's Rule in Jharkhand for second time in two years". The Economic Times. PTI. 1 June 2010. Retrieved 1 May 2012.

105.   Social Science Textbook for Class IX Part-III.. FK Publications. p. 115. ISBN 978-81-89611-19-4. Retrieved 7 May 2012.

106.   Sharma, Kanhaiyalal (2002). Reconstitution of Constitution of India. Deep and Deep Publications. ISBN 81-7629-405-5.

107.   general studies Indian polity. Upkar Prakashan. p. 106. Retrieved 12 May 2012.

108.   "The Presidential and Vice-Presidential Elections Act, 1952". lawmin.nic.in. Retrieved 3 September 2013.

109.   "The President and Vice-President Election rules, 1974". Ministry of Law & Justice, Government of India. Retrieved 31 May 2012.

110.   "Election to the president of India". Election commission of India. p. 16. Retrieved 27 May 2013.

111.   Great Britain. Ministry of Overseas Development. Library; Great Britain. Overseas Development Administration. Library. Public Administration. Upkar Prakashan. pp. 167–. Retrieved 11 May 2012.

112.   "Balance of power in presidential race". NDTV. 22 May 2007. Retrieved 6 May 2012.

113.   Pratiyogita Darpan (October 2007). Pratiyogita Darpan. Pratiyogita Darpan. p. 67. Retrieved 31 May 2012.

114.   "The President(Emoluments And) Pension Act" (PDF). Ministry of Home Affairs, Government of India. p. 2. Retrieved 26 May 2013.

115.   "President gets richer, gets 300 pc salary hike". CNN-IBN. 11 September 2008. Retrieved 9 November 2008.

116. Randhawa, Gurcharan Singh; Mukhopadhyay, Amitabha (1986). Floriculture in India. Allied Publishers. p. 593. ISBN 978-81-7023-057-1.

117. Randhawa, Mohindar Singh; Randhawa, Gurcharan Singh; Chadha, K. L.; Singh, Daljit; Horticultural Society of India (1971). The Famous gardens of India. Malhotra Publishing House.

118. India Foreign Policy and Government Guide. International Business Publications. 1 May 2001. p. 39. ISBN 978-0-7397-8298-9.

119. Article 56 (1) (b) and Article 61 of the Constitution of India.

120. Bhardwaj, A.P. Study Package For CLAT and LL.B Entrance Examinations. McGraw-Hill Education (India). pp. 238–239. ISBN 978-0-07-107468-1.

121. http://164.100.47.5/pres2012/4000rs.pdf

122. Subrahmaniam, Vidya (10 November 2005). "K.R. Narayanan – President who defied stereotype". The Hindu. Retrieved 15 June 2012.

123. "President appoints Manmohan Prime Minister". The Hindu. 20 May 2004. Retrieved 15 June 2012.

124. Sundar Rajan, K.T. (4 December 1996). "Presidential Years". Outlook. Retrieved 13 June 2012

125. Bhattacharjya, Satarupa (12 June 2006). "Show Of Dissent". India Today. Retrieved 13 June 2012.

126. Interview with K. R. Narayanan on Independence day, 15 August 1998; by N. Ram, Editor, Frontline ["K. R. Narayanan in conversation with N. Ram", The Hindu, 10 November 2005. Retrieved 24 February 2006].

127. "Kalam returns Office of Profit Bill". CNN-IBN. 31 May 2006. Retrieved 2 May 2012.

128. "Signing office of profit bill was toughest decision:A P J Kalam". The Economic Times. PTI. 18 July 2010. Retrieved 2 May 2012.

129. "'Kalam erred on Office of Profit bill'". The Times of India. PTI. 22 April 200. Retrieved 2 May 2012.

130. Section 75(5) of the Constitution of India

131. "Prime Minister and the Cabinet Ministers". pmindia.nic.in. Retrieved 2008-06-05.

132. "Ministers of State (Independent Charge)". pmindia.nic.in. Retrieved 2008-06-05

133. "Ministers of State (without Independent Charge)". pmindia.nic.in. Retrieved 2008-06-05.

134. "(Allocation of Business) Rules 1961". cabsec.nic.in. Archived from the original on 30 April 2008. Retrieved 2008-06-05.

135. "Cabinet Secretariat,Govt.of India". cabsec.gov.in. Retrieved 2008-06-05

136. "PM's answers to Parliamentary Questions". pmindia.nic.in. Retrieved 2008-06-05.

137.   "Recent Visit of the Prime Minister". pmindia.nic.in. Retrieved 2008-06-05

138.   "Recent National Messages of the PM". pmindia.nic.in. Retrieved 2008-06-05

139.   Basu, Durga D. (2009). "11". Introduction to the Constitution of India. Nagpur, India: LexisNexis Butterworths Wadhwa Nagpur. p. 199. ISBN 978-81-8038-559-9

140.   The Constitution of India, Article 75-6

141.   "A Raise for Prime Minister Manmohan Singh?". Wall Street Journal. 23 July 2010. Retrieved 14 August 2012

142.   "Leaders of the fee world: How much a country's leader is paid compared to GDP per person". The Economist. 5 July 2010. Retrieved 14 August 2012.

143.   "Pay & Allowances of the Prime Minister" (PDF). pmindia.nic.in/. Retrieved 14 June 2013.

144.   "Council of Ministers". Retrieved 31 January 2012

145.   Council of Ministers | National Portal of India. India.gov.in. Retrieved on 2013-07-18.

146.   Council of Ministers | National Portal of India

147.   Super Admin (27 May 2009). "Manmohan Singh | Cabinet Expansion | UPA | Congress | NCP | Trinamool Congress | List of Ministers". News.oneindia.in. Retrieved 16 December 2011.

148.   "59 new ministers inducted in Manmohan's cabinet, gone up to 79". GroundReport. 28 May 2009. Retrieved 16 December 2011.

149.   59 ministers sworn in to complete India's new government - Monsters and Critics

150.   "Our Parliament". Indian Parliament (parliament.nic.in). Retrieved 19 August 2011.

151.   "The President of India is prativa patil". Presidentofindia.nic.in. Retrieved 14 August 2012.

152.   "Lok Sabha". parliamentofindia.nic.in. Retrieved 19 August 2011.

153.   "Parliament – Government: National Portal of India". Home: National Portal of India. Retrieved 10 May 2011.

154.   "Terrorists attack Parliament; five intruders, six cops killed". 2006. . Rediff India. 13 December 2001

155.   *elearning.vtu.ac.in/P3/CIP71/9.pdf* data retrieved at 03.03.2012

156.   Gerald D. Berreman (1972). Race, Caste, and Other Invidious Distinctions in Social Stratification. University of California, Berkeley. doi:10.1177/030639687201300401

157.   de Zwart, Frank (July 2000). "The Logic of Affirmative Action: Caste, Class and Quotas in India". Acta Sociologica 43 (3): 235–249. doi:10.1177/000169930004300304. JSTOR 4201209.

158.   "List of Schedule Castes". Ministry of Social Justice and Empowerment, Government of India. 2011.

159.   J Smith, Brian K. (2005). "Varna and Jāti". Macmillan Reference USA.

160. Sadangi (2008). Emancipation of Dalits and Freedom Struggle. ISBN 978-81-8205-481-3

161. Jaffrelot, Christophe (2006). "The Impact of Affirmative Action in India: More Political than Socioeconomic". India Review 5 (2): 173–189. doi:10.1080/14736480600824516.

162. 161.. Barth, Fredrik (1962). Leach, E. R., ed. Aspects of Caste in South India, Ceylon, and North-West Pakistan. Cambridge University Press. ISBN 978-0-521-09664-5.

163. Mills, Martin A. (2002). Identity, Ritual and State in Tibetan Buddhism: The Foundations of Authority in Gelukpa Monasticism. Routledge. pp. 40–41. ISBN 978-0-7007-1470-4.

164. Ballhatchet, Kenneth (1998). Caste, Class and Catholicism in India 1789–1914. ISBN 978-0-7007-1095-9.

165. Robin J Moore, Sir Charles Wood's Indian Policy 1853-66, The University Press, University of Manchester, Chapter 10, pp 204-226

166. André Burguière and Raymond Grew (2001), The Construction of Minorities: Cases for Comparison Across Time and Around the World, The University of Michigan Press, ISBN 978-0472067374, pp 215-229

167. The Economist (June 29 2013), Affirmative Action, India Reservations

168. Reservation System And Indian Constitution - Special Refrence To Mandal Commission By Dr. Sunil Kumar Jangir

169. "Spiritual Terrorism: Spiritual Abuse from the Womb to the Tomb", p. 391, by Boyd C. Purcell

170. Constitution of India Government of India (2004)

171. CRIME AGAINST PERSONS BELONGING TO SCs / STs Government of India (2011)

172. How do I obtain caste certificate Protective Discrimination Policies, Government of India (2012)

173. Can't change caste, SC to college student The Supreme Court on Friday said that a person could not be identified to a caste other than those of her parents.

174. Rajendra Shrivastava vs The State Of Maharashtra on 22 January, 2010 Judge observed "It is now well settled that a person acquires caste by birth and not by marriage

175. Ex-India President Narayanan dies BBC News (2005)

176. D. D. Kosambi (Summer 1944). "Caste and Class in India". Science & Society 8 (3): 243–249. JSTOR 40399616.

177. Ronald Inden (2001). Imagining India. Indiana University Press. pp. 56–66. ISBN 978-0-253-21358-7.

178. Dr. Ambedkar and Social Justice, Page 223, by Madan Gopal Chitkara

179. Charles Drekmeier (1962). Kingship and community in early India. pp. 81–90. ISBN 0-8047-0114-8

180. Lawrence Goodrich. Cultural Studies. pp. 205–209. ISBN 1-4496-3728-0.

181. William Pinch (1996). Peasants and Monks in British India. University of California Press. ISBN 978-0-520-20061-6.

182. Cassan, Guilhem (September 2011). "The Impact of Positive Discrimination in Education in India: Evidence from a Natural Experiment". Paris School of Economics and Laboratoire d'Economie Appliquee.

183. Anne Waldrop (2004). "Dalit Politics in India and New Meaning of Caste". Forum for Development Studies 31 (2). doi:10.1080/08039410.2004.9666283

184. Ghurye 1969, pp. 1–2.

185. Ghurye 1969, pp. 2–22.

186. Chapman 1993, pp. 10–14.

187. Gershevitch, Ilya. The Cambridge History of Iran. p. 651.

188. The World Year Book of Education. Columbia University. Teachers College, University of London Institute of Education. p. 226.

189. Origin and Growth of Caste in India by Nripendra Kumar Dutt, p. 39

190. Georges Dumézil (translated by Derek Coltman) (1988). Mitra-Varuna: An Essay on Two Indo-European Representations of Sovereignty. Zone. ISBN 978-0-942299-12-0.

191. A.C. Bhaktivedanta Swami Prabhupada. "4, verse 13". Bhagavad Gita As It Is. BBT press. ISBN 0-89213-123-3.

192. Nicholas B. Dirks (2001). Castes of Mind: Colonialism and the Making of New India. ISBN 978-0-691-08895-2.

193. Michael Ward "Philosophizing Religion: Why so much Debate about Exploitation in the Hindu Caste System" Journal of Human Values vol. 12 no.2 195–201(October 2006)

194. Govt of Haryana, India. 1899.

195. Eric Stokes (July 1980). The Peasant and the Raj: Studies in Agrarian Society and Peasant Rebellion in Colonial India. Cambridge University Press. pp. 38–43 (see other chapters too). ISBN 978-0-521-29770-7.

196. Eric Stokes (February 1973). "The First Century of British Colonial Rule in India: Social Revolution or Social Stagnation?". Past and Present 58: 136–160. JSTOR 650259.

197. Célestin Bouglé. Essais sur le régime des castes (original in French through URL link, see Pocock translation through ISBN link, particularly chapter 2 of part 2). Cambridge University Press. pp. 80–123. ISBN 978-0-521-08093-4.

198. Ian Kerr (2007). Engines of change: the railroads that made India. Praeger Publishers. pp. 89–99. ISBN 0-275-98564-4.

199. David Arnold (January 1983). "White colonization and labour in 19th century India". Journal of Imperial and Commonwealth History XI (2): 133–157.

200. Corbridge, Stuart; Harriss, John (2000). Reinventing India: Liberalization, Hindu Nationalism and Popular Democracy. Polity press. p. 8, 243

201. Omvedt, Gail (2012). "A Part That Parted". Outlook India (The Outlook Group). Retrieved 12 August 2012.

202. James Silverberg (November 1969). "Social Mobility in the Caste System in India: An Interdisciplinary Symposium". The American Journal of Sociology 75 (3): 443–444. JSTOR 2775721.

203. John Keay, India: A History, HarperCollins Publishers Ltd, London, 2000. p. 145.

204. John Keay, India: A History, HarperCollins Publishers Ltd, London, 2000. p. 189.

205. Neil Smelser, Seymour Lipset (2005). Social Structure & Mobility in Economic Development. pp. 8–15, 160–174. ISBN 0-202-30799-9.

206. Srinivas, M.N., Religion and Society among the Coorgs of South India, p. 32 (Oxford, 1952).

207. Caste in Modern India; And other essays: p. 48. (Media Promoters & Publishers Pvt. Ltd, Bombay; first published: 1962, 11th reprint: 1994).

208. Gosal, R. P. S. (September 1987). "Distribution of scheduled caste population in India". Social Science Information 26 (3): 493–511. doi:10.1177/053901887026003002.

209. "Scheduled castes and scheduled tribes population: Census 2001". Government of India. 2004.

210. "Constitution of India". Ministry of Law, Government of India. Retrieved 2012.

211. "Profile: Mayawati Kumari". BBC News. 16 July 2009.

212. 221. "Meira Kumar, a Dalit leader is the new Lok Sabha Speaker". NCHRO. 2009.

213. Deepa Shankar (2007). "What is the progress in elementary education participation in India during the last two decades?". The World Bank

214. Mohanty and Ram (November 2010). "LIFE EXPECTANCY AT BIRTH AMONG SOCIAL AND ECONOMIC GROUPS IN INDIA". International Institute for Population Sciences.

215. Darshan Singh (2009). "DEVELOPMENT OF SCHEDULED CASTES IN INDIA – A REVIEW". Journal of Rural Development 28 (4): 529–542

216. Desai and Kulkarni (May 2008). "Changing Educational Inequalities in India in the Context of Affirmative Action". Demography 45 (2): 245–270. PMC 2474466. PMID 18613480.

217. Reservation in India Dr. B.R. Ambedkar & His People - A Dalit Activism NGO (2004)

218. "India: (Prevention of Atrocities) Act, 1989; No. 33 of 1989". Human Rights Watch. 1989.

219. "About NCST". Government of India. 2011.

220. Marc Galanter, Competing Equalities: Law and the Backward Classes in India. Delhi: Oxford University Press, 1984, 84-85

221. "Caste-based Discrimination in International Human Rights Law", p. 257, by Mr David Keane

222. Akhter, Andalib (5 April 2001). "Justice K. G. Balakrishnan: Rising From Down Under". Retrieved 30 August 2010.

223. National Commission for Backward Classes, Government of India. 2009.

224. "India Journal: The Basic Shortages that Plague Our Schools". The Wall Street Journal. 3 January 2012.

225. Karen Leonard and Susan Weller (August 1980). "Declining subcaste endogamy in India: the Hyderabad Kayasths, 1900–75". American Ethnologist 7 (3).

226. "THE DOLLAR BRIDES—Indian girls marrying NRIs often escape to a hassle-free life". Calcutta, India: The Telegraph. 28 January 2003.

227. "UN report slams India for caste discrimination". CBC News. 2 March 2007.

228. Reply to SC daunting task for government, Tribune India.

229. "Central List of Other Backward Castes". National Commission in Backwards Castes, Government of India.

230. What is India's population of Other Backwards Castes?,Yahoo News.

231. "Cabinet clears caste, BLP census". Thestatesman.net. 20 January 2011. Retrieved 20 January 2013. [

232. "Caste and the Census". The Hindu (Chennai, India).

233. "Caste in doubt". Indian Express. 17 May 2010. Retrieved 20 January 2013.

234. Christian Castes Encyclopædia Britannica.

235. David Cahill (1994). "Colour by Numbers: Racial and Ethnic Categories in the Viceroyalty of Peru". Journal of Latin American Studies 26: 338–342.

236. Magnus Mörner (May 1983). "Economic Factors and Stratification in Colonial Spanish America with Special Regard to Elites". The Hispanic American Historical Review 63 (2): 335–362.

237. Patricia Seed (November 1982). "Social Dimensions of Race: Mexico City, 1753". The Hispanic American Historical Review 62 (4): 569–591. JSTOR 2514568.

238. Forrester, Duncan (1980). Caste and Christianity. Curzon Press. pp. 98, 102.

239. Harold Coward- Hindu-Christian Dialogue: Perspectives and Encounters, Motilal Banarsidass Publ., 1993, ISBN 81-208-1158-5, pp. 14–20 [1]

240. Susan Bayly – Saints, Goddesses and Kings: Muslims and Christians in South Indian Society, pp. 243–253, Cambridge University Press, 2004, ISBN 0-521-89103-5 [2]

241. Fuller, C.J. Indian Christians: Pollution and Origins. Man, New Series, Vol. 12, No. 3/4. (Dec. 1977), pp. 528–529.

242. Amaladass, Anand (1993) [1989 (New York: Orbis Books)]. "Dialogue between Hindus and the St. Thomas Christians". In Coward, Harold. Hindu-Christian dialogue: perspectives and encounters (Indian ed.). Delhi: Motilal Banarsidass. pp. 15–19. ISBN 81-208-1158-5.

243. Aggarwal, Pratap (1978). Caste and Social Stratification Among Muslims in India. Manohar

244. 234. Social Stratification Among Muslims in India by Zarina Bhatty.

245. Ambedkar, Bhimrao. Pakistan or the Partition of India. Thackers Publishers.

246. H. H. Risley (1903). Ethnographic Appendices, in GOI, Census of India, 1901 (see tables on Ajlaf and Arzal, and Risley discussion of these Muslim castes versus Hindu castes) 1. Calcutta: Office of the Superintendent of Government Printing. pp. 45–62. ISBN 978-1-246-03552-0.

247. Web resource for Pakistan or the Partition of India

248. Hamermesh, M. Caste at birth .

249. Chowdhuri Parkash, J. (2012). Caste system, social inequalities and reservation policy in india: Class, caste, social policy and governance through social justice. LAP LAMBERT Academic Publishing.

250. Leach, Edmund Ronald (24 November 1971). Aspects of Caste in South India, Ceylon and North-West Pakistan (p. 113). Cambridge University Press.

251. Muslim Communities of South Asia: Culture and Society Edited by T.N. Madan. New Delhi: Vikas Publishing House, 1976 p. 114.

252. "The Scheduled Castes in the Sikh Community – A Historical Perspective".

253. Harish K. Puri (2004). Dalits in Regional Context. ISBN 978-81-7033-871-0.

254. Durga Prasad, p. 115, History of the Andhras upto 1565 A. D.

255. Nicky Grist (1984). "Land tax, labour and household organisation in Ladakh".

256. Melvyn Goldstein (1988). "Freedom, Servitude and the Servant-serf Nyima: a re-rejoinder to Miller". The Tibet Journal 14 (2): 56–60.

257. T. Grunfeld (1996). The Making of Modern Tibet. ISBN 1-56324-713-5.

258. Herbert Passin (October 1955). "Untouchability in the Far East". Monumenta Nipponica 11 (3). JSTOR 2382914.

259. Martin, Robert Montgomery, p. 216, The History, Antiquities, Topography, and Statistics of Eastern India.

260. P. 586 The East Indian Gazetteer: Containing Particular Descriptions of ..., Volume 1 By Walter Hamilton (M.R.A.S.)

261. Laura Dudley-Jenkins (October 2009). Identity and Identification in India (see review of sociology journal articles starting page 42). Routledge. ISBN 978-0-415-56062-7.

262. C Bates (1995). "Race, Caste and Tribe in Central India: the early origins of Indian anthropometry". Edinburgh Papers In South Asian Studies (3).

263. B.R. Ambedkar (1939). "Essays on Untouchables and Untouchability: Social"

264. "Online Collection (The Riddell Gifts)". National Galleries of Scotland. 1985.

265. B.R. Ambedkar (1917). "CASTES IN INDIA: Their Mechanism, Genesis and Development". Missing or empty |url= (help)

266. B.R. Ambedkar (1935). "THE UNTOUCHABLES WHO WERE THEY AND WHY THEY BECAME UNTOUCHABLES ?". Missing or empty |url= (help)

267. Changes in Mahatma Gandhi's views on caste and intermarriage

268. Trisha Gupta (20 September 2008). "Visual history tells us about repressed histories".

269. Christopher Pinney (1998). Camera Indica: The Social Life of Indian Photographs. University Of Chicago Press. ISBN 978-0-226-66866-6.

270. Sarah Fraser (2010). "The Face of China: Photography's Role in Shaping Image, 1860—1920". Getty Research Journal (2): 39–52.

271. "Caste, Ethnicity and Exclusion in South Asia: The Role of Affirmative Action Policies in Building Inclusive Societies"

272. 271.. "Crime statistics, 87 major countries". UN ODC. 2007.

273. "Crimes and Crime Rates by Type of Offense: 1980 to 2009". Census—US. 2010.

274. "31.28 million cases pending in various courts". The Times of India. 6 May 2010.

275. Danny Yee. "Book review of Caste, Society and Politics in India: From the Eighteenth Century to the Modern Age". Retrieved 11 December 2006.

276. Bhattacharya, Amit. "Who are the OBCs?". Archived from the original on 27 June 2006. Retrieved 19 April 2006. Times of India, 8 April 2006.

277. "Caste-Based Parties". Country Studies US. Retrieved 12 December 2006.

278. India's caste system discriminates.

279. Singh and Roy (2011). Indian Political Thought: Themes and Thinkers. Pearson. pp. 82–90. ISBN 978-81-317-5851-9

280. "Essays, speeches, addresses and writings", by Naoroji, Chunilal Lallubhai Parekh, p. 493

281. Swami Vivekananda (1952). The Complete Works of Swami Vivekananda (8 vols., Calcutta) V. pp. 25–30. ISBN 978-81-85301-46-4.

282. Gopal Guru, with Shiraz Sidhva. India's "hidden apartheid"[dead link].

283. William A. Haviland, Anthropology: The Human Challenge, 13th edition, Thomson Wadsworth, 2010, ISBN 978-0-495-81084-1, p. 536 (see note 9).

284. The Constitution of India by P.M. Bakshi, Universal Law Publishing Co, ISBN 81-7534-500-4.

285. Mendelsohn, Oliver & Vicziany, Maria, "The Untouchables, Subordination, Poverty and the State in Modern India", Cambridge University Press, 1998.[page needed]

286. Kevin Reilly, Stephen Kaufman, Angela Bodino, Racism: A Global Reader P21, M.E. Sharpe, 2003 ISBN 0-7656-1060-4.

287. Excerpts from The Constitution of India.

288. E. Venizelos (26 April 2008). "Human Rights in India: the issue of the casts and namely of the Untouchables". Introductory speech at the "Scientific Conference on caste" hosted by the Centre for European Constitutional Law. Centre for European Constitutional Law. Retrieved 6 July 2012. [dead link]

289. "An Untouchable Subject?". Npr.org. 29 August 2001. Retrieved 20 January 2013.

290. Ambedkar, The Annihilation of Caste. p. 49 of his Writings and Speeches, vol.1, Education Dpt., Government of Maharashtra 1979.

291. Andre Beteille (3 October 2001). "Race and Caste". Chennai, India: The Hindu. Retrieved 6 July 2012.

292. Cahill, David (1994). "Colour by Numbers: Racial and Ethnic Categories in the Viceroyalty of Peru". Journal of Latin American Studies 26: 325–346.

293. María Elena Martínez (July 2004). "The Black Blood of New Spain: Limpieza de Sangre, Racial Violence, and Gendered Power in Early Colonial Mexico". The William and Mary Quarterly 61 (3): 479–520. JSTOR 3491806.

294. Martínez, M. E. (2002). The Spanish concept of Limpieza de Sangre and the emergence of the 'race/caste' system in the viceroyalty of New Spain (PhD dissertation). University of Chicago.

295. María Elena Martínez (2010). "Social Order in the Spanish New World". Public Broadcasting Service, United States.

296. India – A Country Study, USA Library of Congress, 1995, Chapter 5.

297. Hanstad (2005). "Improving land access to India's rural poor". The World Bank.

298. Haque (2006). "IMPROVING THE RURAL POORS' ACCESS TO LAND IN INDIA". DARPG, Government of India.

299. Swaminathan S. Anklesaria Aiyar (July 2011). "The Elephant That Became a Tiger, 20 Years of Economic Reform in India"

300. "The God of Small Things Background".

301. "Obscenity case slammed against Arundhati Roy". Rediff.com. Retrieved 20 January 2013.

302. Caste, Society and Politics in India from the Eighteenth Century to the Modern Age, Cambridge University Press ,2001

303. Ed. Lesley Brown. Clarendon Press, Oxford,1993 304. M Narasimhachary, The Caste System: An Overview, 'Indian Culture in the Modern World'. 23rd October 2002, London

304. 305 The cohesive role of Sanskritization and other essays, Delhi, 1989

305. Hasan Z. 2000. Representation and redistribution: the new lower caste politics of north India.

306. Jaffrelot C. 2003. India's Silent Revolution: The Rise of the Low Castes in North Indian Politics. Delhi: Permanent Black

307. Jain M. 1996. Backward caste and social change in UP and Bihar.

308. Brass P. 1997. The politicization of the peasantry in a north Indian state.

309. Manor J. 1997. Caste and class in a cohesive society.

310. Blair H. 1980. Rising kulaks and backward classes in Bihar: social change in the late 1970s. Econ. Pol. Wkly. 15:64–74

311. ShashankKela, Caste, Class and Politics in Contemporary North India, pp1-10

312. Zelliot E. 1970. Learning the use of political means: the Mahars of Maharashtra. In Caste in Indian Politics, ed. R Kothari. Delhi: Orient Longman

313. Omvedt G. 2001. Ambedkar and after: Dalit movement in India.

314. Guru G. 2001. The language of Dalit- Bahujanpolitcial discourse.

315. Burra N. 1996. Buddhism conversion and identity: a case study of village Mahars. See Srinivas 1996

316. Vora R. 2004. Decline of caste majoritarianism in Indian politics. InIndian Democracy: Meanings and Practices, ed. R Vora, S Palshikar. New Delhi: Sage

317. Yadav Y. 2001. Understanding the second democratic upsurge: trends of Bajhujan participation in electoral politics in the 1990s.

318. PradiptaChaudhury, Political Economy of Caste in Northern India, 1901-1931, pp1-51

319. Sekhon, Joti. Modern India. Boston: McGraw- Hill, 2000. Print.

320. download.nos.org/srsec317newE/317EL19.pdf